Macroeconomics, Prices, and Quantities

Essays in Memory of Arthur M. Okun

JAMES TOBIN, EDITOR

THE BROOKINGS INSTITUTION
Washington, D.C.

Library of Congress Cataloging in Publication data:

Main entry under title:

Macroeconomics, prices, and quantities.

  Includes bibliographical references and index.
  1. Macroeconomics—Addresses, essays, lectures.
2. Okun, Arthur M.   I. Okun, Arthur M.   II. Tobin,
James, 1918–.
HB172.5.M336   1982   339   82-17671
ISBN 0-8157-8486-4
ISBN 0-8157-8485-6 (pbk.)

9 8 7 6 5 4 3 2 1

THE BROOKINGS INSTITUTION is an independent organization devoted to nonpartisan research, education, and publication in economics, government, foreign policy, and the social sciences generally. Its principal purposes are to aid in the development of sound public policies and to promote public understanding of issues of national importance.

The Institution was founded on December 8, 1927, to merge the activities of the Institute for Government Research, founded in 1916, the Institute of Economics, founded in 1922, and the Robert Brookings Graduate School of Economics and Government, founded in 1924.

The Board of Trustees is responsible for the general administration of the Institution, while the immediate direction of the policies, program, and staff is vested in the President, assisted by an advisory committee of the officers and staff. The by-laws of the Institution state: "It is the function of the Trustees to make possible the conduct of scientific research, and publication, under the most favorable conditions, and to safeguard the independence of the research staff in the pursuit of their studies and in the publication of the results of such studies. It is not a part of their function to determine, control, or influence the conduct of particular investigations or the conclusions reached."

The President bears final responsibility for the decision to publish a manuscript as a Brookings book. In reaching his judgment on the competence, accuracy, and objectivity of each study, the President is advised by the director of the appropriate research program and weighs the views of a panel of expert outside readers who report to him in confidence on the quality of the work. Publication of a work signifies that it is deemed a competent treatment worthy of public consideration but does not imply endorsement of conclusions or recommendations.

The Institution maintains its position of neutrality on issues of public policy in order to safeguard the intellectual freedom of the staff. Hence interpretations or conclusions in Brookings publications should be understood to be solely those of the authors and should not be attributed to the Institution, to its trustees, officers, or other staff members, or to the organizations that support its research.

Foreword

ARTHUR M. OKUN's posthumously published book, *Prices and Quantities: A Macroeconomic Analysis* (Brookings, 1981), was an attempt to explain the perplexing coexistence of high inflation and high unemployment. This condition—often termed stagflation—has become a fact of life for most modern industrialized economies, and economists have been struggling to understand its causes and to devise methods of curing it. The quest has led them to reexamine the *micro*economic structure and behavior underlying the *macro*economic phenomena of inflation and unemployment. Okun's work emphasized that conventional microeconomic theories, most of which assume that markets are cleared by flexible prices and wages, are not applicable to most sectors of industrialized economies. Instead, he argued that analytical models emphasizing long-term relationships between buyers and sellers are more realistic.

In Okun's analysis, business firms establish long-term relations with their employees and customers through implicit as well as explicit contracts. Such contracts, though consonant with the basic interests of all parties, reduce the sensitivity of wages and prices to short-run changes in the demand for labor and goods. One result is that restrictive macroeconomic policies reduce output and increase unemployment in the short run without having much immediate effect on inflation.

Economic developments in the early 1980s seem to confirm Okun's prediction that the economic cost of moderating inflation by relying exclusively on general monetary and fiscal policies is very large. Okun believed that it could be substantially reduced by a combination of government cost-reducing measures (for example, cutting indirect taxes and eliminating unnecessary regulations) and some form of government-sponsored policies to slow the growth of wages and prices.

Okun hoped that his work would stimulate new thinking among economists and policymakers both about the structure of realistic microeconomic and macroeconomic models and about methods of fighting stagflation. The essays in this book, which are related to various aspects of Okun's theory and policy prescriptions, are a first installment on the discussion he hoped to provoke.

The essays were originally presented at a conference sponsored by Columbia University, Yale University, and the Brookings Institution—the institutions where Arthur Okun pursued his undergraduate and graduate studies, taught and practiced economics, and later undertook the research that ultimately was brought together in *Prices and Quantities*. The idea of the conference originated with Edmund S. Phelps, a former student and colleague of Okun's at Yale and now professor of economics at Columbia. The conference was planned by Phelps, James Tobin of Yale University, and Joseph A. Pechman of the Brookings Institution. It was held at Columbia University in September 1981; the Brookings Institution undertook to edit and publish the proceedings.

The risk of error in this book was minimized by the work of Ellen W. Smith. Elizabeth H. Cross edited the manuscript; Florence Robinson prepared the index.

The sponsors of the conference are grateful to Procter and Gamble, Inc., Greenwich Research Associates, and the Georges Lurcy Charitable and Educational Trust for providing funds to help support the project.

The views expressed here are solely those of the authors and should not be ascribed to the persons or organizations whose assistance is acknowledged above, or to the trustees, officers, or other staff members of the Brookings Institution.

BRUCE K. MACLAURY
President

January 1983
Washington, D.C.

Contents

PRODUCT MARKETS

ASSET MARKETS

MACRO POLICY

Tables

Figures

JOSEPH A. PECHMAN and JULIE A. CARR

Introduction and Summary

THIS VOLUME follows the outline of Arthur Okun's *Prices and Quantities: A Macroeconomic Analysis,* with papers on labor markets, product markets, asset markets, and macroeconomic policy.

The labor market papers deal with what Okun called "the invisible handshake," the informal understandings that establish the long-term relationships of firms, workers, and customers. The first paper attempts to determine whether these implicit contracts help to explain the rigidity of wages during the Great Depression. The second argues that the use of efficient forecasting schemes, or rational expectations, would reduce the output and employment costs of disinflation brought about by fiscal and monetary policies.

The product market papers discuss the stickiness of prices and other market imperfections that occupied such a prominent place in Okun's analysis. The first paper measures the variability of prices (and wages) in the United States, the United Kingdom, and Japan during the last hundred years and discusses the implication of this record for Okun's theory. The second examines the nature of equilibria in markets in which there are imperfections because of the scarcity of information about prices and quantities and suggests that such markets can be improved through government intervention.

The asset market papers are concerned with the conduct of monetary policy and real interest rates. The first compares the relationship between economic activity and money balances, which are now the intermediate target for monetary policy, with the relationship between economic activity and outstanding credit liabilities. The second tests whether nominal interest rates in the United States have been equal to the sum of the real interest rate plus the inflation rate, as many economists, beginning with Irving Fisher, have suggested.

The first of three papers on macroeconomic policy discusses the major competing macroeconomic theories of the day and evaluates their

1

ability to explain and remedy the economic problems of the 1980s. The remaining two papers discuss methods of achieving a stable and predictable monetary standard and the costs of eliminating inherited wage and price inflation.

Labor Markets in the Great Depression

Because the major macroeconomic issues have not been resolved on the basis of post–World War II data, interest has increased in earlier economic history. In his paper Martin Neil Baily attempts to develop a theory of wage and employment adjustment that is consistent with the events of the depression. He describes the central features of the labor market during the 1930s and then asks whether the behavior of individuals and markets can be explained within some framework of rational decisionmaking.

Baily begins by sketching what happened to the labor market from 1929 to 1941. He finds that nominal wages did vary substantially over the period, falling between 1929 and 1933 and rising fairly rapidly after that. Wages did not begin to decline until well after prices and employment had begun to fall, however, and real wages actually rose strongly in manufacturing after 1933, despite persistently high unemployment.

Monthly turnover data of production workers for 1929 show that the economic downturn quickly and dramatically affected accessions, layoffs, and quits. Baily points out that the quit rate began to drop in the same month in which the layoff rate began to rise, indicating that workers realized very early that employment prospects were worsening. Annual turnover data for 1930–41 show both a high layoff rate and a high accession or hiring rate for the early years of the depression, with high turnover rates persisting throughout the depression.

A description of output and productivity completes the economic picture of the period. Between 1929 and 1933 labor productivity dipped only slightly as output and employment fell substantially. This suggests that, when firms fear for their existence, they do not conserve excess workers, but encourage managers and production workers alike to increase efficiency in order to prevent bankruptcy.

Baily then asks whether the classical model of the labor market is consistent with this description of the 1930s. According to this model, the decline in the supply of money in the 1930s induced a decline in the price level, which in turn induced a reduction in output and employment. The model requires that employment depend on the real wage alone, after allowing for the costs of adjusting labor supply in the short run. The employment and wage data for the period 1929–37 suggest that rising real wages could have caused some decline in employment, but the short-run rise in unemployment was much too large to be explained in this way. Furthermore, adjustment costs cannot account for the wage-employment relationship after 1933. Baily finds, then, that adding adjustment costs to the classical model does not overcome the problems of the model in explaining the labor market of the depression.

Baily then turns from a consideration of the classical model to an evaluation of the importance of wage contracts. A substantial body of opinion holds that explicit contracts prevent the downward adjustment of wages after a fall in aggregate demand. From the size of union membership and the duration of union contracts during the 1930s Baily concludes that explicit contracts played at most a minor role in the behavior of wages from 1929 to 1936. However, an implicit contract theory—along the lines developed by Baily and by Arthur Okun—does better. Misperceptions on the part of both employers and their workers about the seriousness of the business decline, standards of fairness for wages, and the practice of laying off low-wage workers first are all part of the explanation of wage behavior from 1929 to 1933. Baily concludes that, though the labor market in the early 1930s cannot be said to provide clear independent support for the implicit contract theory, wage developments during this period are consistent with that interpretation. He argues that this consistency does require dropping the assumption of perfectly competitive product markets.

Misperceptions and implicit contracts do not fully explain why persistent high levels of unemployment after 1933 did not exert more downward pressure on wages. This persistent disequilibrium implies that unclaimed economic rents existed for several years, and the presence of such rents violates the basic postulate that competition will eliminate them in a market economy. Competition might have been expected to eliminate the excess unemployment and the associated economic rents either through an increase in employment and output by existing firms or through the entry of new firms. The former did not occur because by 1935 there was a general belief that wage and price reductions would not work to expand output, and the latter because entry was not attractive to firms during the depression.

Other factors also may have limited competition and so affected the adjustment process in the labor market. Baily believes that the increased level of support given the unemployed under the New Deal may well have influenced the layoff behavior of firms and allowed the economic system to operate despite the large number of hard-core unemployed and nonemployed. New Deal legal changes, particularly the National Industrial Recovery Act (followed later by the National Labor Relations Act), may have affected the behavior of wages after 1933. Baily believes this to be an appealing explanation but also finds some problems with it. He suggests that it is not the legal and institutional changes in themselves but their interaction with a labor market where wages were being determined by implicit contracts (rather than by short-term market conditions) that explains the situation in the 1930s.

Thus although Baily criticizes the classical model of the labor market because of its insistence on competition and equilibrium, he does find the misperceptions component of the model to be useful in explaining wages and employment during the depression. He also concludes that an "eclectic version" of contract theory, considering the legal and institutional environment of the time, is fairly acceptable as an explanation of wage rigidity from 1929 to 1941. And he comes away from this examination of the period impressed anew that money wages do not seem to respond much to excess unemployment, even to large and persistent excess unemployment.

The Role of Expectations in Implicit Wage Contracts

Arthur Okun maintained that the long-term relationships of firms, workers, and their customers make it extremely costly in terms of lost output and employment to eliminate inflation by fiscal and monetary measures. John B. Taylor argues that it is not the relationships themselves, but the expectations of individuals involved, that generate the costs. He suggests that by introducing agreements to use efficient forecasting schemes, or rational expectations, into implicit contracts, the macroeconomic inefficiencies of adapting prices and wages to changing economic circumstances can be reduced.

Implicit contract theory of labor markets generally assumes an arrangement whereby firms stabilize fluctuations in the real wage as part of a risk-sharing agreement with workers. Contracted changes in relative wages are likely to occur in an unsynchronized and staggered fashion because firms will find they can achieve their desired relative wage with more certainty if the prevailing wage is predetermined. Taylor points out that an efficient wage contract would be unlikely not to entail some variation in the relative wage in response to changes in the economic conditions facing the firm. Thus unsynchronized nominal wage contracting, he explains, *can* generate macroeconomic inefficiencies.

Okun considered two alternative wage-setting rules for such a model. These rules are based on the assumption that workers want to maintain the average prevailing wage, which depends on future wage decisions by other workers during the life of the contract. The alternatives differ according to the expectations assumption used, and in each case the assumption about the next-period wage decision is based on an extrapolation rather than on rational forecasts. One assumption is that the reference wage, defined by Okun as the average of existing wages at the time the wage is determined, is expected to grow at the same rate over the next year as it did over the year past. The other mechanism suggested by Okun is simply to increase the current wage relative to its previous level by the same amount that the reference wage was most recently adjusted (that is, by the same amount as that obtained by workers who most recently had a wage adjustment). Okun's analysis does allow for changes in these forecasting rules, but the changes will be gradual because they depend on workers' observing that they are performing poorly relative to the prevailing wage and then demanding a change in the forecasting rule implicit in their contract.

As relative wages must move when the labor market conditions facing the firm change, to understand wage and employment dynamics it is necessary to specify how wages respond to such changes. To do this, Taylor suggests adding the unemployment rate as a proxy for labor market conditions to the equations describing the wage-setting rules. He then shows that these wage-setting rules can lead to real output loss even under a credible monetary disinflation program because, again, changes in contracts will occur only after a period of observation. Taylor thus confirms that macroeconomic inefficiencies are generated in Okun's model.

To analyze the effects of the expectations themselves in the contract model, Taylor replaces the extrapolative wage-setting rules with a rational forecasting scheme. In other words, the forecast of the next-period wage decision is an unbiased forecast, given information about policy. Taylor finds that in the case of a monetary disinflation program the rational expectations version of the model results in considerably less output loss than the nonresponsive expectations version. He also considers the case in which unforeseen events, such as a price shock, force a change in the program either before or after the disinflation. If monetary authorities do not accommodate or only partially accommodate this shock, the employment effects will be smaller with rational expectations than with the extrapolative model. However, the rational expectations version of the model is less than conclusive when it is assumed that authorities accommodate the price shock or that the contract mechanism itself will adapt when policy is less accommodative.

Finally, Taylor shows how the important assumption that workers and firms are forward-looking (that is, they base their behavior on expected future conditions rather than on past relationships) in their wage-setting goals might be tested. If they were not forward-looking, disinflation would be costly in either the extrapolative version or the rational expectations version of the model. Taylor considers only the rational expectations assumption and (though his research is not yet completed) concludes that probably workers and firms are generally forward-looking.

Though there is evidence of forward-looking in wage determination, Taylor points out that there is no proof that this is through rational forecasts. He suggests that surveys of the wage-setting process are necessary to determine whether or not rational expectations are part of the forecasting process. His results lead Taylor to believe that it is important to begin thinking about how expectations in wage formation might be made more rational.

Variability of Prices and Wages

The differences in the stickiness of prices and wages over time and across countries are the focus of Robert J. Gordon's paper. From an empirical analysis of the last century in the United States, the United Kingdom, and Japan, Gordon finds that Arthur Okun's theory does not explain the variability in the responsiveness of prices and wages to changes in aggregate demand and to supply shifts. He suggests that macroeconomic research be concerned with this variability, and discusses problems that must be treated in theoretical models before the variability can be explained.

Okun's book was an attempt to provide the missing theory needed to explain the stickiness of prices and wages. Gordon claims that Okun's analysis is not complete because it considers only the postwar economy; he believes that Okun's product and labor market models cannot explain historical and cross-country differences in behavior.

To identify differences in responsiveness, Gordon develops a simple reduced-form equation that describes the response of price and wage changes to demand disturbances and supply shocks. Using identical specifications, he fits the equation to annual price and wage data in each of the three countries over a period beginning in the late nineteenth century and extending to 1980. Parameter shifts in each equation indicate shifts in responsiveness or variability.

Gordon's results provide evidence that nominal aggregate demand influences wage changes through three channels: current changes in nominal spending, the ratio of actual to potential real GNP, and the feedback from lagged product prices. He finds that in Britain and Japan postwar prices and wages have been more responsive to aggregate demand, and less characterized by inertia, than in the United States and that inertia in U.S. prices and wages is entirely a postwar phenomenon.

Gordon's characterization of historical price and wage behavior differs substantially from that of Okun. First, Okun's wage equation assumes that the inflation process is propelled by a wage-wage inertia, while Gordon's results suggest that postwar wage changes in the United States exhibit feedback from lagged product prices, not lagged wage rates. Second, in Okun's model, the influence of aggregate demand on prices and wages operates through a "rate-of-change" effect (that is, how rapidly demand is rising or falling), whereas Gordon finds that there is also a "level effect," except for the periods 1929–41 in the United States and 1924–38 in the United Kingdom. Third, Gordon finds that U.S. data reject Okun's assumption that current changes in customer market prices are the same as lagged changes in wage rates. Finally, there is no room in Okun's model for the major parameter shifts that occur in Gordon's equations. The results for Britain and Japan only compound the conflict between Gordon's empirical findings and Okun's theory.

Since Okun's theory cannot explain the results obtained in Gordon's analysis, Gordon discusses some points that should be considered in the development of a complete and acceptable model. He first focuses on labor markets. Because the U.S. institution of three-year overlapping wage contracts is often cited as an explanation for some or all of the differences between postwar wage adjustments in Britain and Japan and those in the United States, an explanation of the differences in the length and form of union wage contracts among countries is needed, and obstacles to full indexation of the contracts must be identified. The lack of full indexation of labor contracts, Gordon believes, is a central issue in explaining macroeconomic fluctuations. Turning to product markets, Gordon notes that the absence of complete indexation of product prices to nominal demand disturbances opens the way to output fluctuations. For this reason, theorists need to explain the presetting of product prices and the varying responsiveness of prices to changes in nominal demand, which Gordon finds in his empirical analysis for the United States, Britain, and Japan and which has occurred in other countries and in various hyperinflations. He believes that the source of price stickiness is the tendency of firms to wait for price cuts from their suppliers before cutting their own prices in response to a reduction in aggregate demand, and that the responsiveness of prices to demand changes is relatively high when firms and suppliers share common outside information—for example, that a war has broken out.

Gordon grants that the results he obtains from parameters estimated from a century of annual data for three countries should be regarded as suggestive rather than definitive and urges further research to improve our understanding of the price and wage adjustment process.

Competition in Imperfect Markets

The modern view of industrial organization is that the market sector is characterized by imperfections resulting from the scarcity of information about prices and quantities among market participants. Given these imperfections, competition among firms will not eliminate pure profit and therefore will not yield an optimal allocation of resources (the Walrasian outcome without intervention by government). This result is based only on partial-equilibrium models, which treat product demand as being independent of industry income and assume that the real interest rate and the real wage rate are exogenous. The paper presented by Guillermo A. Calvo and Edmund S. Phelps extends the analysis to a general-equilibrium model in which these restrictions are removed. They examine the resulting equilibrium to see whether it can be improved through government intervention. They conceive of an equilibrium as a path along which all events and parameters pertinent to the decision-making of households and firms conform to their expectations.

In the Calvo-Phelps model, all families are identical in tastes and productivity and all firms are identical in costs and competitiveness. The labor and share markets are perfect. Thus at every point in time, a uniform wage rate is established in the labor market and a uniform price is set in the product market by firms, and each family plans a sequence of employment and consumption, based on the expected course of prices, that maximizes its utility. A feature of this model is that the labor and product markets are continuously cleared if goods prices, the real wage, consumption, and employment are positive. Calvo and Phelps point out that in this model the achievement of market clearing is neither necessary nor sufficient for the attainment of equilibrium.

Calvo and Phelps conjecture that all equilibria are stationary states in the model. Accordingly, they attempt to determine the characteristics of the plans of households and of firms in a stationary equilibrium. It turns out that the household plan selected is such that labor time and consumption are positive constants, while firms plan price paths to maximize the present discounted value of their profits, subject to an expected customer-flow relation. Under these conditions each firm's optimal price is constant and the existing price equals the optimal price at all times.

Next, Calvo and Phelps present a general-equilibrium analysis of the model. The conditions for an equilibrium are reduced to two: that firms correctly anticipate the going (optimal) price and households correctly predict their cash flow, particularly their dividends. Calvo and Phelps find that more than one equilibrium may exist in the model, though an ideal allocation of time and resources (the Walrasian outcome with no intervention) is not one of the possibilities.

To examine the welfare aspects of the model, Calvo and Phelps consider the equilibrium giving greatest utility. They find that this equilibrium is not optimal in the sense that there are technologically possible allocations of labor time and consumption that give higher utility for every family (that is, the equilibrium is not "Pareto-optimal"). Compared with the ideal or Walrasian allocation, the non-Walrasian equilibrium yields underemployment and underproduction, a result that Arthur Okun would have expected.

Calvo and Phelps then consider the possibility that the equilibrium in their model is a constrained Pareto-optimum, that any Pareto-superior allocation with only the institutions envisioned by the model is not feasible. They argue that it is not, since if a non-Walrasian equilibrium exists without intervention, there will exist *some* Pareto-superior non-Walrasian equilibrium supportable *with* intervention. Using the model, they show that a subsidy to firms per unit of labor employed would support such a Pareto-superior equilibrium, given the tax rate on pure profit implied by the condition of budget balance in the model.

Calvo and Phelps note that their findings have no literal policy implications because they are not derived from a model designed to provide policy recommendations. However, they believe that, if the characteristics of their model were embedded into a policy model, a tax on pure profit would be justified. Without such a tax, the government would be discarding its means of reducing the wedge between the reward for and the marginal productivity of industry and thrift.

Money and Credit in Macroeconomic Analysis

Economists have traditionally incorporated the prices of financial assets (usually measured inversely by yields) in macroeconomic analysis, but the role of financial quantities remains much less developed. Few analyses have included financial variables other than money to describe the relationship between nonfinancial economic activity and financial market activity. And money is the primary focus of monetary policy in most of the industrialized Western countries. Benjamin M. Friedman presents an empirical case for a redirection of this emphasis in macroeconomic research and in the formulation of monetary policy away from this exclusive focus on money. Friedman's argument is based on the view that the liability side, as well as the asset side, of the public's balance sheet contains useful information and that credit aggregates, as well as asset aggregates, need to be considered.

Because economic theory provides no a priori reason for the greater significance of money holdings than credit liabilities for macroeconomic analysis, the emphasis on money must be based on a set of presumptions about the empirical relationships connecting money and the key measures of nonfinancial economic activity, including especially income and prices. Friedman shows, however, through a series of tests for the United States during the period since 1951, that the relationship between economic activity and outstanding credit liabilities exhibits the same degree of regularity and stability as the relationship between economic activity and money balances.

Friedman first calculates the ratio of year-end credit market indebtedness to fourth-quarter gross national product for all U.S. financial borrowers, and for five different categories of borrowers that make up the total, for 1946–80. He finds that the total nonfinancial debt ratio is much more stable than the ratios for individual sectors.

Next, he examines the stability of the ratios to GNP of ten financial aggregates, including five liability groupings and five asset groupings, for 1953–78. Total net assets, total debt, and total nonfinancial debt are, in that order, the most stable aggregates in relation to GNP. The monetary base, private nonfinancial liabilities, and the money stock are the least stable. As a possibly better test of stability, Friedman estimates ten regression equations, in each case relating the growth of nominal GNP to a moving average of the growth of one of the ten financial aggregates previously used and a moving average of a fiscal policy measure. Total net assets performs best in this test and bank credit performs worst. Total nonfinancial debt is about in the middle. To improve on this form of regression analysis, Friedman next tests the relationship of each of three of the financial aggregates to income following an unanticipated movement in the aggregate (or in income). The results show that the three asset ratios and the total nonfinancial debt ratio are the most stable. To account for the distinction between the real and price components of nominal income variation, Friedman reestimates the equations and includes real GNP and the price deflator. The results don't change much.

The evidence suggests, then, that among the various liability measures considered there is something unique about total nonfinancial debt and that at least this aggregate measure of credit liabilities consistently exhibits just as much stability in relation to U.S. economic activity as the more familiar asset aggregates do. Simply put, the credit-income relationship is clearly important for understanding economic behavior. Given this evidence, the one remaining rationalization for including the money market but excluding credit markets in macroeconomic analysis would be the presumption that money is central to nonfinancial decisions while credit is not.

Friedman proceeds to test this presumption by regression analysis. By estimating two three-variable systems, each including real GNP, the price deflator, and either the money stock or total nonfinancial debt, he finds that neither money nor credit helps explain real income. When both money and credit are added to real GNP and the price deflator in a four-variable system, each one does incrementally explain real income. Friedman points out that what appears to matter for the explanation of real income is neither money nor credit, but instead the interrelation of the two. Together with the earlier analysis, therefore, these regressions show that there is no empirical basis for focusing on money to the exclusion of credit in macroeconomic analysis.

Friedman next considers what kind of structural economic model would be consistent with these empirical observations. The results indicate that a plausible model for determining real income should include three markets: for goods and services, for credit, and for money. This framework corresponds to the four-variable system just described, where the quantity of credit represents the relevant aspects of behavior in the credit market and the remaining three variables represent the quantities in the other two markets and the rate of exchange between them. Friedman suggests that neither the nominal interest rate nor the quantity of credit can, by itself, be an adequate representation of the credit market. Thus macroeconomic analysis should not only explicitly incorporate the credit market into its models, but it should do so with a quantity and a relative price (here, nominal interest rate) variable.

Finally, Friedman notes that his evidence provides no support for the exclusive use of the money supply as the intermediate target for monetary policy. Instead, the evidence supports either abandonment of the intermediate target procedure for monetary policy altogether or adoption of a two-target policy based on both money and credit.

Inflation and Interest Rates

Lawrence H. Summers's paper studies the long-run relationship between interest rates and inflation and finds that interest rates do not respond to inflation in the way the classical theories suggest. Summers concludes that economic models of fully informed and rational agents do not fit the empirical evidence. To explain the puzzle, he suggests that the concept of money illusion may help to clarify the behavior of interest rates and inflation.

Summers first considers the theoretical relationship between rates of interest and inflation in both the short and long run using a simple general-equilibrium macroeconomic model. According to the model, the relationship between movements in inflation and interest rates will depend on the nature of the shocks—the exogenous forcing variables—affecting the system. Summers points out that, while there is little reason to expect any stable relation between short-term movements in interest rates and inflation, the model yields more explicit long-run predictions. The nonneutrality of the tax system having been taken into account, the parameter measuring the long-run effect of a change in the rate of inflation on interest rates is estimated at greater than one. The model can be manipulated to yield predictions about this long-run relationship, because it implies that in the long run the level of inflation is determined only by the rate of money growth. Since there is no obvious reason for expecting the rate of money growth to be determined by any real factors, inflation is in effect determined exogenously in the long run.

Summers next examines historical data on the relationship between interest rates and inflation. Neither ten-year averages of the rates of inflation and nominal interest rates for the United States for the period 1860–1979 nor regression analyses using these data show a clear relationship between inflation and nominal interest rates. Nor does using average rates of inflation and interest rates over the course of business cycles change the results. Summers points out that the traditional approach to the study of the relationship between interest rates and inflation, which involves the estimation of equations relating short-term interest rates to the expected rate of inflation, may not be meaningful because of the existence of simultaneity in such equations. For this reason it is not surprising to him that such analyses have not borne out the relationship between inflation and interest rates observed by Irving Fisher and that the results are highly unstable through time. (In the appendix to his paper, Summers shows that recent attempts to reestimate the relationship and provide evidence of the Fisher effect also yield unsatisfactory results for most sample periods.)

According to the standard model previously described, the relationship to be determined is that between steady state inflation (generated by the rate of money growth) and interest rates. As the model exhibits approximate superneutrality in the absence of taxes, real interest rates should be essentially unaffected by changes in the rate of inflation and the coefficient for the expected rate of inflation should equal one. Using spectral regression techniques that allow the user to filter out high-frequency movements in the variables (and, here, to represent a steady state), Summers tests the hypothesis that the long-run (low-frequency) relationship between interest rates and inflation is stronger than the high-frequency relationships that dominate movements over the course of the business cycle.

Focusing first on the 1860–1940 period, Summers begins by replicating Fisher's work in order to estimate the effect of changes in the expected rate of inflation on interest rates. The results do not demonstrate the empirical validity of what has become known as the Fisher effect (although Fisher's conclusions were overstated by later authors). Summers then estimates equations describing the relationships between inflation and short- and long-term interest rates, at various frequencies. For the entire 1860–1940 period, the highest estimate of the effect of inflation is only 0.12, and for 1870–1900 the relationship is actually negative. (The failure of interest rates to adjust to changes in inflationary expectations is confirmed in the appendix with the use of more standard techniques.) Summers notes that the strong evidence against the Fisher proposition for the prewar period is particularly striking because rigidities in the economy were virtually nonexistent and taxes were negligible. This suggests that the failure of interest rates to fully adjust to inflation reflects something more fundamental than the effect of institutional nonneutralities.

Turning to the postwar period, Summers estimates for various intervals the parameter that measures the effect of the expected rate of inflation on both short- and long-term interest rates. There is little or no evidence that, as predicted in the model, this parameter is greater than, or even equal to, one. It appears that almost all the power in the Fisher relationship comes from the acceleration of inflation during the 1960s. However, the coefficient on inflation does increase as the length of the cycle increases; it rises from 0.24 to 0.73 in the long-term interest-rate regressions.

In the standard model, one potential explanation of the behavior of interest rates is that steady state (low-frequency) movements in the rate of inflation are associated with other factors, or variables, that also affect real interest rates. The Fisher effect should hold if these variables are taken into account. Though Summers estimates a large number of equations, he does not find any such variables.

Another potential explanation of the nonadjustment of interest rates to inflation is the existence of some unmeasurable variable which is correlated with inflation and which affects required returns. Summers, then, examines by regression the low-frequency relation between inflation and alternative indicators of the real interest rate: rates of return and earnings and dividend price ratios for various periods. The results indicate that there is no strong relation between inflation and any of the three variables. In further examining the puzzling behavior of the interest rates and the stock market, Summers finds that inflation has substantially widened the spread between the expected return on debt and equity. This finding supports the view that investors suffer from money illusion, or confuse nominal and real interest rates in valuing stock.

The hypothesis that some form of money illusion exists in financial markets could explain the observed relationships between inflation and interest rates. According to this hypothesis, prewar-period agents ignored inflation in making financial calculations, and as the average inflation rate increased during the postwar period, investors' sophistication increased and the market partially but not fully reflected the impact of changes in inflation. Finally, Summers explains that some form of inflation illusion is plausible in financial markets and that it is not readily susceptible to elimination by market forces.

Macroeconomic Theories

In his paper, William Nordhaus discusses the prominent macroeconomic theories of the day in relation to the key policy issues of the 1980s. Nordhaus holds that the "neo-Keynesian synthesis"—the synthesis of Keynesian and neoclassical economics—is the best way to understand the puzzles of the economy as well as the dilemmas of policy.

Before discussing the theories and corresponding policy implications, Nordhaus enumerates the central problems for macroeconomic theory: slow productivity growth, chronic inflation, high unemployment, and vulnerability to volatile oil and foreign exchange markets. In achieving the major goals of economic policy, economic performance over the last decade in the United States has been poor in all respects. The problems for theory, about which there is little consensus, are to explain the causes of these economic problems and to devise policy solutions.

As appropriate policy depends on the theory, Nordhaus first identifies the chief elements of the neo-Keynesian synthesis and then compares it with the major competing paradigms—monetarism, rational expectations, and supply-side economics.

He describes four central elements in the neo-Keynesian synthesis, the first being the distinction between actual and potential output. Actual output can be thought of as "demand" and potential output as "supply." One central element of the neo-Keynesian synthesis is that distinct forces determine supply and demand and that both sides require attention from economic policy. The second feature is that potential output is determined by a production function with labor, capital, energy, and other, material inputs. Assuming that the rate of technological change is exogenously given, policy can affect potential output growth by altering the growth of inputs. However, empirical evidence indicates that the growth rate of potential output is not easily affected by policy. Though the determination of potential output is not subject to much debate (even by the critics of this theory), the various paradigms differ in explaining how *actual* output is determined. The third feature of the neo-Keynesian synthesis is that actual output is determined by aggregate spending, which in turn depends on fiscal and monetary policies. Both types of policy have substantial impacts on actual output, but there is much more uncertainty about money multipliers than about the fiscal multipliers. The final feature concerns the division of the growth of nominal GNP between prices and quantities. Nordhaus notes evidence indicating that around 90 percent of the first-year response to a spending shock shows up in output and 10 percent in prices, a finding that was repeatedly emphasized by Arthur Okun.

Nordhaus next discusses the other macroeconomic paradigms, again emphasizing only those aspects of the theories that relate to economic policy. He interprets monetarism as a special case of the neo-Keynesian synthesis. The major differences between the two concern output determination and the inflation process. In the strict monetarist view money velocity is interest-inelastic, so nominal GNP is determined by the money stock. Prices adjust relatively rapidly to demand or supply shocks, so that inflation can be cured with little cost simply by reducing the growth rates of the money supply. Nordhaus argues that there is little empirical support for these propositions and that there is still a wide divergence among monetarists about the costs of disinflation.

The rational expectations, or new classical macroeconomics, view rests on two premises: economic agents form expectations on the basis of all available information and all markets clear in the very short run (that is, prices are perfectly flexible). According to this view, actual output never deviates from potential except for random shocks, while 100 percent of the anticipated changes in nominal GNP go into prices.

Policy therefore cannot affect the real economy, but disinflation is an easy and costless process, merely involving an announced and credible reduction in aggregate demand. Nordhaus acknowledges that these views have been influential with the economics profession, but the idea that policy cannot affect the real economy is strange to economic practitioners and policymakers.

Supply-side economics holds that economic activity responds quickly to changes in relative prices, particularly to changes in tax rates, but that aggregate income effects are unimportant. If this view of the world is correct, growth in potential output can be readily enhanced by personal and business tax cuts, without worry about what happens to aggregate demand. The major problem with this theory, Nordhaus explains, is the failure to distinguish between actual and potential output, which leaves supply siders without a consistent view of the inflation process.

Finally, Nordhaus discusses five issues that must be faced by policymakers over the coming years. The first is whether economic policy should be subject to strict legal constraints. The recent trend toward "economic constitutionalism" is intended to impose stricter economic discipline on economic decisionmakers, who are regarded as untrustworthy and lacking credibility. Nordhaus believes that the use of rigid rules is a second-best solution to stabilizing the economy or reaching the appropriate balance between the public and private sectors.

The second issue, which Nordhaus labels "deficism," is the call for a balanced federal budget as a cure for high interest rates, high inflation, and swollen government. Nordhaus argues that deficism is a highly imperfect instrument for controlling economic activity and is fundamentally flawed as an economic doctrine.

Nordhaus discusses the issue of monetarism only briefly because the debate is so well known. Most striking to him is that the debate continues, given the weaknesses of monetarist doctrine—the evidence of interest-sensitivity of the demand for money, the instability of the definition of money, and the unreliable nature of the relationship between interest rates and output.

Though supply siders and neo-Malthusians (those who believe that limitations of resources and energy constrain economic growth) dissent, there is otherwise a consensus about the appropriate policy to spur productivity, the fourth issue. Virtually all economists have called for one of an assortment of pro-saving or pro-investment tax and monetary policies to increase the growth of potential output.

The final issue is how to solve chronic inflation. Most of the recent inquiry into the mechanics of the inflation process and the dilemmas of policy has been undertaken in the framework of the neo-Keynesian synthesis. It is widely agreed that the orthodox way of slowing chronic inflation—inducing slack in product and labor markets—is extremely costly. Nordhaus points out that accepting inflation as the major constraint on high levels of utilization of labor and capital requires the development of new and more efficient anti-inflation policies. He identifies two such classes of policies—cost-reducing policies such as cutting indirect taxes and promoting productivity, and incomes policies to moderate the pace of price and wage increases—which were prominent elements in Arthur Okun's program to combat inflation and achieve a satisfactory rate of economic growth.

Macroeconomic Policies

The volume ends with contributions by Robert A. Mundell and James Tobin on macroeconomic policy. Mundell argues that macroeconomists of both the Keynesian and monetarist schools neglected to take into account the effect of the international monetary system on domestic policies. According to Mundell, no country can disassociate its monetary system from that prevailing elsewhere in the world. To achieve a stable and predictable monetary standard, he advocates a return to the gold standard with fixed exchange rates, a budget policy that preserves internal balance, and reductions in key tax rates with an accommodating monetary policy to promote stable economic growth.

James Tobin attacks the widely held view that the inherited wage and price inflation can be eliminated without much economic pain by the public announcement of a resolute irreversible policy of monetary inflation. He recalls Arthur Okun's warning that the era of chronic inflation will end with a deep and prolonged recession and points out that Okun has been vindicated by recent developments in both Great Britain and the United States. He endorses Okun's view that the heavy cost of disinflation can be moderated only if an incomes policy is adopted and is made credible by a consensus of labor and management engineered by the president.

Labor Markets

MARTIN NEIL BAILY

The Labor Market in the 1930s

ALTHOUGH he was probably best known as an adviser on economic policy issues, Arthur Okun was also a keen student of macroeconomic theory. His firm grasp of the analytical foundations of economics enabled him to provide sound policy advice. In the first six chapters of his *Prices and Quantities* he "focused on the descriptive and analytical aspects of price and quantity adjustments."[1] He felt strongly that good macro policy should be grounded in a believable theory of wage and employment adjustment. He regarded neither the post-Keynesian analysis nor the new classical or equilibrium models as satisfactory, but constructed his own institutionally oriented version of implicit contract theory to explain observed behavior.

Because it has proven hard or impossible to resolve major theoretical and policy issues from postwar data, interest in macroeconomic history has recently increased. This paper is such an attempt to learn from earlier times. No one doubts that the Great Depression was a turning point for economic theory and policy, yet despite its importance no generally accepted theory of wage and employment adjustment has emerged from that period. Keynesians have criticized Robert Lucas, arguing that his model is inconsistent with the depression. And Lucas has conceded that his "theory postulated lags in the adjustment of price-wage expectations as the *only* source of 'rigidity' or of the persistence of unemployment. In fact, other important sources of rigidity were present in the Great Depression."[2] But he counters that the depression creates a problem not only for his model but for any theory. "Once one attempts to obtain a quantitative explanation for wage-price rigidity in terms of individual

My thanks to Lesley Kalmin and Suzanne M. Wehrs for excellent research assistance.

1. Arthur M. Okun, *Prices and Quantities: A Macroeconomic Analysis* (Brookings Institution, 1981), p. 263.

2. Robert E. Lucas, Jr., and Leonard A. Rapping, "Unemployment in the Great Depression: Is There a Full Explanation?" *Journal of Political Economy*, vol. 80 (January–February 1972), p. 190.

and market behavior, there *is* no traditional theory to return to."[3] And Okun sounds a similar note when he argues that Keynesian analysis is faulty: "Of the various empirical shortcomings of the Keynesian wage-floor model, its predictions about productivity, real wages, and factor shares over the cycle are glaringly inaccurate. . . . [This leaves] the *General Theory* without a microeconomic underpinning or a macroeconomic distribution theory."[4]

In this paper I describe the central features of the labor market during the 1930s and then ask if the behavior of individuals and markets is explicable within some framework of rational decisionmaking. The standard of rationality applied, however, is not that markets will show rational expectations as this concept is now understood. The hypothesis that labor and product markets are "efficient," so that widely available information about monetary disturbances has no effect on output or unemployment, has not been supported by the empirical work of the proponents of the hypothesis.[5] Rather, the concept of rationality used here is that the decisions made by individuals had a sound economic basis, given their own past experience and the extent of their understanding of the workings of the system as a whole—bounded rationality, if you like.

A Description of the Labor Market

Compensation and Weekly Hours

Table 1 shows hourly compensation in current dollars and the average number of weekly hours for all employees and for production workers in manufacturing from 1920 to 1945. Also shown are consumer prices and wholesale finished goods prices. Table 2 shows rates of growth of nominal and real wages. The series for manufacturing earnings was

3. Ibid., p. 191.

4. Okun, *Prices and Quantities*, p. 16.

5. Thomas J. Sargent, "Rational Expectations, the Real Rate of Interest, and the Natural Rate of Unemployment," *Brookings Papers on Economic Activity, 2:1973*, pp. 429–72; Robert J. Barro, "Unanticipated Money Growth and Unemployment in the United States," *American Economic Review*, vol. 67 (March 1977), pp. 101–15; and John F. Boschen and Herschel I. Grossman, "Tests of Equilibrium Macroeconomics Using Contemporaneous Monetary Data," Working Paper 558R (National Bureau of Economic Research, October 1981).

Table 1. *Hourly Earnings and Weekly Hours, 1920–45*

Year	Average earnings (dollars per hour)		Average hours worked per week		Whole-sale price index, finished goods[d]	Con-sumer price index, all goods[d]
	All employees[a]	Production workers, manufacturing[b]	All employees (full-time-equivalent)	Production workers, manufacturing[c]		
1920	0.519	0.537	49.7	47.4	158	117
1921	0.499	0.464	47.3	43.1	109	104
1922	0.475	0.435	48.2	44.2	102	98
1923	0.502	0.479	48.9	45.6	105	100
1924	0.512	0.498	48.6	43.7	102	100
1925	0.517	0.497	49.0	44.5	106	102
1926	0.525	0.503	49.3	45.0	106	103
1927	0.542	0.510	49.0	45.0	100	101
1928	0.544	0.513	49.0	44.4	101	100
1929	0.563	0.526	48.6	44.2	100	100
1930	0.560	0.526	47.6	42.1	93	97
1931	0.532	0.503	46.8	40.5	81	89
1932	0.485	0.446	45.2	38.3	74	80
1933	0.457	0.441	44.9	38.1	75	76
1934	0.512	0.527	41.7	34.6	83	78
1935	0.524	0.542	42.5	36.6	87	80
1936	0.534	0.553	43.6	39.2	87	81
1937	0.566	0.633	44.4	38.6	92	84
1938	0.576	0.639	43.0	35.6	87	82
1939	0.583	0.638	43.7	37.7	85	81
1940	0.597	0.670	43.8	38.1	86	82
1941	0.655	0.737	44.2	40.6	94	86
1942	0.758	0.864	45.0	43.1	104	95
1943	0.838	0.975	46.3	45.0	106	101
1944	0.903	1.050	46.6	45.2	107	103
1945	0.984	1.060	44.8	43.5	108	105

Sources: Bureau of the Census, *Historical Statistics of the United States: Colonial Times to 1970* (Government Printing Office, 1975), pp. 164, 169, 174; Edward F. Denison, *The Sources of Economic Growth in the United States and the Alternatives Before Us* (New York: Committee for Economic Development, 1962), p. 37; and Albert Rees, "Patterns of Wages, Prices and Productivity," in American Assembly, *Wages, Prices, Profits and Productivity,* Background Papers and the Final Report of the Fifteenth American Assembly (American Assembly, 1959), pp. 15, 27.

a. Full-time-equivalent employees' earnings, plus supplements to wages and salaries. Pre-1929 series is Lebergott's earning series "when employed," excluding armed forces and without wage supplements.

b. Increases in paid holidays, vacations, and sick leave will increase average hourly earnings. The years 1929–45 include wage supplements—old-age and survivors insurance, unemployment insurance, workmen's compensation, and private pension, welfare, and insurance plans. Pre-1929 supplements are mostly workmen's compensation and are considered negligible.

c. Hours include paid vacations and holidays, considered insignificant before 1940.

d. 1929 = 100.

Table 2. *Average Annual Growth of Nominal and Real Wages,*
1920–41

Percent

Period	Hourly earnings, all employees			Hourly earnings, production workers, manufacturing		
	Nominal	Real (WPI)	Real (CPI)	Nominal	Real (WPI)	Real (CPI)
1920–22	−4.50	17.38	4.50	−10.53	11.35	−1.53
1922–29	2.44	2.72	2.10	2.71	3.00	2.38
1929–33	−5.20	1.99	1.86	−4.41	2.79	2.66
1933–37	5.35	0.24	2.70	9.04	3.93	6.39
1937–41	3.63	3.09	3.05	3.80	3.27	3.22

Sources: Same as table 1.

constructed by Albert Rees; the series for all employees is the same as that used by Robert Lucas and Leonard Rapping in their model of the business cycle.[6] The latter series is derived by taking the annual earnings of workers when fully employed and dividing by the annual average hours of full-time-equivalent workers, estimated by Edward Denison.

The fall in nominal wages from 1929 to 1933 was pronounced for both series, totaling 17.6 percent in manufacturing and 20.8 percent overall.[7] The depression gives no support whatsoever to the hypothesis that a given level or rate of change of money wages has special significance. For neither series was the nominal decline enough to create a decline in real wages. The consumer price index fell 28.2 percent and the wholesale price index 31.2 percent over the same period, so real wages actually rose by between 7 and 11 percent. For neither series is any appreciable decline in nominal wage rates observed between 1929 and 1930 despite the sharp rise in unemployment and the rapid decline in industrial production that had begun in the fall of 1929.

The two wage series do move against each other quite noticeably. Nominal compensation for manufacturing production workers was actually lower in 1929 than in 1920. Between 1920 and 1922 compensation per hour dropped 21 percent and only 19 percent of this had been regained by 1929.

6. Robert E. Lucas, Jr., and Leonard A. Rapping, "Real Wages, Employment, and Inflation," in Edmund S. Phelps and others, *Microeconomic Foundations of Employment and Inflation Theory* (Norton, 1970), pp. 257–305.

7. All percentages are computed as 100 times logarithmic changes. Rates of growth or decline between two years, t and $t + T$, are these changes divided by T.

The growth of both real and nominal wages after 1933 is remarkable. For example, for manufacturing production workers average real compensation measured against consumer prices rose by 25.6 percent between 1933 and 1937, a period when the unemployment rate averaged 19.6 percent. The growth in average real compensation for all workers was much lower at 10.8 percent, but that is still pretty high. Almost all of the increase in real compensation came in two years. Real compensation for manufacturing workers rose by 14.6 percent in 1933–34 and by 10.2 percent in 1936–37. Since the wholesale price index rose relative to the CPI over these years, the rise in the producer real wage was much smaller. In fact, the producer real wage for all employees was flat in 1933–37. The sharp increases in wages in two years strongly suggest the importance of institutional changes, particularly the National Industrial Recovery Act and the growth of unions. But making the case that such institutional changes can cause these dramatic increases in nominal and in consumer real wages despite massive unemployment is not going to be easy.

After 1937 nominal wage growth did slow; it equalized in the two series but remained high relative to the period up to 1929. In 1941 real compensation was up from 1937 a full 12.8 percent in manufacturing and 12.2 percent overall. The real economy was growing during the 1937–41 period, of course, but unemployment still averaged 15 percent, and there was a sharp recession in 1938.

The figures for average weekly hours show a marked cyclical pattern implying that average weekly earnings in nominal dollars fell somewhat more than nominal wages in the early years of the depression. Full-time workers in the whole economy experienced a decline in weekly earnings of 28.7 percent in nominal dollars. This was about the same as the fall in the consumer price index, so that persons who were fully employed throughout the 1929–33 period maintained their real incomes, but no more than this. In manufacturing, average weekly hours fell more than in the economy as a whole (by 16.6 percent) so that real weekly earnings fell even for those who remained fully employed.

Weekly hours fell sharply in 1933–34, 7.5 percent overall and 9.6 percent for manufacturing. This meant that over half the increase in hourly wages from 1933 to 1934 did not translate into real weekly earnings increases. By 1937, however, hours had returned to their 1933 level, and by 1941 they were actually equal to or above their 1933 level; weekly earnings thus grew as fast as or faster than hourly earnings after 1933.

Table 3. *Indexes of Employment, Total Hours, and Unemployment, 1920–45*
1929 = 100 unless otherwise specified

Year	Employment			Hours				Unemployment rate[a]
	Total civilian	Private non-farm	Production workers, manufacturing	All employees	Private non-farm	Manufacturing	Production workers, manufacturing	
1920	84.9	88.6	101.0	89.1	85.3	107.3	108.3	5.2
1921	80.2	78.3	77.3	80.5	76.2	75.4	75.4	11.7
1922	85.8	85.5	85.5	86.2	82.9	84.7	85.5	6.7
1923	91.8	94.5	97.9	92.9	91.7	99.3	101.0	2.4
1924	91.0	91.7	90.9	91.0	88.4	89.2	89.9	5.0
1925	94.6	95.4	94.1	94.3	92.2	93.4	94.7	3.2
1926	97.0	98.1	95.9	97.5	96.3	96.4	97.6	1.8
1927	97.1	97.4	93.8	97.1	96.6	95.2	95.5	3.3
1928	97.7	97.3	94.0	98.1	97.3	94.2	94.4	4.2
1929	100.0	100.0	100.0	100.0	100.0	100.0	100.0	3.2
1930	95.6	92.9	87.1	93.5	91.5	85.0	93.0	8.9
1931	89.4	82.7	73.5	85.5	80.9	69.3	67.4	16.3
1932	82.3	72.2	62.5	75.6	69.4	55.4	54.1	24.1
1933	82.4	72.7	69.1	76.0	68.4	59.4	59.6	25.2
1934	87.2	80.1	80.6	76.8	69.6	62.6	63.1	22.0
1935	90.2	83.4	86.1	81.1	73.8	70.4	71.3	20.3
1936	95.2	89.9	93.5	89.3	82.1	81.7	83.0	17.0
1937	99.7	96.4	102.6	93.2	86.7	88.4	89.6	14.3
1938	95.5	89.6	87.3	86.8	78.7	70.4	70.3	19.1
1939	99.0	94.2	97.1	90.6	84.1	81.5	82.8	17.2
1940	102.8	99.6	104.4	94.5	89.2	89.9	90.0	14.6
1941	109.0	112.8	128.6	104.5	99.8	115.5	118.1	9.9
1942	116.3	122.5	151.7	116.3	108.5	141.8	147.9	4.7
1943	117.9	128.6	176.8	131.4	113.6	168.9	180.0	1.9
1944	116.8	126.8	172.1	134.2	111.8	166.8	175.9	1.2
1945	114.3	121.8	151.9	125.8	106.1	142.9	149.4	1.9

Sources: Bureau of the Census, *Historical Statistics: Colonial Times to 1970*, pp. 126, 138, 169; Denison, *Sources of Economic Growth*, pp. 35, 37; and Bureau of Economic Analysis, *Long Term Economic Growth, 1860–1970* (GPO, 1973), p. 193.
a. As percent of civilian labor force.

Employment, Total Hours, and Unemployment

The paths of employment, hours, and unemployment (table 3) move in a way that is mutually consistent and follows the known pattern of the cycle during the depression, and there is less to be said here. In fact, the unemployment numbers are derived from the employment series because there was no comprehensive survey of unemployment during the 1930s. Census figures for 1920, 1930, and 1940 provide benchmark years for labor-force estimation.

Private nonfarm employment fell 32.6 percent between 1929 and 1933; production worker employment in manufacturing fell 47.1 percent through 1932. Denison's total hours measure fell 27.9 percent from 1929 to 1932 and stayed flat through 1934. Hours of production workers in manufacturing fell an astounding 61 percent from 1929 to 1932 (a 20 percent rate of annual decline) and by 1934 were still down 46 percent from their 1929 level. Total hours in manufacturing, which include hours of white-collar workers, stayed very close to the hours for production workers alone. Unlike the typical cycle of recent years, it seems that white-collar workers did not benefit from greater job security than blue-collar employees.

Both hours and employment rose rapidly after 1933. Private nonfarm employment rose 28.3 percent between 1933 and 1937. The figure for production workers in manufacturing was 49.6 percent between 1932 and 1937. This means that all or almost all of the employment lost from 1929 to 1932 or 1933 had been regained by 1937. Total hours had not fully regained their 1929 level by 1937 because weekly hours remained below their 1929 level. Total hours and all employee hours in manufacturing remained 7.0 percent and 12.3 percent, respectively, below their 1929 levels.

The economy turned down into the second dip of the depression in 1938, with nonfarm employment falling 7.4 percent and the employment of production workers in manufacturing falling 16.2 percent in one year. Weekly hours also fell. The recovery was rapid after 1938, however, with employment and total hours both exceeding their 1929 level by 1941 and continuing to grow during World War II.

Population and labor force growth continues whether the economy is depressed or not, so the unemployment rate remained very high in 1937 and was still high in 1941 even though the 1929 levels of employment had been reached or exceeded in those years. Since the census years of 1930 and 1940 missed the worst years of the depression, it is possible that some workers became discouraged in their job search and withdrew from the labor force. If so, the official unemployment rate overstates the amount of open unemployment, because no adjustment has been made for discouragement.[8] Also, as Michael Darby has pointed out, workers employed on government WPA (Works Progress Administration) projects are counted as unemployed.[9] Such employment reached 2.5 million, plus about another 1.2 million in various other public works programs, in 1936, a year when about 9 million were counted as unemployed. In 1940 WPA employment was about 2 million (plus 0.8 million in other works programs), out of 8 million who were unemployed.

Turnover in Manufacturing

Beginning in 1926 surveys of manufacturing establishments were made (by the Metropolitan Life Insurance Company) that measured the turnover of production workers, with turnover rates expressed per 100 workers per month. Retrospective surveys were then used to estimate turnover back to 1919. The rates were calculated as unweighted medians through 1929 and as average values thereafter. The Bureau of Labor Statistics (BLS) took over the survey in 1929. The data are shown in table 4. They are not fully comparable with postwar series even after 1930 because only production workers are counted and intercompany transfers are excluded.[10]

From 1920 to 1929 the reported layoff rate was very low. The highest, 1.8, was for 1921, a year in which the unemployment rate had jumped to 11.7 percent. (In 1958, when the unemployment rate was 6.8 percent, the layoff rate was 2.6.) In his 1942 study of labor turnover, W. S. Woytinsky gave turnover data for 1930 from the Metropolitan Life

8. For a discussion of this point, see Robert M. Coen, "Labor Force and Unemployment in the 1920's and 1930's: A Re-examination Based on Postwar Experience," *Review of Economics and Statistics,* vol. 55 (February 1973), pp. 46–55.

9. Michael R. Darby, "Three-and-a-Half Million U.S. Employees Have Been Mislaid: Or, an Explanation of Unemployment, 1934–1941," *Journal of Political Economy,* vol. 84 (February 1976), pp. 1–16.

10. Beginning in 1943, all employees are included, and intercompany transfers are included from 1959 on. The 1929 figure is for January to May only.

Table 4. *Labor Turnover in Manufacturing, 1920–45*[a]
Average monthly rate per 100 employees

| Year | Accessions | Separations | | |
		Total	Layoffs	Quits[b]
1920	10.1	10.3	0.8	8.4
1921	2.8	4.4	1.8	2.2
1922	8.0	5.3	0.4	4.2
1923	9.0	7.5	0.3	6.2
1924	3.3	3.8	0.6	2.7
1925	5.2	4.0	0.4	3.1
1926	4.5	3.9	0.5	2.9
1927	3.3	3.3	0.7	2.1
1928	3.7	3.1	0.5	2.2
1929	5.1	3.9	0.4	3.0
1930	3.8	5.9	3.6	1.9
1931	3.7	4.8	3.5	1.1
1932	4.1	5.2	4.2	0.9
1933	6.5	4.5	3.2	1.1
1934	5.7	4.9	3.7	1.1
1935	5.1	4.3	3.0	1.1
1936	5.3	4.0	2.4	1.3
1937	4.3	5.2	3.5	1.5
1938	4.7	4.8	3.9	0.8
1939	5.0	3.7	2.6	1.0
1940	5.4	4.0	2.6	1.1
1941	6.5	4.7	1.6	2.4
1942	9.3	7.8	1.3	4.6
1943	9.1	8.6	0.7	6.3
1944	7.4	8.1	0.7	6.2
1945	7.7	9.6	2.6	6.1

Source: Bureau of the Census, *Historical Statistics: Colonial Times to 1970*, pp. 181–82.
a. Beginning in 1930, averages are arithmetic means; before that, they are unweighted medians. Pre-1943 data pertain to production workers only.
b. Data before 1940 include miscellaneous separations.

survey and also from the BLS survey, and reported the following monthly rates per 100 workers:[11]

	Accessions	Separations	Layoffs	Quits
Metropolitan Life	1.6	2.4	1.2	1.1
BLS	3.1	5.0	3.0	1.6

11. W. S. Woytinsky, *Three Aspects of Labor Dynamics*, Report Prepared for the Committee on Social Security (Washington, D.C.: Social Science Research Council, 1942), p. 44.

There is some discrepancy between Woytinsky's BLS numbers and those for 1930 in table 4, even though the BLS is the original source of the table 4 numbers. But the main divergence occurred when the BLS took over the survey. The early surveys showed turnover rates only about one-half of the later, more comprehensive results. The small sample and the use of a median value presumably account for this.[12]

The turnover data for the period 1930–41 show a pattern of considerable interest. As one would expect, the layoff rate in the early years of the depression was very high, averaging 3.8 per 100 workers per month over the three years 1930–32, when employment was tumbling. But the accession, or hiring, rate was also very high during these years, averaging 3.9, a figure that is about the same as the layoff rate. Until 1940 the quit rate included miscellaneous separations such as retirements, deaths, and military duty. The quit rate, thus defined, averaged 1.3 over the period 1930–32, while discharges added another 0.2 to the separation rate. The decline in employment then comes about because total separations, including layoffs, quits, and discharges, exceeded accessions by an average of 1.4 over the three years. This compounds to an annual rate of employment decline of about 18 percent—roughly consistent with, but a little higher than, that shown by the employment series.

Monthly turnover data are also available for 1919–40 from Woytinsky. Through 1929 the figures are from Metropolitan Life and hence suspect. But the month-to-month changes for 1929 are interesting and probably indicative of the true monthly pattern:[13]

	Accessions	*Layoffs*	*Quits*
January	5.2	0.3	2.9
February	5.2	0.4	2.5
March	5.2	0.4	3.1
April	5.4	0.5	3.0
May	4.6	0.5	3.0
June	4.6	0.4	3.0
July	5.0	0.5	2.9
August	4.1	0.5	2.8
September	4.2	0.7	2.3
October	3.4	0.9	2.3
November	2.3	1.1	2.0
December	1.8	1.2	1.7

12. I am guessing that the distribution of layoffs across firms is skewed so that the median is below the mean.

13. I seasonally adjusted the original series presented by Woytinsky. The figures for

The first signs of the downturn appear in August, as the accession rate dropped. The layoff rate began to rise in September and the quit rate dropped in the same month. By December the accession rate was one-third of its January to July average, while the layoff rate was nearly three times the size and the quit rate only about one-half of their levels early in the year. The downturn shows up quickly and dramatically in all the turnover series. Perhaps the most striking of the three is the quit rate. It seems that workers realized very quickly that alternative job opportunities had deteriorated.

Monthly BLS data after 1929 show no big surprises not seen in the annual data. The layoff rate peaked and began to decline in the summer of 1932 and accessions began to pick up about the same time. Accessions did surge dramatically in the summer of 1933, the rate averaging 8.9 a month for May through August.[14]

The annual or monthly series thus show a very large labor turnover relative to the changes in the stock of workers. This has also been a distinctive feature of the postwar labor market, but I was surprised that the same pattern was so pronounced during the depression. The high turnover rates persisted right through the depression, with the layoff rate averaging 3.2 from 1933 to 1937 and 2.7 from 1938 to 1941. Employment security did not occur even when the level of employment began to rise after 1932 for manufacturing production workers. The difference between the phases of the cycle, of course, came about because accessions exceeded separations in every year after 1932 except 1937 and (marginally) 1938.

Turnover among the Unemployed

Although comprehensive and regular unemployment surveys were not conducted before World War II, there were periodic small surveys. Many of these are reported and analyzed by Woytinsky. It is difficult to know exactly how to compare the findings of these surveys with modern

---

1929 shown in table 4 are consistent with the monthly data shown here, since the average is for January through May only. Bureau of the Census, *Historical Statistics of the United States: Colonial Times to 1970* (Government Printing Office, 1975), pt. 1, p. 160, states that the BLS took over the survey in July and implies Metropolitan Life stopped at that point. Woytinsky, however, reports Metropolitan Life figures for all of 1929 and 1930, as reported here.

14. This figure is not seasonally adjusted.

analyses of transition probabilities and the durations of spells of unemployment, because the methods and definitions were different. Some early surveys made no attempt to distinguish people unemployed according to today's definition from those retired or otherwise out of the labor force. The unemployed were those looking for jobs or those who had had jobs at one time. And the distinction remained fuzzy in surveys taken in the 1930s. Old-age assistance came in with the New Deal, but it is likely that some of the recipients were counted as unemployed by surveys.

But the survey evidence still leaves a strong impression that part of the labor force experienced high turnover and rapid reemployment and part consisted of hard-core unemployed with very long spells of unemployment. In a surprisingly modern-sounding dual-labor-market framework, Woytinsky suggests "the existence of two contrasting groups among the unemployed: persons who have a fair chance of reemployment in the near future, and those who remain out of jobs for considerable periods of time."[15]

The empirical evidence for his assertion comes from surveys of unemployment duration taken annually during the 1930s in Buffalo, Lincoln (Nebraska), and Philadelphia. These duration distributions record spells still uncompleted at the time and show a bimodal pattern with many short spells and many very long spells.[16] The proportion of very long spells increases among survey respondents through the middle 1930s. To give a striking example: in 1937, 61.7 percent of the unemployed males in Philadelphia reported uncompleted spells in excess of one year (21.6 percent in excess of five years), and 28.3 percent reported uncompleted spells of less than six months (18.7 percent less than two months).

In other years or other cities the bimodality is less evident—any dual-labor-market model is somewhat oversimplified. And one may wonder how someone unemployed for over five years or even over one year would be counted in today's Current Population Survey.[17] But the basic idea is surely correct. The establishment turnover data show frequent layoffs and hirings and the survey data show many unemployed for short spells. Unless the surveys are spurious, however, long-term unemploy-

15. *Three Aspects,* p. 67.
16. Ibid., pp. 86–103.
17. The Philadelphia survey showed an overall unemployment rate of 27.1 percent in 1937, when the estimated national rate was 14.3 percent. The latter figure is based on employment and estimated labor-force figures.

ment was contributing a major fraction of the total number of weeks of unemployment, at least after 1932.

Output and Productivity

The figures for real output shown in table 5 complete the picture of what happened to the real economy and need no further comment. The figures for average labor productivity are of interest because they show that, unlike postwar business cycles, the extent of labor hoarding was

Table 5. *Indexes of Output and Productivity, 1920–45*
1929 = 100 unless otherwise specified

Year	Real GNP (billions of 1958 dollars)	Output		Output per worker-hour	
		Private non-farm	Manufac-turing	Private non-farm	Manufac-turing
1920	140.0	71.9	66.0	79.5	61.5
1921	127.8	70.6	53.5	86.1	71.0
1922	148.0	74.7	68.0	83.9	80.4
1923	165.9	85.7	77.0	87.8	77.3
1924	165.5	89.2	73.5	93.3	82.3
1925	179.4	90.7	82.0	92.6	87.7
1926	190.0	97.6	86.2	95.0	89.4
1927	189.8	98.2	87.0	95.4	91.5
1928	190.9	99.7	90.0	96.1	95.6
1929	203.6	100.0	100.0	100.0	100.0
1930	183.5	87.8	85.5	97.0	100.6
1931	169.3	78.0	72.0	98.5	103.8
1932	144.2	63.6	53.8	95.4	97.1
1933	141.5	62.0	62.7	93.2	105.6
1934	154.3	70.3	69.0	103.3	110.4
1935	169.5	77.7	82.8	106.7	117.7
1936	193.0	91.2	96.7	111.3	118.5
1937	203.2	96.2	103.2	110.4	116.7
1938	192.9	88.9	81.0	113.5	115.2
1939	209.4	98.6	102.5	117.6	125.8
1940	227.2	109.0	118.8	122.2	132.1
1941	263.7	127.2	158.0	124.2	136.9
1942	297.8	138.7	197.2	123.3	139.2
1943	337.1	149.4	238.3	124.6	141.2
1944	361.3	158.3	232.5	134.4	139.4
1945	355.2	156.4	196.5	142.0	137.5

Sources: Bureau of Economic Analysis, *Long Term Economic Growth, 1860–1970*, pp. 185, 211; and Bureau of the Census, *Historical Statistics: Colonial Times to 1970*, p. 224.

small and short-lived. Joseph Schumpeter said that the depression had been an "efficiency expert," claiming that average labor productivity had actually risen between 1929 and 1932 in manufacturing.[18] Subsequent estimates do not confirm this strong assertion, but his basic idea seems correct. Labor productivity dipped only slightly as output and employment fell substantially. By 1934 productivity was growing rapidly; this growth continued into the 1940s, with the 1937–38 recession having only a modest effect. When firms fear for their own existence they do not conserve excess workers. Instead they encourage managers and production workers alike to increase efficiency and prevent bankruptcy.

The Fall in Aggregate Demand

Recent literature on the depression concentrates on the reasons aggregate demand fell so much and failed to recover fully. More specifically, whether the Federal Reserve can be blamed for causing the depression has been the subject of a lively, even acrimonious debate.[19] The purpose of this paper is to ask how the labor market responded to the fall in demand, not why the fall occurred. But some discussion of demand is essential because the demand for labor is a derived demand.

Peter Temin looks at the events of the 1930s against the background of a conventional IS-LM analysis. Although he discusses the role of price movements, IS-LM is the basic paradigm. Within this framework he makes a persuasive case that monetary forces played at most a very minor role in the decline in demand from 1929 to 1931. He points out that a reduction in the supply of money should have resulted in an increase in nominal interest rates, whereas in fact these rates fell (or at least risk-free rates fell). This means that shifts in the IS curve must have dominated any shifts in the LM curve.

Allowing for the decline in the price level, he argues, does not change this conclusion. It is true that once the price level had started declining, the result could conceivably have been high expected real interest rates,

18. Joseph A. Schumpeter, *Business Cycles: A Theoretical, Historical, and Statistical Analysis of the Capitalist Process*, vol. 2 (McGraw-Hill, 1939), p. 928.

19. Milton Friedman and Anna Jacobson Schwartz, *A Monetary History of the United States, 1867–1960* (Princeton University Press, 1963); Peter Temin, *Did Monetary Forces Cause the Great Depression?* (Norton, 1976); and Karl Brunner, ed., *The Great Depression Revisited* (Martinus Nijhoff, 1981).

despite the low nominal rates. But there should still have been a period of high nominal rates precipitating the fall in demand and prices. Moreover, he notes that, since the real money supply actually rose between 1929 and 1931, allowing for price changes weakens the argument that monetary forces were crucial.

The vigorous argument that followed the publication of Temin's book focused on the question of whether his argument had demolished the monetarist view, given that IS-LM is not accepted as the appropriate frame of reference.[20] The most interesting aspect of the discussion was that it revealed a potential inconsistency in different monetarist approaches to the business cycle.

The equation $MV = PQ$ is the central relation of monetarism.[21] With V constant, it implies that a change in M must either change P or change Q, or both. In general, for any given change in M, the larger the change in P, the smaller the change in Q will be. This is because the quantity equation is an aggregate demand relation, of course, and it accords with the idea that price flexibility assists the stability of real output. Provided prices adjust, real output need not.

In their analysis of the labor market and the aggregate supply curve, however, the monetarists' view of the impact of price changes is different. A recession is a period when a falling price level is interpreted by each individual firm as a falling relative price. Finding their own real wages too high, firms then reduce output and employment. But it is the fall in prices in this model that has caused the reduction in output. The bigger the change in P, presumably the bigger the change in Q will be.

It is not at all clear that these aggregate demand and supply relationships have been put together in a consistent way. This is revealed by the quotations and counterquotations used by Temin and his critics. Temin quotes from monetarist discussions of the demand side. His critics reply by quoting discussions of supply. The inconsistency also shows up in the different strands of the rational expectations literature. Robert Barro started from the quantity equation and divided up changes in the money stock into anticipated and unanticipated changes. The former change P but not Q, and vice versa for the latter.[22] For Barro, an unanticipated change in money does not change the price level but does change output.

20. Brunner, *The Great Depression Revisited.*

21. Here M is the money supply, V is velocity, P is the price level, and Q is real output.

22. Robert J. Barro, "Unanticipated Money, Output, and the Price Level in the United States," *Journal of Political Economy,* vol. 86 (August 1978), pp. 549–80.

But in the classical models of Lucas and Sargent unanticipated changes in the money supply change real output *because they change the price level*. Nevertheless, Lucas and Sargent have cited Barro's work as supportive of their models.[23]

For this paper it seems sensible to work with the classical supply side, which says that the decline in the supply of money in the 1930s induced a decline in the price level. This decline in prices then induced a reduction in output and employment. The quantity equation can be ignored.[24]

Nonmonetarists propose no clear alternative cause of the depression. Perhaps there should not be one. Expenditure-oriented business-cycle models describe endogenous sources of instability in the economy, particularly multiplier-accelerator interactions. Whether some disturbance of the economy will provoke unstable growth or decline depends rather sensitively on the parameters. This makes it likely that sometimes the economy will react unstably, sometimes not. Nobody today would take multiplier-accelerator models literally, but a self-perpetuating cycle of output decline, inducing a reduction in consumption and investment

23. See Robert E. Lucas and Thomas J. Sargent, "After Keynesian Macroeconomics," in *After the Phillips Curve: Persistence of High Inflation and High Unemployment*, Conference Series 19 (Federal Reserve Bank of Boston, 1979), pp. 49–72. I have oversimplified Barro's findings somewhat for expositional purposes. His actual results are just as difficult to reconcile with the Lucas supply curve, however. In "Unanticipated Money, Output, and the Price Level" Barro finds that current and three lagged values of unanticipated money growth have powerful effects on real output, while the anticipated part of money growth has no effect (equations 3 and 4, pp. 555–56). Equation 4 on page 562 shows that an anticipated change in the money supply changes the price level almost exactly in proportion. But the same equation shows that an unanticipated change in the money supply has a much smaller effect on the price level in the same year (a 1 percent unanticipated increase in the money supply raises the price level by only $1.02 - 0.74 = 0.32$ percent). Over the next three years the price level actually moves in the opposite direction from the movement in the money supply (the negative coefficients on the next three lagged terms all exceed unity).

These results mean, for example, that an unanticipated increase in the money supply causes a small increase in the price level in the same year, followed by slightly larger decreases in the price level in the next three years. At the same time real output has been increased for the whole four years. It is not obvious how this fits with the Lucas supply curve.

24. Probably there are consistent ways to combine the quantity equation and the labor-market model. Monetarism has already dealt with the problem of a variable velocity (V changed more than M from 1929 to 1933) and has done so rather cleverly by attributing changes in V to past and expected future monetary policy. Presumably, if wages move relative to prices over the cycle, the volume of transactions will change relative to PQ, and hence V will change. Still, some rethinking of the role of price adjustment in monetarist and rational expectations analysis and its role in either causing or preventing quantity adjustment seems to be needed.

demand, inducing in turn further declines in output, is consistent with the depression years. What got the process started is not clear. Certainly the Federal Reserve was following a tightening monetary policy in 1929 to restrain the boom in the real economy and the speculation in the stock market, and this probably helped tip the economy downward.[25] In the wake of the stock market crash a "wait-and-see" attitude toward further purchases of durable goods—both consumer and producer goods— probably set in even though no one anticipated the disaster to come. Given the very high levels of investment preceding 1929, the stocks of durables were such that only anticipation of continued rapid growth could have sustained continued high investment.

The Classical Labor Market Model

The classical labor market model described above was used subsequently by Keynes. There was a famous exchange between Keynes, Dunlop, Tarshis, and Ruggles over the cyclical behavior of wages after the *General Theory* appeared.[26] Dunlop and the others argued that the countercyclical movement of real wages required by the classical model of labor demand was not in fact observed. Keynes himself abandoned that part of his model, although some Keynesian textbooks retained it.[27] It makes more sense to consider the new classical versions of this same story than to pursue an old discussion directly. The major difference this introduces is that contract rigidity and adjustment lags used by classical or monetarist authors are replaced by the misperceptions hypothesis.

The New Classical Models

In their 1970 paper Lucas and Rapping specify a CES production function (their equation 16) and then write down the marginal productiv-

25. The role of money in precipitating the depression is analyzed by Robert J. Gordon and James A. Wilcox, "Monetarist Interpretations of the Great Depression: An Evaluation and Critique," in Brunner, ed., *The Great Depression Revisited*, pp. 49–107.

26. John Maynard Keynes, "Relative Movements of Real Wages and Output," *Economic Journal*, vol. 49 (March 1939), pp. 34–51; John T. Dunlop, "The Movement of Real and Money Wage Rates," *Economic Journal*, vol. 48 (September 1938), pp. 413–34; Lorie Tarshis, "Changes in Real and Money Wages," *Economic Journal*, vol. 49 (March 1939), pp. 150–54; and Richard Ruggles, "The Relative Movements of Real and Money Wage Rates," *Quarterly Journal of Economics*, vol. 55 (November 1940), pp. 130–49.

27. See, for example, William H. Branson, *Macroeconomic Theory and Policy* (Harper and Row, 1972).

ity condition (equation 17), given "profit maximization under competition."[28] Although in developing their equations for estimation they make employment (or labor input) depend on the wage and output, it is certainly possible in principle to solve the production function and marginal product conditions for output or employment as a function of the real wage *alone* (with capital fixed or adjusting slowly). The only reason given for these two relations to be violated in the short run is that labor is costly to adjust. Employment would thus be "too high" when output and employment were falling and "too low" when they were rising.

Sargent recognizes that the logic of the new classical model requires that employment depend on the real wage alone without adding output as an independent determinant. As before, he assumes that there are adjustment costs. He ends up with a "demand model [that] makes employment depend inversely on the appropriate real wage . . . [but introduces] a potentially rich dynamic structure . . . into that dependence because firms are assumed to face costs of rapidly adjusting their labor force and so find it optimal to take into account future expected values of the real wage in determining their current employment."[29]

Sargent then develops his dynamic model and tests it on postwar data. He confirms the earlier finding of Neftçi that real wages "Granger cause" employment, with the relation being an inverse one.[30] He obtains results for his model that he finds "moderately comforting" and concludes, "The simple contemporaneous correlations that formed the evidence in the original Dunlop-Tarshis-Keynes exchange and also in much of the follow-up empirical work done to date are not sufficient to rule on the question of whether the time series are compatible with a model in which firms are always on their demand schedules for employment."[31]

Now everyone agrees that, ceteris paribus, higher real wages discourage labor demand, so that if postwar data (1948–72) uncover that negative relation, all to the good. The question is whether the employment fluctuations of the 1930s can be explained solely or even principally as responses to real wage changes. Adjustment costs do imply that lags

28. Lucas and Rapping, "Real Wages," p. 270.

29. Thomas J. Sargent, "Estimation of Dynamic Labor Demand Schedules under Rational Expectations," *Journal of Political Economy*, vol. 86 (December 1978), p. 1012.

30. Salih N. Neftçi, "A Time-Series Analysis of the Real Wages–Employment Relationship," *Journal of Political Economy*, vol. 86 (April 1978), pt. 1, pp. 281–91.

31. Sargent, "Estimation of Dynamic Labor Demand Schedules," p. 1041.

and expectations will modify the contemporaneous relation between wages and employment. Nevertheless, I fail to see how the addition of adjustment costs overcomes the problems of the classical model. In explaining the sharp decline in employment at the outset of the depression, adjustment costs make things worse, implying a smaller reduction in employment for any given wage change. The best classical case can probably be made from the "all employees" series. Between 1922 and 1941 the producer real wage rose at an annual rate of 2.1 percent. Since 1929 had high employment, which had risen above its 1928 level, this should mean the real wage was not above its equilibrium trend level in 1929. Assume, therefore, that the ratio of the actual to the equilibrium real wage in 1929 was 1.00 and that the equilibrium grew at 2.1 percent a year after that. The ratios of actual to equilibrium real wages in subsequent years are then:

1929	1.00	1934	0.99
1930	1.05	1935	0.95
1931	1.11	1936	0.94
1932	1.09	1937	0.92
1933	1.00		

This wage series can be compared to the index of total hours, which showed labor input falling from 100 in 1929 to 75.6 in 1932 and then rising to 93.2 by 1937. With a suitable distributed lag one could certainly find a correlation or "causal" relation between wages and employment.[32] The wage was above trend from 1929 to 1932, when labor input was falling, and below trend from 1933 to 1937, when it was rising. Over the three years 1930–32 the wage was 8.3 percent above trend on average. Labor input was down 28 percent by 1932, yielding an elasticity of 3.4. This is a very high short-run elasticity. If there were smooth short-run capital-labor substitutability (Cobb-Douglas, for example) and no adjustment costs, such an elasticity might be reasonable. But the prevalence of idle capital as well as idle labor in the downturn attests to the difficulty of short-run substitution, and if it is costly to reduce labor input, the elasticity is further reduced.

32. The articles by Dunlop, Tarshis, and Ruggles cited in note 26 examined manufacturing wages, where the rapid rise in employment after 1933 coincided with rapid growth in the real wage. Thus using the "all employees" wage series rather than manufacturing wages gives the classical model a better chance.

The biggest problem for the model, however, occurs after 1933. From 1933 to 1937 the wage was at or below trend, but labor input remained below its 1929 level throughout, being down 21 percent in 1935 even though the wage had not been above trend for three years, and still down 7 percent in 1937 after five years. I know of no evidence suggesting that adjustment costs are large enough to account for such a slow recovery. This is particularly true when firms could resume former work practices, rehire former employees and reclaim lost firm-specific human capital, or simply stop putting so many employees on periodic temporary layoff.

Labor Supply

New classical models imply that, drawn against the actual real wage, the labor supply curve will shift upward as the price level declines. The new classicists do not appeal to contractual commitments. Instead workers construct a "normal wage" or expected wage and compare the actual wage to this. For example, in Lucas and Rapping the normal wage in 1932 is estimated to have been $0.55 though the actual average wage was $0.48.[33] By assumption, there is supply-demand equilibrium in all years, so the 28 percent decline in labor input in 1932 relative to 1929 reflects not only a reduction in labor demand, but also a reduction of labor supplied in response to the gap between the actual wage and the normal wage.

One line of criticism of the new classical model is that workers in the 1930s did not describe themselves as voluntarily unemployed. Certainly descriptions of what it was like in the 1930s do not suggest a model where workers rejected job offers because of the wage. If a job opened up, hundreds of applications were received. But anecdotal or impressionistic evidence is tricky. Even in the Lucas and Rapping model workers would be expected to be distressed by what they think are sharp real wage cuts. If workers are generally disappointed in the wage offers that have been made them, one would expect high-wage vacancies to draw many applicants.

The more forceful criticism is that the implied elasticity of labor supply is much too great. The Lucas and Rapping model suggests that an 11.8 percent decline in the ratio of the actual wage to the normal wage between 1929 and 1932 can explain the 28 percent decline in labor input. The implied elasticity is 2.4. The conventional microeconomic estimates

33. "Unemployment in the Great Depression," p. 189.

of the response of labor supply to a change in the wage are close to zero for males and small for females. But since by the assumptions of the model the wage decline is viewed as temporary, it can be argued that the relevant elasticity is the compensated or substitution elasticity. The income maintenance experiments for Denver and Seattle found wage elasticities that can be taken as substitution elasticities since the experiments were temporary. Based on Gary Burtless and David Greenberg's coefficient estimates, the three-year elasticities were roughly 0.11 for men, 0.37 for wives, and 0.18 for unmarried women.[34] Another recent study of labor supply is that of Jerry Hausman, who has developed new labor supply estimates using the University of Michigan Panel Survey on Income Dynamics. He finds a substitution elasticity of roughly 0.54 for males.[35] This is a very high estimate, which may be due in part to the constraints imposed on the estimation procedure, but it is still much too low for the Lucas and Rapping model.

Moreover, the assumption that the compensated elasticity is the correct one is questionable. The argument is that a decline in the wage that is seen as temporary alters the decision on when to work but does not change a worker's estimate of his permanent income. This also implies, however, that consumption should not be reduced in the short run because consumption depends on permanent income. It is true that savings fell sharply from 1929 to 1933: permanent income was above actual income. But consumption did fall substantially, so permanent income must have fallen.

Marginal versus Average Wages

In their reply to Albert Rees's criticism of their model,[36] Lucas and Rapping suggest in a footnote that looking at the behavior of average wage rates over the cycle may be deceptive because

the abnormally low wage offers which lead to unemployment are not evenly

---

34. Gary Burtless and David Greenberg, "Inferences Concerning Labor Supply Behavior Based on Limited-Duration Experiments," *American Economic Review*, vol. 72 (June 1982), pp. 488–97.

35. Jerry A. Hausman, "Labor Supply," in Henry J. Aaron and Joseph A. Pechman, eds., *How Taxes Affect Economic Behavior* (Brookings Institution, 1981), pp. 27–72. Burtless's comments on pages 76–77 indicate that the labor supply equation for a median prime-age male was $h = 2,663 + 11.3W - 0.113Y$. If the after-tax wage is roughly \$4.50 and the hours of work are 1,900, then the substitution elasticity is 4.5 (11.3/1,900 + 0.113) = 0.535.

36. "On Equilibrium in Labor Markets," *Journal of Political Economy*, vol. 78 (March–April 1970), pp. 306–10.

distributed over the labor force. The figure $0.46 [the reported average wage in 1933] is the average wage of those who found jobs *and* accepted them. Presumably the average "best offer" for those who did not work was considerably lower. For a labor market model similar in concept to ours but which captures some of the important effects of labor-force heterogeneity, the reader is referred to Mortensen.[37]

This marginal wage idea is mentioned by Peter Diamond in his comment on this paper (also in a footnote). Referring to the same Lucas and Rapping piece, he argues that beneath their explicit model of intertemporal labor substitution is a more complicated search model that can be tested only with a wage series for marginal workers.

The implication here is that an alternative wage series would validate the classical model. This needs to be considered explicitly. First, the average wage series discussed in this paper is precisely the one used by Lucas and Rapping in their own empirical work. If there is a better wage series, it should be used, but macroeconomic models cannot be tested on the basis of hypothetical evidence.

Second, job search may provide a use of time distinct from the normal concept of leisure, and this may raise one's estimate of the likely short-run labor-supply elasticity a bit. But the search model has very serious problems of its own when tested against the experience of the 1930s.[38] I will come back to this later on. There is, in fact, no treatment of labor-force heterogeneity in the Mortensen model: all workers are alike.

The third and most basic issue is whether the reported average wage is a biased indicator during a recession. It may be. Probably a disproportionate number of those unemployed during the depression were low-skill workers whose wages had been below average when employed or whose best job offers were below the reported average wage. But this shift effect may not be very large. The agricultural sector increased its share of total employment from 1929 to 1933, which biases downward the reported average wage. The data in table 3 show that total hours in manufacturing fell by as much as the hours of production workers,

37. Lucas and Rapping, "Unemployment in the Great Depression," p. 189, n. 3. The reference is to Dale T. Mortensen, "A Theory of Wage and Employment Dynamics," in Phelps and others, *Microeconomic Foundations,* pp. 167–211.

38. Robert E. Lucas, Jr., argues forcefully against the job-search model: "There is little evidence that much time is spent in job search, that search is less costly when unemployed than when employed, or, for that matter, that measured unemployment measures any *activity* at all." Lucas, "Understanding Business Cycles," in Karl Brunner and Allan H. Meltzer, eds., *Stabilization of the Domestic and International Economy* (North-Holland, 1977), pp. 7–29. The quotation is from p. 18.

indicating that the labor input of the high-wage white-collar workers fell by as much as that of the low-wage blue-collar workers.

Moreover, it is an illusion to suggest that the classical model as a whole is helped by showing an upward bias in the average wage series when employment fell. Such a bias might help one deal with labor supply but gets one in trouble with labor demand. The classical model requires the producer real wage to rise substantially in the 1929–33 period. If the reported nominal wage has an upward bias, then the observed real wage increase in that period disappears and so does the motivation for the decline in labor demand.

Conclusions on the Classical Model

Explaining the decline in employment between 1929 and 1932 or 1933 within a model of competitive market-clearing is extremely hard. The model works by specifying that the producer-real-wage rises while the worker-real-wage falls. But with any reasonable assumptions about supply and demand elasticities, the gap between the two has to be enormous, given the very large decline in labor input. It is virtually impossible to construct a plausible model that creates such a gap.

That said, however, not all parts of the classical story should be discarded. The reported real wage did rise sharply in 1931 and 1932 as the price level fell, and unless this was entirely a mix effect, it surely hurt employment. It is likely that workers, who had become used to a stable price level, failed to realize in those early years of the depression that a money wage cut did not mean a real wage cut relative to 1929. This is an idea to be carried forward.

Contract Theory and the Early 1930s

Explicit Wage Contracts

Many people argue that explicit contracts prevent the downward adjustment of wages following a fall in aggregate demand. Were such contracts important in the 1930s?

In 1930 (a census year) the civilian labor force numbered 48.5 million people, of whom 44.2 million were employed. Only 33.8 million of the employed were not in agriculture (roughly 70 percent of the civilian labor force). There were 3.2 million union members that year, making up 7.2 percent of all civilian employment or 9.3 percent of nonagricultural employment. Unions had been much stronger in 1920, but a hostile political and legal environment had hurt their membership. Between 1930 and 1936 there was a moderate swing in union membership, with the total declining to 2.8 million in 1933 and rising to 3.9 million by 1936. In 1936 union membership was 7.4 percent of the civilian labor force and 11.6 percent of nonagricultural employment.[39] As far as I know, union contracts were of only one year's duration during the 1930s, further limiting their effect.

From these figures it is clear that explicit contracts between firms and unions played at most a minor role in the behavior of wages from 1929 to 1936. Most firms and workers were not locked into wage contracts that prevented wage adjustment. If contract theory has a role in explaining wages, it must be some version of informal or implicit contract theory.

Implicit Contract Theory and Wages, 1929–33

Contract theory comes in a variety of forms, but a common theme is that firms will avoid short-run fluctuations in the wage rate. Okun makes a general argument about what policies or what implicit wage contracts are seen as "fair" in order to explain why workers prefer a stable wage. Risk aversion by workers is another reason given. In any case, the central feature of the theory is that, by assuming that the wage and employment decision is made as part of a long-term relationship between a firm and its workers, the theory eliminates or reduces an employer's incentive to lower wages as a result of *temporary* demand fluctuations or increases in aggregate unemployment.[40] That feature is common to most of the contract-related literature, even the part that offers alternative specific reasons for wage stickiness.

39. Union membership figures from Leo Troy, *Trade Union Membership, 1897–1962*, Occasional Paper 92 (Columbia University Press for the National Bureau of Economic Research, 1965), p. 1. The employment and labor force figures are from Bureau of the Census, *Historical Statistics: Colonial Times to 1970*, p. 126, and differ from Troy's figures. Hence his percentages differ from those given here.

40. The clearest development of this idea is in Robert E. Hall, "Employment Fluctuations and Wage Rigidity," *Brookings Papers on Economic Activity, 1:1980*, pp. 91–123. See also Martin Neil Baily, "On the Theory of Layoffs and Unemployment," *Econometrica*, vol. 45 (July 1977), pp. 1043–63.

Two important issues arise in trying to match the contract framework with wage behavior in the early 1930s. The first is how to explain why real wages rose substantially above trend in 1931 and 1932. The second is explaining the decline in employment. Consider the behavior of wages first. Perhaps the obvious way to reconcile the movement in wages with the contract framework is to combine this framework with the misperceptions feature of the Lucas and Rapping model. One can argue that employers were providing real wage stability, but both they and their workers were using a normal or expected price level that lagged behind the actual price level.

Another way to explain the stickiness of money wages as the price level fell is by a relative wage approach. Firms were maintaining a standard of fairness relative to other wages, as Okun argues, or they were providing the insurance that their own workers would not suffer relative to other comparable workers. Concern about relative wages introduces inertia into the wage adjustment process that will tend to raise the average real wage during a period of falling prices.

A final possible explanation of wage behavior is that the composition of the employed changed. This point was discussed earlier when evaluating the classical model.

The Decline in Employment with a Competitive Product Market

The second issue that arises with the implicit contract approach is to explain the decline in employment in a way that is consistent with the explanation of wage stickiness. It is important here to distinguish different versions of the model. There is an efficient markets or pure version of contract theory that shares assumptions with the new classical model. It retains perfect competition in the product market and implies that firms always maintain equality between the value of the marginal product and the opportunity cost of workers' time. This maintains the equality of the supply of and demand for labor that is a crucial feature of the classical framework. The pure version of the contract approach could be a big help to the classical model by loosening the link between labor demand and supply and the wage rate.

It turns out, however, that the earlier problems with the classical model resurface in an only slightly modified form. The contract framework provides an independent reading of the extent to which the fall in the price level was misperceived. If firms were trying to maintain a stable real wage, the rise in the real wage in 1931 and 1932 should be attributed to misperceptions. This means that each firm, on average, thought its own relative price was down by 9 to 11 percent. This decline then has to be enough to induce a 28 percent decline in labor *supply*. The implied elasticity of labor supply (roughly 2.8) is even less plausible than the figure obtained using Lucas and Rapping's 11.8 percent gap between the actual and the normal wage. After 1932 wage goes back to trend (and prices stop falling), so the analysis gets even tougher.

Pure contract models emphasize income support programs, since if such programs were generous, this would help to explain why the decline in employment was so large. Income support for the unemployed was not large enough in 1929–33 to change one's mind about the plausibility of a labor-supply elasticity of 2.8. But such support may have been more important from 1933 on.

The Decline in Employment and the Pricing Decision

The crucial step in understanding the employment decline is to throw out the assumption of a perfectly competitive product market. This step does not mean embracing the arbitrary assumption that nominal prices are fixed, which in any case is factually incorrect for the 1930s, nor does it mean assuming that firms have monopoly power in the long run. It simply means recognizing that the marginal revenue product fell much more than the price times the marginal physical product in the 1930s.

The rational expectations assumption has had a profound impact on macroeconomics, but (in the spirit of Charles Schultze's recent paper[41]) I would argue that the lesson for microeconomic pricing models has not been absorbed. The rational expectations assumption means that even industries with a large number of firms will not mimic a perfectly competitive market. Any firm with even halfway rational expectations should know that cutting a price will induce similar price cuts by other firms in the industry. In the early 1930s there certainly was some price cutting in an attempt to gain an advantage over rivals or to drive out high-cost producers altogether. But most firms learned that the price elasticity of demand they faced, *given their competitors' responses,* was much less than infinity and probably quite small.

41. Charles L. Schultze, "Some Macro Foundations for Micro Theory," *Brookings Papers on Economic Activity, 2:1981,* pp. 521–76.

Once the price-taking assumption is dropped, it is plausible that a cumulative fall in aggregate demand would sharply depress firms' estimates of marginal revenue at a full-employment level of output and would therefore result in a cutback of labor input and output. To my knowledge no one has started with a model of fluctuations in aggregate demand and followed through to an analysis of price and wage setting consistent with the contract approach. This means that it is not possible to test directly the efficiency of the labor input decision, given the fall in demand. The textbook theory of the firm says that equality is maintained between the marginal revenue product and the wage. Contract theory implies instead that there is equality between the marginal revenue product and the shadow wage or opportunity cost of workers' time. It is a pity that the test cannot be made because it would help evaluate the role of contract theory in explaining sticky wages. However, the test is probably not important otherwise, because even if the labor market response to the fall in demand is efficient, the unemployment is still socially inefficient, given the pricing assumption.

Job Search

The models of the business cycle that emphasize job search take roughly the same approach as the new classical models. Unemployment above the natural rate occurs only because of misperceptions, and product markets are usually assumed to be perfectly competitive. The main difference is in the labor supply analysis. If workers refuse to accept wage cuts because they believe better-paid jobs are available, a large elasticity of labor supply may be more plausible.

The search model does provide an empirically important perspective. Many of the unemployed were looking hard for new jobs. When many firms were laying off workers, they could not foresee when they could rehire all those released, or even if they would do so. A fall in demand always hits unevenly across the economy, resulting in excessive "structural" unemployment as workers move to other sectors. And certainly many laid-off workers were overoptimistic about their own job prospects. The search model thus opens up fruitful lines that are by no means inconsistent with contract theory. On the contrary, a model with only permanent jobs and temporary layoffs is not empirically valid, so job search and job changing need to be included.

The big problem with the job-search model is persistence. The new classical models and the contract model have trouble with this too, but in these the question is whether a downturn was believed to be temporary. The search model comes close to asserting that workers do not really see the recession at all. Workers offered continued employment at a lower wage refuse to accept it because they believe their alternative job options have not worsened. But information about a deterioration in job prospects spreads quickly. It is especially likely that in such an uncertain environment as the 1930s workers faced with a wage cut would have kept their jobs while looking around for new ones. I had always thought that one could make a case for the search-misperceptions model in the first months of the downturn, or even the first year, when wage cuts might have provoked quits. After that the case would be hard to make. But the fact that the monthly turnover data show that the quit rate declined as early as the fall of 1929 makes me doubt that misperceptions about job prospects lasted even that long.

Postwar turnover data show that about two-thirds of all layoffs are rehired. Comparable data for the 1930s are not available. But turnover data for the 1930s disaggregated by industry provide further support for the hypothesis that layoffs followed by rehires (the contract theory or labor pool model) were very important relative to layoffs followed by search and labor mobility. Industries with high average separation and layoff rates also had high accession rates.[42] Although there certainly was some worker mobility, most of the turnover does not seem to have been associated with movements of workers among industries. Manufacturing establishments maintained their labor pool and reduced labor input in the short run by temporary and indefinite layoffs. Zenith Radio Corporation in Chicago, for example, made radios for the consumer market. In the early 1930s it closed its factory on Christmas Eve and reopened at Easter.

Conclusions on the Early 1930s

Contract theory argues that, in order to maintain worker morale and to promote a stable work force, firms try to provide a stable wage or adopt fair wage and employment practices. Money wages did fall

42. Woytinsky, *Three Aspects,* pp. 232–35. The comparison between the search and labor pool models made here is only for the short-term unemployed. The hard-core unemployed in the later years of the depression cannot be described as part of a labor pool or as engaged in efficient, productive search.

substantially in the early 1930s, but wages did not lead the deflation; they lagged behind the declines in prices, which in turn were led by the competitive auction market commodities.

Peter Temin has documented the fact that in the early stages of the depression few people anticipated how severe it would be and it is unlikely that anyone realized how prolonged it would be.[43] There had been periodic business cycles before, the most recent in 1920–22, when a very sharp downturn was followed by a quick recovery. Firms and workers facing the decline in demand had every reason to think that laid-off workers would be rehired, that the recession was temporary, and that firms that led the way as aggressive wage cutters would acquire an adverse reputation that could be costly when full employment was restored.

The turnover data for manufacturing support this interpretation. The combination of a very high layoff rate and a very high accession rate could in principle be consistent with workers constantly leaving one establishment and moving to another. But, more plausibly, a pattern of constant layoffs and rehires is suggested. The generally poor business conditions meant that laid-off workers were more likely to return than would be true of temporary layoffs in a boom.

The behavior of the labor market in the early 1930s cannot be said to provide independent support for the contract theory interpretation. But provided one stays away from the assumption of perfectly competitive product markets, this period is consistent with that interpretation.

Wages and the Persistence of Unemployment

The manufacturing sector bottomed out in 1932 and unemployment peaked in 1933. Conditions were never again so bad, but full employment was not restored before the outbreak of World War II. Prices stopped falling—in fact, consumer prices rose in all years after 1933, except for a very mild decline in 1938–39. By 1933 the real money stock had exceeded its 1929 level, but it fell slightly after that as prices rose. Robert Gordon and James Wilcox have argued that movements in the nominal money supply did "cause" some part of nominal GNP movements, which is plausible enough.[44] But with short-term, risk-free interest rates

43. *Did Monetary Forces Cause the Great Depression?*
44. Gordon and Wilcox, "Monetarist Interpretations of the Great Depression."

close to zero from 1933 to 1939 and prices rising, real interest rates were very low. It is hard to see a shortage of money as the principal factor holding down demand. I do not know of a detailed income-expenditure model that explains why aggregate demand recovered so slowly and erratically. The overhang of excess capacity discouraged investment and housing expenditure, and continued high unemployment reduced permanent income and consumption.

The question at issue here, however, is why the persistent high level of unemployment did not put more downward pressure on wages.[45] The fundamental paradox of the 1933–41 period is the apparent persistence of disequilibrium, which implies that unclaimed economic rents existed for several years. And the presence of such rents violates the postulate that competition will eliminate rents in a market economy. The existence of excess unemployment must have been obvious to both firms and workers. It makes no sense to argue that by the middle 1930s anyone was unaware that the unemployment rate exceeded the natural rate. Contract theory argues that wages adjust to the climate, not the weather, and apparently the climate had changed. Nevertheless, firms were not willing to take advantage of the excess supply of labor to lower wages.

The ways in which competition could have been expected to eliminate the excess unemployment and the associated economic rents are by existing firms expanding employment and increasing output or by the entry of new firms. Since employment and output did expand rapidly after 1933, we are not looking for an explanation of stagnation but rather of why the adjustment process was not more forceful and complete.

Income Support Programs

Herbert Hoover reportedly argued that one reason there was so much unemployment was that selling apples in the street was so profitable. Despite the intuitive grasp of efficient labor market theory he revealed, this is a hard story to swallow. But certainly if workers classified as unemployed were receiving a substantial income from other sources, this would explain or help explain why the competition of the unemployed for jobs was not great.

Tables 6, 7, and 8 give the basic data on income support programs.

---

45. Whether such pressure, had it existed, would have helped restore full-employment equilibrium is a question I shall not tackle.

Table 6. *Total Unemployed and Recipients of Income Support,*
Selected Years, 1929–40

Thousands; annual averages

		Recipients of income support			
Year	Total unem-ployed	Total[a]	General relief	Work Projects Administra-tion[b]	Old-age assistance
1929	1,550	334[c]	n.a.	0	n.a.
1931	8,020	1,288[c]	n.a.	0	n.a.
1933	12,830	5,014	4,227	427[d]	108
1934	11,340	6,587	4,415	992[d]	142
1935	10,610	6,319	4,606	482	303
1936	9,030	5,746	1,666	2,544	737
1937	7,700	5,196	1,445	1,793	1,369
1938	10,390	6,461	1,700	2,761	1,692
1939	9,480	6,283	1,661	2,407	1,852
1940	8,120	5,550	1,410	1,912	1,983

Sources: Theodore E. Whiting and T. J. Woofter, Jr., *Summary of Relief and Federal Work Program Statistics, 1933–1940* (GPO, 1941), pp. 45–49; Bureau of the Census, *Relief Expenditures by Governmental and Private Organizations, 1929 and 1931,* Special Report (GPO, 1932), p. 15; and Bureau of the Census, *Historical Statistics: Colonial Times to 1970,* p. 126.

n.a. Not available.

a. Also includes National Youth Administration, Civilian Conservation Corps, Public Works Administration, Aid to Families with Dependent Children, Aid to the Blind, Farm Security Administration Grants, earnings on regular federal construction projects, Federal Emergency Relief Administration special programs, and emergency funds from other federal agency projects.

b. Until 1939, when it was renamed, this was the Works Progress Administration.

c. Data are not comparable to those for later years. Figures are for families outside institutions receiving relief from public and private sources. Coverage is of cities and towns containing 89 percent of the total population. Average is for the first quarter of the year.

d. Civil Works Program.

Table 7. *Total Expenditures on Income Support and Average*
Annual Earnings, Selected Years, 1929–40

Year	Expenditure on all pro-grams[a] (billions of dollars)	Expenditure as percent of wages and salaries	Annual re-ceipt per full-time recipient (dollars)	Expenditures on WPA[b] (billions of dollars)	Average an-nual earnings per full-time WPA worker (dollars)
1929	0.22[c]	0.48[c]	n.a.	0.0	0
1931	0.73[c]	2.15[c]	n.a.	0.0	0
1933	1.22	5.10	244	0.21[d]	503[d]
1934	2.38	8.62	361	0.50[d]	507[d]
1935	2.53	8.38	401	0.24	494
1936	3.12	9.15	543	1.59	626
1937	2.65	6.87	511	1.19	662
1938	3.24	9.31	501	1.75	634
1939	3.19	8.46	507	1.57	650
1940	2.72	6.57	491	1.27	664

Sources and notes: Same as table 6.

Table 8. *Average Annual Earnings of Full-Time Employees,*
by Sector, 1933–40
Current dollars

Year	All employees	Agriculture[a]	Manufacturing	Wholesale and retail trade
1933	1,048	232	1,086	1,183
1934	1,091	253	1,153	1,228
1935	1,137	288	1,216	1,279
1936	1,184	308	1,287	1,295
1937	1,258	360	1,376	1,352
1938	1,230	369	1,296	1,352
1939	1,264	385	1,363	1,360
1940	1,299	407	1,432	1,382

Source: Bureau of the Census, *Historical Statistics: Colonial Times to 1970*, pp. 164, 166, 167.
a. Includes Forestry and Fisheries.

Income support for the unemployed did not begin with the New Deal.
On the average 334,000 families were being supported by various forms
of public and private relief in the first quarter of the boom year of 1929.
By the first quarter of 1931 this figure had risen to 1.3 million. In addition
to this support to families, in the first quarter of 1931, 4.2 million meals
were served per month (the soup kitchens) and 1.5 million nights of
lodging per month were given to homeless men (what happened to
homeless women?).[46]

The New Deal programs took over the state, local, and private relief
programs that were unable to cope with the flood of unemployed. The
numbers receiving assistance were greatly expanded. By 1934 the
number of people receiving some form of income assistance equaled
about two-thirds the number of unemployed. Some of those receiving
assistance, however, were not unemployed. In table 7, the expenditure
figures are shown. After 1933 the total expenditure on all forms of relief
was at the rate of 8 to 9 percent of the wage bill. At the level of the
individual, the incentives are shown by calculating how much would be
received a year by a full-time recipient of relief. These figures can be
compared with the annual earnings of full-time employees in table 8.

To a worker comparing the amount available on relief or in a WPA
job with the amount of earnings in an average full-time job, the WPA
would have looked pretty bad. This holds even more strongly for the

46. Bureau of the Census, *Relief Expenditures by Governmental and Private Organizations, 1929 and 1931*, Special Report (GPO, 1932), p. 15.

average worker in manufacturing or wholesale and retail trade. To those in certain classes of low-paying jobs, however, relief or WPA income would have seemed more attractive. The payment was actually higher than the average for agricultural workers. There may have been some disincentive effect on agricultural employment from the WPA, but I was unable to find it in the data.

Michael Darby has suggested that the Lucas and Rapping model can be reconciled with the persistence of high unemployment because of the WPA; WPA workers should have been counted as employed, not unemployed, he argues.[47] The first response to this is that the Lucas and Rapping model has great difficulty even with the early years of the depression. And income support will not help much because only a small fraction of the unemployed can have been receiving relief and the payments were low. Second, it is a mistake to single out the WPA. This program was introduced as an alternative to emergency relief. The purpose, in part, was to discourage those who were collecting relief without being needy, much as "workfare" is intended to discourage people on welfare today.

Nevertheless, it is clear that a nontrivial level of support to the unemployed was supplied under the New Deal. Such support may well have influenced the layoff behavior of firms and, in a sense, allowed the economic system to operate despite the presence of a large group of hard-core unemployed and nonemployed. Without such support the competitive pressure on wages would probably have been much greater. The other alternative is that there would have been even more serious social upheaval than actually occurred.

The National Industrial Recovery Act and the National Labor Relations Act

The next explanation of the slow or perverse adjustment of wages after 1933 is that New Deal legal changes prevented wage adjustment and encouraged wage increases. The National Industrial Recovery Act (NIRA), passed in June 1933, was a sweeping attempt to promote economic recovery. For purposes here the most important provision of the act was that it proposed setting up "codes of fair competition" in 450 industries. In practice these codes were designed to promote cartels

47. "Three-and-a-Half Million U.S. Employees Have Been Mislaid."

among employers and the formation of unions. A minimum wage, varying between 25 and 40 cents an hour, was established for industrial workers. Restrictions were placed on the number of hours to be worked by a single employee; usually it was thirty-five to forty hours a week.

In a detailed analysis Michael Weinstein has argued that the NIRA codes (and their precursor, the President's Reemployment Agreement) can account for the perverse behavior of wages and prices in the mid-1930s and hence that "no support is provided for any theory that attributes wage and price rigidity to the private economy of the early and middle 1930s."[48] I find it tempting simply to accept his conclusion. I could then argue that implicit contract theory can handle the 1929–33 period and government intervention explains the rest. Maybe that is even the correct answer, but there are some tricky questions.

The basic evidence Weinstein uses is not overwhelming—a Phillips curve wage equation with dummy variables for the beginning and the end of the NIRA codes. The dummies indicate that the introduction of the codes was responsible for a 26 percent increase in wage rates, and their removal for a 14 percent decrease in wage rates. This means that a legacy of excessive nominal wages was left behind by the codes—about 12 percent. A somewhat smaller net effect of 7 percent on prices is found, so that real wages were raised by about 5 percent. The wage series used is average hourly earnings from a selection of manufacturing industries.

First, the interpretation of this finding needs to be changed, even if it is accepted as correct. The Phillips curve already implies wage rigidity in the private economy. Even if wages had simply followed a normal Phillips curve, why persistently high unemployment induced such a sluggish wage response would still have to be explained.

Second, it is difficult to explain why a government intervention in the wage- and price-setting process, which was in force for only twenty-three months and enforced only loosely, should have had such a dramatic and permanent impact. After all, the Phillips curve econometricians have been quick to state that temporary interventions in wage and price setting, such as the Nixon controls program, have had at most a temporary effect. The bounce-back of inflation after controls have been removed is now a matter of conventional wisdom.

48. Michael M. Weinstein, *Recovery and Redistribution under the NIRA*, Studies in Monetary Economics, vol. 6 (North-Holland, 1980), p. 29.

Even the casual econometrician can see the jump in the wage series in 1934. I think there is no doubt that this jump was engineered by Roosevelt. Even though the President's Reemployment Agreement that preceded the passage of the industry-specific codes was not legally binding and even though about 16,000 complaints of violation of the NIRA were on hand through 1934, a great majority of law-abiding employers felt they were required to raise wage rates and did so. The question is why wages did not sag rapidly once the NIRA was declared unconstitutional. There is really no sign of this downward bounce-back in the data, as Cagan noted in his comments on Weinstein's hypothesis.[49]

One possible reason for the absence of a wage decline when the NIRA ended is that it was succeeded by the National Labor Relations Act. This act took over the provisions of the NIRA that favored union membership. Perhaps the most important of these is that firms must "bargain in good faith," that is, an employer must not go out among the unemployed and replace his existing work force. Trade union membership did grow rapidly under the provisions of the NIRA and the NLRA, from 2.8 million in 1933 to 3.4 million in 1934 and 3.9 million by 1936. A big organizing drive in 1937 raised membership to 5.6 million, and by 1941 the figure was 8.4 million. As a percentage of nonfarm employment, however, union membership remained fairly small, reaching only 15 percent by 1937 and 20 percent by 1941. Moreover, many consider the impact of unions to be on relative wages rather than on the wage level.

Once again, however, the simple evidence looks very strong. The big jump in unionization in 1937 coincided with a big jump in nominal wages, especially in manufacturing, where the unions were strongest. And if one looks at data for before 1929, it is noticeable that the relative decline of manufacturing wages in 1920–22 coincided with a decline both in union membership and in the threat of unionization.

The final legal restriction on adjustment comes from the existence of minimum wages. The NIRA included elaborate minimum wage codes, but once these were declared unconstitutional, there was no effective minimum wage until 1938, when the Fair Labor Standards Act was passed. This mandated a 25-cent minimum as of November 1938 covering 43.4 percent of nonsupervisory, nonfarm employees. This figure was 41.7 percent of the average wage in manufacturing. By way of compari-

49. Phillip Cagan, "Comments on 'Some Macroeconomic Impacts of the National Industrial Recovery Act, 1933–35,' " in Brunner, ed., *The Great Depression Revisited*, pp. 282–85.

son, the 1968 minimum covered 72.6 percent of workers and was 55.6 percent of the average manufacturing wage, and the 1978 figures were 83.8 percent and 48.4 percent, respectively.[50] It is clear that a minimum wage at this level cannot account for much unemployment, and there was no minimum from May 1935 until November 1938 in any case.

The Effect of Legal Restrictions

It is surely true that the NIRA and the growth of the union movement had an impact on wages. But it is equally true that the legal and institutional changes in themselves are too narrow in terms of timing or labor-force coverage to explain the whole picture. Some interaction effects or spillover effects of the legal changes must have been occurring.

The Economic Climate in the Middle 1930s

The legal changes had an impact that went beyond the narrow coverage of union membership or the narrow time-horizon of a given statute because they interacted with a labor market where wages were not being set according to short-term market conditions. The legal changes offset the change in the economic climate that persistent high unemployment would have caused.

Okun emphasized that employers must follow personnel practices perceived as fair. While in force, the NIRA prevented wage cutting. An employer who came to his workers the day after the NIRA was declared unconstitutional and told them he was cutting wages purely to raise his own profits, with no offsetting benefit of more employment, would have had a considerable morale problem. Moreover, unionization, though small, had been growing; disgruntled employees were likely to join unions. Any entrepreneur likely to cut wages aggressively probably regarded unions as a cancer to be avoided if at all possible.

To some extent employers did try to increase their share of the pie in the 1930s, and this may have shown up more in other conditions of employment than in wages. But the legal and institutional changes

50. Finis Welch, *Minimum Wages: Issues and Evidence* (American Enterprise Institute for Public Policy Research, 1978), p. 3.

limited this process. It is not that fluctuations in the legal environment caused fluctuations in employment, but that these changes as they worked in a contract labor market limited the adjustment of wages in response to persistent unemployment.

Even though employers may not have felt it worthwhile to fight with their workers over the shares of the given economic pie, firms might have been expected to try to expand output in order to decrease the frequency of temporary layoffs of their employees and increase their own profits. And potential entrants to an industry would face no morale problems if they hired from the pool of unemployed at lower than prevailing wages.

The reason that existing firms did not exploit the labor market disequilibrium more fully is because by 1935 there was a general belief that using wage and price reductions to expand output had not worked. This belief was reinforced by the fact that after 1933, when prices stopped declining, output and employment rose rapidly.

In rational expectations macroeconomic models it is assumed that an equilibrium price level exists, a level that eliminates excess unemployment or economic rents. Economic agents form an unbiased estimate of this and then make decisions using the equilibrium price level as a benchmark. This assumption is of a rational market, but this will only evolve if the individual agents find that behavior consistent with a rational market response is reinforced during a learning or adjustment process. As I argued earlier, firms learn in practice that price-cutting wars during slack demand periods tend to leave every firm worse off. This means that, even with persistent slack, individual firms see a gain or economic rent to be exploited only to the extent that industry profits can be raised—or from a contract theory perspective, only to the extent that both firms and workers can be made better off. And as long as marginal revenue products were down relative to full-employment levels because aggregate demand remained depressed in 1933–41, persistent excess labor was the privately efficient outcome.

This leaves the entry of new firms as the final mechanism that might have exploited unclaimed rents. Entry and the threat of entry have played an important role in oligopoly theory, but variations in the threat of entry over the business cycle have not been given enough attention. In fact, these variations play an important part in determining cyclical pricing behavior and hence in the derived demand for labor. Oligopoly theorists have argued correctly that the threat of entry prevents the exercise of (much) monopoly power.[51] But this result should be applied to industries in long-run equilibrium. Even better, it should be restated that entry makes it unlikely that capital will earn an above-normal rate of return in the long run.

The condition that capital earns a normal rate of return has already played a crucial role in the argument that was given earlier. It means that prices will be close to competitive levels when demand is at normal levels. And it therefore follows that when an industry demand curve shifts left it will generally be true that a cut in the price of the industry's product relative to the general price level will reduce the industry's profits. Only if the demand curve shifts to the point where the new short-run monopoly price is below the old long-run equilibrium price will firms in the industry find that industrywide price cutting actually increases profits.

In a recession, with excess capacity and idle capital, the threat of entry is greatly diminished. A potential entrant would believe he could earn an above-normal rate of return on new investment only because there are idle workers willing to take jobs at wages below those prevailing in existing firms in the industry. But making a profit from entry is a long-run proposition; few new plants or companies make money in the short run.[52] The entrant has to believe that his work force will accept wages lower than those prevailing in the industry long enough for him to earn above-normal returns on his investment in an industry that already has too much capital relative to current levels of demand. As long as the wage and price decisions of the firms in an industry are in line with long-run competitive equilibrium, it is unlikely that a recession or even a persistent period of slack will make entry attractive.

Over time, the capacity of the system to absorb the unemployed grows despite the obstacles described above. The development of new industries looks more attractive when excess labor is readily available. At full employment such development requires bidding workers away

51. For a recent example, see Sanford J. Grossman, "Nash Equilibrium and the Industrial Organization of Markets with Large Fixed Costs," *Econometrica*, vol. 49 (September 1981), pp. 1149–72.

52. The classic study of entry barriers is Joe S. Bain, *Barriers to New Competition: Their Character and Consequences in Manufacturing Industries* (Harvard University Press, 1956).

from other firms. This creates upward pressure on wages that does not exist when there is excess labor. Unemployment, after all, does have some effect on wages.

Conclusions about Wages and Employment

My strongest criticisms have been of the classical model of the labor market, because of its insistence on competition and equilibrium even in the short run. This makes it difficult to explain the observed employment variations, given realistic elasticity estimates. It is important not only to use formal statistical analysis of a problem, but also to do an order-of-magnitude calculation. If this does not come out correctly, rethink the problem. It is hard to get the order-of-magnitude calculation to come out right for the classical model.

But the misperceptions component of classical and search models probably played an important part in explaining the early years of the depression. People continued to believe that the economy would soon return to normal. The high rates of hiring revealed in the turnover data indicate that well-paid jobs were available to some workers. Some unemployed were unwilling to undercut the employed or to accept menial jobs because they hoped for positions that offered terms comparable to those available in 1929.

The narrow risk-sharing version of implicit contract theory cannot provide a complete explanation of wage rigidity from 1929 to 1941. That lasted too long to be perceived as a temporary change in the economic situation. And many firms were unable or unwilling to act risk neutrally. Nevertheless, an eclectic version of contract theory seems to me to be on the right track. Concerned about their own survival, firms could not provide full protection. Because price cutting was seen as a beggar-thy-neighbor policy that would provoke retaliation and leave everyone worse off in the end, output and employment were cut back instead. The basic message of contract theory is that a policy of aggressive wage cutting is not used because of its effects on morale and reputation. Firms, even when laying workers off, consider their reputations because they anticipate future hiring or rehiring. The turnover data indicate that even in the worst years of the depression firms were continually hiring or rehiring workers.

Without a change in the legal and institutional environment after Roosevelt's election, the importance of the reputation effects described in contract theory would not have kept real wages up or caused the rapid real wage gains in manufacturing. However, the permanent effects of the NIRA would have been much less, or nonexistent, if the labor market were more like an auction market. The two combined made a big difference, with the threat of unionization providing an important spur to the use of "fair" labor relations policies. The general recovery of employment and output after 1933 and the acceptance of responsibility for income maintenance of the hard-core unemployed also reinforced the stable wage policies.

Conclusions for Policy Today

This paper was not intended as new historical research into the depression. Rather, I hope that some light has been cast on current macroeconomic thinking by appealing to historical evidence. One comes away from an examination of this period impressed anew by the fact that, even though money wages change a great deal, they do not seem very responsive to excess unemployment, even to persistent excess unemployment. I have argued that there was a basis in rational decision-making and in the institutional environment for this observed behavior. But I do not conclude that the 1930s necessarily demonstrate fundamental wage inertia in all circumstances.

The simple fact is that falling wages and prices do not work very well, if at all, to restore full-employment aggregate demand. An expansionary monetary and fiscal policy is the correct remedy for a depression. Current economic difficulties are different. If unemployment above the natural rate did cause a rapid slowing of wage growth, full employment could and would be restored quickly through aggregate demand control. Even though I have argued that the new classical model of the business cycle is badly flawed, I still think there is something to the argument advanced by its proponent, Thomas Sargent, that a regime change could break the inertia in wages. I even had some hope that Margaret Thatcher's experiment would work.

Sargent has argued that the preconditions for a successful regime change are that the proposed change be widely accepted, understood, and believed to be permanent.[53] I see only a slim connection between these conditions and the business cycle theory he uses, but they may be quite correct anyway. They may also be the conditions necessary for a successful incomes policy. If wages were sticky in the depression because people did not believe wage cutting would work, wages might not be sticky if everyone believed a new policy would work. The trick, of course, is to figure out how to establish the preconditions. Mrs. Thatcher clearly did not have it figured out. Time will tell about the current U.S. experiment with tight money, but few economists of any persuasion are hopeful that the costs of restraining inflation will be avoided.

Comment by Peter A. Diamond

MARTIN BAILY starts by taking us on a tour of statistics about the 1930s. These are interesting, particularly the high rate of accessions. It is too bad that data showing the split between recalls and new hires are not available. One suspects that the new hire rate was substantial. It would be nice to know.

Then Baily looks at the relationship between these data and two theoretical frameworks—intertemporal labor substitution with market clearing and implicit contracts with sticky wages.[54] (Here he allows misperceptions.) In both cases he finds that the theories are not plausibly consistent with the data, particularly after 1932.[55] That is, neither of these theories fits the data when combined otherwise with conventional competitive equilibrium and estimates of the reasonable size of both misperceptions and elasticities of labor supply and demand. At least in some years, additional (or alternative) mechanisms must have been at

53. Thomas J. Sargent, "Stopping Moderate Inflation: The Methods of Poincaré and Thatcher" (University of Minnesota and Federal Reserve Bank of Minneapolis, May 1981).

54. He takes the market model as set up by Lucas and Rapping in "Real Wages."

55. The poor fit of market clearing and intertemporal substitution with part of the 1930s is acknowledged by Lucas and Rapping, "Unemployment in the Great Depression." They use a model of a representative household to derive econometric equations. It is clear from their discussion, however, that they have in mind a more complicated model with search. The relevant wage series for this latter theory needs to reflect the wages faced by the marginal workers, which is not the same as the published average wage series.

work. Baily explicitly draws the conclusion that a fully successful macroeconomic model cannot have a competitive output market.

Baily tests an implication of implicit contracts (sticky real wages) but no other aspect of implicit contracts. Thus his findings hold also for alternative theories implying sticky wages. While I agree that firms are concerned with workers' morale and their own reputation when setting wages or wage negotiation positions, I think one needs to be careful in the use of implicit contract theory. In some situations the isomorphism between a distribution over time and a distribution across states of nature is helpful. However, when the situation is changing and the firm is concerned with contemporary and future expectations (not past expectations), the isomorphism may break down. This is particularly true of a time like the 1930s when implicit contracts were being broken, as witnessed, for example, by the cancellation of pension programs.

Sticky wages and prices did not prevent the depression; wage and price cuts were seen as not helping and may not have been able to help much. This suggests the need for using models that focus on the problem of trade coordination rather than on wages and prices. The Walrasian model has trade coordinated by a fictitious auctioneer and instantaneous reactions to events. In macroeconomics it seems to me important to recognize the difficulty of coordinating trade and the fact that everything takes time. Thus I would go further than Baily and argue for the necessity not only of dropping the assumption of a competitive output market, but also of dropping the Walrasian model for one where the allocation process occurs over time. Naturally I think the most promising approach lies along the line of search equilibrium, which I have been pursuing lately.

JOHN B. TAYLOR

Rational Expectations
and the Invisible Handshake

CAN long-term career or customer relationships, which improve the
economic welfare of individuals at the microeconomic level, have
harmful macroeconomic side effects that make even a credible monetary
disinflation program extremely costly? That they can, and do, is the
theme of Arthur Okun's comprehensive theoretical investigation, *Prices
and Quantities*. The policy implications of this study are of particular
interest today as policymakers appear to have implemented a program
of monetary restraint to disinflate the U.S. economy. If accurate, Okun's
prediction that "the dynamics of inflation are embedded in the process
of wage and price determination and cannot be eliminated solely by fiscal
and monetary measures without incurring great losses of output and
employment"[1] raises serious doubts about the sustainability of such a
program of monetary restraint.

While long-term relationships—invisible handshakes—between
workers, firms, and their customers are the main subject of Okun's
study, the *expectations* of individuals involved in these relationships
also figure prominently in the analysis. This should not be surprising,
for long-term relationships do not diminish the importance of expectations in macroeconomic analysis. On the contrary, expectations of the
future significantly affect the terms of contractual arrangements. They
are of greater quantitative importance in contractual situations than they
are in more flexible auction market situations. Okun's analysis certainly
recognizes the importance of expectations, but it breaks ranks with
much current macroeconomic research by deliberately avoiding the use
of *rational* expectations, or efficient forecasting, in the investigation of

I am grateful to Robert E. Hall and George L. Perry for helpful comments.

1. Arthur M. Okun, *Prices and Quantities: A Macroeconomic Analysis* (Brookings
Institution, 1981), p. 234.

long-term arrangements. Instead of relying on rational forecasts, the implicit contracts in Okun's analysis have a rigid forecasting clause that is just as slow to adapt to economic change as more conventional aspects of the long-term relationships: "prices and wages are not the result of precise forecasts: indeed, they reflect arrangements that people have sensibly adopted to reduce their dependence on forecasts."[2] Why is it sensible to avoid the use of precise forecasts in implicit contracts? At least in the wage-setting decision, "forecasting the wages of other firms is complex and costly, and communicating the validity of the forecast to workers may be equally challenging."[3]

While such a treatment of expectations may be empirically accurate in some cases, it runs counter to recent research on macro models with long-term contractual arrangements where rational expectations have been the benchmark assumption.[4] It also runs counter to much of the early and more recent microeconomic theory on implicit contracts,[5] where agents are assumed to know the distribution of possible outcomes and forecast these outcomes efficiently even though their information sets may be asymmetric. This difference raises the question of whether Okun's conclusions about macroeconomic side effects are due to inefficient forecasting rather than to the invisible handshake per se. Would replacing the rigid forecasting clause in the implicit contracts with an agreement to use an efficient forecasting scheme reduce the macroeconomic inefficiencies or eliminate them entirely?

In this paper I examine this question by introducing rational expectations into Okun's macro model with long-term contracting, as presented in *Prices and Quantities*. The analysis indicates that this change in the expectations assumption significantly reduces the macroeconomic inefficiencies. In other words, it is not the invisible handshake that causes many of the macroeconomic difficulties, but rather the forecasting clause in the implicit contract. I make use of results developed in recent

2. Ibid., p. 356.
3. Ibid., p. 97.
4. For example, Stanley Fischer, "Long-Term Contracts, Rational Expectations, and the Optimal Money Supply Rule," *Journal of Political Economy*, vol. 85 (February 1977), pp. 191–205; and Edmund S. Phelps and John B. Taylor, "Stabilizing Powers of Monetary Policy under Rational Expectations," *Journal of Political Economy*, vol. 85 (February 1977), pp. 163–90.
5. For example, Costas Azariadis, "Implicit Contracts and Underemployment Equilibria," *Journal of Political Economy*, vol. 83 (December 1975), pp. 1183–1202; and Sanford J. Grossman and Oliver D. Hart, "Implicit Contracts, Moral Hazard, and Unemployment," *American Economic Review*, vol. 71 (May 1981, *Papers and Proceedings, 1980*), pp. 301–07.

research on rational expectations models with unsynchronized wage setting.[6] I proceed by showing that the Okun model (at least by my interpretation) closely resembles the staggered wage-setting model considered in this research. The primary differences are in the expectations assumptions, as is shown in some detail below.

How should these results be interpreted in practice? What do they suggest about an appropriate research strategy in this area? One approach is to dismiss the rational expectations assumption as empirically inaccurate or too speculative for practical policy analysis and continue to rely on rigid extrapolative forecasting rules. A second approach is to dismiss the wage- and price-setting model as too simplistic or just incorrect: something must be wrong with the model if merely changing an expectations assumption eliminates the costs of disinflation. A third approach—which is emphasized here—is to recognize that there may indeed be serious barriers to the use of optimal forecasts of wages and prices that are responsive enough to achieve the macro efficiencies that the rational expectations approach suggests are feasible, but also to recognize that these barriers might be lowered or removed through public policy. Rational forecasting may indeed be too costly to justify implementation by individual firms and workers, or even by large corporations or labor unions. Moreover, it may not be wise for firms or workers to expect that other firms or workers are using the *same* forecasting model that they are using. And the macro policy that underlies the rational forecast may not be credible. This credibility barrier to rational expectations has already received serious attention in practical policy discussions, usually taking the form of monetary reform proposals that would force the macroeconomic policymakers to be credible. The analysis that follows suggests that attention should also be placed on the first two barriers if significant improvements in macroeconomic efficiency are to be achieved.

A Macro Model with Long-Term Contracts

In chapter 3 of *Prices and Quantities* a simple macro model of aggregate wage dynamics and unemployment fluctuations is introduced to illustrate the process of inflation in a world of long-term contracts.

6. Edmund S. Phelps, "Obstacles to Curtailing Inflation," in James H. Gapinski and Charles E. Rockwood, eds., *Essays in Post-Keynesian Inflation* (Ballinger, 1979), pp. 179–93; and John B. Taylor, "Aggregate Dynamics and Staggered Contracts," *Journal of Political Economy*, vol. 88 (February 1980), pp. 1–23.

Unsynchronized, or staggered, wage setting in which wage decisions are made relative to a prevailing wage is a central feature of the dynamics of this model, which seems to capture much of the microtheoretic rationale for implicit contracts. As this model is the target of my rational expectations treatment, some brief discussion about how it relates to recent work on contract theory is in order.

Contract Theory and Staggered Wage Setting

Implicit contract theory of labor markets has generally been cast as an arrangement whereby firms stabilize fluctuations in the real wage as part of a risk-sharing agreement with workers, which potentially takes account of asymmetric information and moral hazard. Hall has argued persuasively that such long-term arrangements are empirically relevant and that their micro efficiency (given the shifts in firms' productivity) should be taken seriously.[7] As Hall, Grossman and Hart,[8] and others have pointed out, however, such "real" contracting cannot explain why changes in the money supply have real effects, as would be the case in a costly disinflation. Accordingly, contract theory apparently cannot explain the macroeconomic inefficiencies with which I am concerned here.

Although these issues are still unresolved, there is a reinterpretation of the contract-theoretic results that is appropriate for the type of model of staggered wage setting considered here. It does not seem to violate the spirit of the implicit contract model to reinterpret it as an insurance arrangement that provides stability of the wage *relative* to the going wage received by similar workers. If workers are at all mobile, the current wage received by other similar workers represents the appropriate opportunity cost of working in the current firm. If moving is costly (or if threatening to move in order to capture the appropriate market wage is costly), firms will be ready to provide an implicit contract benchmarked to this going wage. An advantage of relative wage insurance is that the circumstances under which the firm must renege on its contract correspond to the situation where the firm must leave the business: if the firm cannot meet the going wage (cannot fulfill its contract) and generate positive profits, then it will not be in business. Real wage

7. Robert E. Hall, "Employment Fluctuations and Wage Rigidity," *Brookings Papers on Economic Activity, 1:1980,* pp. 91–123.

8. Ibid.; and Grossman and Hart, "Implicit Contracts."

stabilization does not have this feature. A renegotiation of the contract is called for when the guaranteed real wage does not generate positive profits while a wage payment at the prevailing wage does. Relative wage contracting is therefore more sustainable.

These contracted changes in relative wages are likely to occur in an unsynchronized and staggered fashion, because firms will find they can achieve their desired relative wage with more certainty if the prevailing wage is predetermined. In a situation where each firm would like to go last a competitive equilibrium could plausibly evolve in which wage setting was fairly evenly staggered over time. Okun mentions that this temporal equilibrium is much like a spatial equilibrium in location theory, although this has not yet been worked out formally.

An efficient *relative* wage contract would probably entail some variation in the relative wage even if that variation was less than in the auction market. For example, Arnott, Hosios, and Stiglitz have developed an implicit contract model with layoffs, quits, and job search.[9] They show that the optimal contract will stipulate a reduction in the wage relative to the expected prevailing wage when marginal productivity is low, as in the case of a slump in the demand for the firm's product. An analogous argument suggests that, when unemployment is low and expected search costs are accordingly reduced, firms will find it efficient to bid up their wage relative to the expected prevailing wage.

How can such a setup generate macroeconomic inefficiencies? Relative wage contracting can generate a path for the *nominal* wage that is not directly related to current economic conditions. If nominal wage payments require some transactions medium, there will be a direct demand relationship between these payments and the quantity of transactions balances—much like Keynes's demand for money in terms of wage units. Hence, changes in the nominal wage path can reduce total expenditures if the supply of money does not change by the same percentage. Moreover, reductions in the growth of the money supply will have real effects because the path of nominal wages is given at any point by the recently set relative wage contracts. Real wage movements are not a central part of this mechanism. Prices can be determined as stable markups over costs, as implied by Okun's customer relations model, in which case the aggregate price level will follow the aggregate

9. Richard J. Arnott, Arthur J. Hosios, and Joseph A. Stiglitz, "Implicit Contracts, Labor Mobility, and Unemployment," working paper (Princeton University, 1980).

nominal wage fairly closely, reinforcing the contractionary effects of a decline in the growth of the money supply. In that case real wage movements play no role in the analysis. Although this approach is considerably different from the mechanism in the "neo-Keynesian synthesis," it does generate results consistent with the insignificant empirical role of real wages in the business cycle. In this framework an increase in the nominal wage reduces aggregate employment simply by reducing real balances (measured in terms of both the aggregate price level and the aggregate wage level), assuming a less than fully accommodative monetary response. This differs from the "neo-Keynesian synthesis" explanation where an increase in the nominal wage would increase the real wage and reduce firms' demand for labor.

Alternative Wage-setting Rules

To simplify the algebraic treatment of this unsynchronized nominal wage contracting, assume that there are annual wage changes with half the workers changing their wages in January and the other half in July (Okun's tabular example has one-fourth of the contracts changing each quarter). Let x_t be the log of the contract wage set in period t to last through period $t + 1$. The log of the geometric average wage is given by $w_t = \frac{1}{2}(x_t + x_{t-1})$. The framework and notation correspond with that in my earlier work,[10] except that the procedure for setting the contract wages and the corresponding expectations mechanism has yet to be specified.

Okun considered two different wage-setting rules for this model. Each depends on the expectations assumption used. To describe these rules one must introduce Okun's notion of the "reference" wage, which is the average of existing wages outstanding at the time the wage is determined. Note that the reference wage is different from the "prevailing" wage relevant to wage decisions made in period t. The prevailing wage for a given contract decision will depend partially on the upcoming wage decision of other workers, while the reference wage is simply a function of past wage decisions. In this two-period version of the model the reference wage for workers or firms deciding on wages in period t is

10. Taylor, "Aggregate Dynamics."

x_{t-1}, the wage determined six months earlier. The prevailing wage is $\frac{1}{2}(x_{t-1} + x_{t+1})$.

The wage-setting rules considered by Okun (in the absence of a motivation for a relative wage change) are given in the form

(1) $$x_t = x_{t-1} + \tfrac{1}{2}g,$$

where g is the forecast of the change in x_t over the length of the contract. By definition,

(2) $$g = x^e_{t+1} - x_{t-1},$$

where x^e_{t+1} is the forecast of the wage decision in the next period, x_{t+1}. According to equation 1, the wage decision is to raise the current wage over the reference wage by one-half of the projected increase in the reference wage. That rule 1 makes sense when no relative wage change is desired is most easily shown by substituting equation 2 into 1. This gives

(3) $$x_t = \tfrac{1}{2}(x_{t-1} + x^e_{t+1}).$$

Thus rule 1 is a way for workers to match the average prevailing wage over the life of the contract. (The second six months of the wage, x_{t-1}, is in effect during period t, and the first six months of the wage, x_{t+1}, is in effect during period $t + 1$.) According to equation 3, workers can expect to stay even on average, although they will be ahead in the beginning and behind at the end.

Note that x^e_{t+1} is not a rational expectation in Okun's model. Okun's two wage-setting rules are derived by placing specific extrapolative assumptions on x^e_{t+1} or equivalently on g. One extrapolative assumption is that the reference wage is forecast to grow at the same rate over the next year as it did over the past year. This results in the wage-setting rule given by

(4) $$x_t = x_{t-1} + \tfrac{1}{2}(x_{t-1} - x_{t-3}).$$

Equation 4 will keep workers even under a steady inflation rate in which it is rational to extrapolate next year's increase in the reference wage as equal to this year's increase. But if inflation of the reference wage is expected to increase or decrease, equation 4 will not be rational.

Another wage-adjustment mechanism suggested by Okun is simply to increase the current wage relative to its previous level by the same amount that the reference wage was most recently adjusted. Algebraically this procedure is represented by

$$(5) \qquad\qquad x_t = x_{t-2} + (x_{t-1} - x_{t-3}).$$

That is, workers setting wages today get an increase $(x_t - x_{t-2})$ equal to the increase $(x_{t-1} - x_{t-3})$ obtained by workers who most recently had a wage adjustment. Equation 5 is of particular interest because it corresponds with many casual interpretations of wage change. That is, unless there is a shift in labor market conditions caused, say, by a recession, workers will continue to match the wage gains of workers who immediately preceded them. Equation 5 has the interesting property that it preserves the differential between the current wage and the *reference* wage under any inflation pattern. That is, if workers were d percent above the reference wage when they previously changed their wage, they will remain d percent above the reference wage by using 5. If

$$(6) \qquad\qquad x_{t-2} - x_{t-3} = d,$$

equation 5 implies that

$$(7) \qquad\qquad x_t - x_{t-1} = d,$$

regardless of the path of wage rates. It is therefore possible to see how 5 could become a rule of thumb incorporated in an implicit contract. Under a steady inflation workers might get used to the idea of always jumping ahead of the reference wage by a fixed percent, and for a time under a higher rate of inflation they might not change this clause of the contract. But eventually workers would see that their wage relative to the more relevant *prevailing* wage was not constant and would attempt to change their contract. Okun's analysis does not rule out such changes. It does argue that they will occur only gradually, however. If the consensus forecast was that the rate of inflation would change in the future, Okun's analysis would not predict any change in equation 4 or 5. Only by observing over a period of time that they were doing poorly relative to the prevailing wage would workers insist on a change in the forecasting rule implicit in their contract.

    To generate wage and employment dynamics it is necessary to consider shifts in one of these two wage-setting rules. Wage-setting mistakes or shocks, for example, could be captured by adding a random disturbance term to these rules. More important, relative wages will have to move when the labor market conditions faced by the firm change.

This can be captured algebraically by adding the unemployment rate as a proxy for these labor market conditions to any of the three equations. (It may be plausible to add the *expected* unemployment rate over the life of the contract to these equations, but for the purposes of this analysis the addition of only the current unemployment rate will do just as well.)

Macro Efficiency Issues

It is easy to see how the wage-setting equations 4 and 5 can lead to real output loss even under a credible monetary disinflation program. Suppose that the rate of money growth is reduced steadily from recent levels in order to disinflate the economy. According to either 4 or 5, wage inflation will not be reduced unless the rate of unemployment (which is now envisioned as a term on the right-hand side of these equations) rises, causing firms to attempt to bid down their wages relative to the prevailing wage. There is, of course, a natural mechanism in the model to generate the rise in unemployment. As money growth is reduced relative to the given growth rate of wages and prices, real balances will fall and interest rates will rise, cutting off the demand for goods and forcing firms to lay off workers. Equations 4 and 5 show that this loss in employment is inevitable. Only changes in these equations—changes in the contract—will prevent it, and according to the interpretation of these equations, this can only occur after a period of observation.

Now suppose that expectations are rational so that x^e_{t+1} in the basic wage-setting equation 3 is an unbiased forecast, given information about policy. It is important to note that no other changes have been made in the model—only the extrapolative rules have been replaced with a rational forecasting scheme. To make the effect of this change as dramatic as possible, suppose it becomes generally known that wage levels starting in period $t + 1$ will be stabilized at the current level of the most recently set wages. For example, suppose that a wide commodity standard is introduced whereby the monetary authorities are expected to stabilize the aggregate price level in period $t + 1$ at the current level. By the markup assumption, this means that the rational expectation of x_{t+1} will equal x_{t-1}, assuming credibility of the program. According to equation 3, the appropriate wage adjustment for workers setting their wage in period t, the date the plan is announced, is simply to match $x_{t-1} = x^e_{t+1}$. They adjust their wage from x_{t-2} to x_{t-1}. If inflation has been proceeding at a 10 percent annual rate, workers in period t will receive a 5 percent wage adjustment, and workers in all subsequent periods will experience zero wage inflation. The disinflation process lasts no longer than the length of the longest contract (one year) and requires no increase in unemployment—equation 3 holds as an identity throughout. Phelps has shown how this same possibility exists in a more general model.[11] Of course, this price-standard example is probably too extreme. I have shown that a gradual program of *monetary* restraint will generate some output loss, but because of the adjustments in x_{t+1}^e (which are feasible with rational expectations), this loss will be considerably less than in the nonresponsive expectations case.[12] By announcing the monetary disinflation far enough in advance, it is possible to make these losses negligible. The analogy with these previous results can be made under the interpretation that Okun's model reduces to equation 3, which with rational expectations is identical to the staggered contract model used in this earlier research.

A Qualification Concerning Policy Accommodation

Both of the simple policy examples of the previous section avoid the issue of unforeseen random events that force a change in the program either before or after the disinflation. Suppose, for example, that during the monetary disinflation there is an unanticipated price shock (for example, a run-up of energy prices). In both the extrapolative and the rational expectations versions of the simple macro model, the monetary authorities will have to make a decision about whether to accommodate this shock. If they do not accommodate, or if they only partially accommodate, both models suggest that there will be a decline in employment and output as real balances are reduced when this shock first bids up the price level and is then forced out of the system. Although the rational expectations version of the model indicates that (if this nonaccommodative strategy in response to future shocks is correctly anticipated) the employment effect will be smaller than without rational expectations, the macro side effects do not disappear. When future price shocks are included, therefore, a trade-off between output and price fluctuations remains if policy is committed to maintaining a price target consistent with zero average inflation in the long run. Evidently some of the macro efficiencies persist.

The difference between this example, where the price target is

11. Phelps, "Obstacles to Curtailing Inflation."
12. Taylor, "Aggregate Dynamics."

maintained (even if deviations are permitted in the short run), and the disinflation example of the previous sections is that the *level* of wages and prices must be maintained. With a positive shock, this requires a *decline* in average nominal wages or prices toward their long-run targets, which is not required for disinflation. This return to the target wage or price levels requires a temporary deviation of employment from full-employment levels, which is unavoidable with the long-term contracts of the previous section, even with rational expectations.

One resolution to this qualification is to forget the notion of a price-*level* target for future policy and to stipulate that policymakers aim only for a zero inflation rate: that they fully accommodate any price shock by ratifying the new price or wage level but then commit themselves to remaining at this new price level. The difficulty is that the policy is unable to distinguish between exogenous shocks that bid up wages and prices and endogenous increases in wages and prices that are made in expectation of a fully accommodative strategy. If policymakers are expected to accommodate price and wage shocks, they will also be expected to accommodate endogenous increases in wages and prices. Hence it does not seem possible to discard the notion of a price- or wage-*level* target and maintain credibility about a zero inflation target.

Another resolution is to argue that the implicit contract mechanism itself will adapt and thereby offset any macroeconomic inefficiencies that result from a less than fully accommodative strategy. Perhaps the contracts will change to permit larger relative wage adjustments, for example, so that employment fluctuations do not increase with the less accommodative strategy. Implicit contract theory and the simple macro models that try to reflect this theory are not yet sophisticated enough to predict whether such an outcome is possible. But such adaptation requires changes in the implicit contracts themselves rather than changes in the forecasting schemes considered in previous sections. These changes in the long-term relationships could make them less efficient at the micro level. But this is an open question.

Testing for "Forward-looking" Wage Setting

The model outlined above requires that firms and workers be forward-looking in their wage settlements so that they keep even with the prevailing wage during the term of the settlement, unless changes in the relative wage are desired for economic reasons. In the extrapolative version of the model firms and workers look forward by looking backward, and in the rational expectations version they look forward by using rational forecasts. In both models, however, workers and firms are assumed to be forward-looking in their wage-setting goals. In this section I show how this assumption might be tested, given an expectational assumption. Although the tests could be carried out conditional on an expectational assumption, only the rational expectations assumption is dealt with here. The test procedure is directly analogous to that used by Sargent to test the expectations theory of the term structure of interest rules using the rational expectations assumption.[13]

A more general form of equation 1 or 3 that leaves open the forward-looking assumption is given by

$$(8) \qquad x_t = (1 - f)x_{t-1} + fx_{t+1}^e + h_t,$$

where f represents how forward-looking wage settlements are, and h is a proxy for expected labor market conditions during the period of the set wage. In empirical applications h_t could be related to the employment rate. Suppose for the purposes of conducting the test that $h_t = -\gamma(u_t^e + u_{t+1}^e)$, where γ is a parameter and u_t is the unemployment rate. The main concern here is with testing the null hypothesis $H_0: f = \frac{1}{2}$, which is the assumption made in the previous section. Obviously, if $f = 0$, there is no forward looking and, whether expectations are rational or not, disinflation will be costly.

The test procedure is to estimate an unconstrained time series process, such as a vector autoregression, for x_t and u_t. Equation 8, under the assumption of rational expectations, will place constraints on this estimated time series process. The constrained versus the unconstrained version can be compared with a standard F-statistic. In research that is still under way I have run tests of this kind using quarterly data from Canada, where contract wages corresponding to the contracts x_t are available for much of the postwar period, and have found that it is generally difficult to reject the hypothesis that $f = \frac{1}{2}$. But the point I wish to raise here is that this result is quite general and is unlikely to be specific to a particular country. The unconstrained vector autoregression for x_t and u_t generally has a form where the lagged cross effects between u_t and x_t are small and the lagged dependent variable coefficients in each

13. Thomas J. Sargent, "A Note on Maximum Likelihood Estimation of the Rational Expectations Model of the Term Structure," *Journal of Monetary Economics,* vol. 5 (January 1979), pp. 133–43.

equation are large. Moreover, when x_t is entered into the equations in first difference form, the lagged dependent variable is very close to 1. To a first-order approximation, therefore, the unconstrained vector autoregression has the form

$$(9) \qquad\qquad x_t - x_{t-1} = x_{t-1} - x_{t-2},$$

and

$$(10) \qquad\qquad u_t = \alpha u_{t-1},$$

where for the sake of illustration only one lagged term is considered in the unemployment equation. The approximation in 9 and 10 has simply set the coefficient of the lagged unemployment rate in the wage equation and the coefficient of the lagged contract inflation rate in the unemployment equation to zero, since these are generally small and do not significantly affect the results. According to equation 9, the rational forecast of future x_t conditional on past observations is given by

$$(11) \qquad\qquad x_t^e = 2x_{t-1} - x_{t-2},$$

and

$$(12) \qquad\qquad x_{t+1}^e = 3x_{t-1} - 2x_{t-2}.$$

These can be substituted into 8 to obtain

$$(13) \quad 2x_{t-1} - x_{t-2} = (1 - f)x_{t-1} + f(3x_{t-1} - 2x_{t-2}) + \gamma\alpha(1 + \alpha)u_{t-1}.$$

In this example, the parameter f is identified and can be obtained by equating the coefficients of either x_{t-1} or x_{t-2} on both sides of equation 13. Both equations yield $f = \frac{1}{2}$. The value of α does not matter. As long as the joint process for x_t and u_t is a form that is close to 9 and 10, the value of f is close to $\frac{1}{2}$, the assumed value in the preceding section. This illustration explains why the result $f = \frac{1}{2}$ is likely to be quite general: equations 9 and 10 are close approximations of the wage and unemployment dynamics in many countries.

The Usefulness of the Rational Expectations Assumption

While the previous section gives some evidence of forward looking in wage determination, it does not prove that this forward looking is not achieved by simple extrapolation. In fact, the autoregressive model of equation 9, which is taken to be representative of postwar time series data, is perfectly consistent with the extrapolative rule suggested by Okun and shown here in equation 5. The correspondence between equations 5 and 9 illustrates the difficulty of testing for rational expectations in this context. There seems to be no substitute for direct evidence on *how* firms and workers arrive at their forecasts of future wages relevant to their wage decision. This requires careful survey studies to examine the forecasting *process,* not merely surveys of the forecasts themselves. The forecasts reached are subject to the same identification problems that the comparison of 5 and 9 suggests.

An alternative, perhaps more constructive, approach that may generate large social benefits, given the discussion in the first section, is to begin thinking about how the expectations process in wage formation might be made more rational. Little would be lost by such a strategy if firms and workers were already behaving as if they were rational forecasters, but much would be gained if they were not.

Recent efforts to make macro policy, and particular monetary policy, more credible can be interpreted as efforts to encourage firms and workers to be more accurate in their forecasting by paying attention to the future implications of a credible policy. For example, one group of economists has recently suggested that the members of the Board of Governors of the Federal Reserve System submit their resignation to the president if they miss their announced deceleration program. [14] Those who argue for a gold or general commodity standard have similar aims. Recent discussions about balancing the federal budget seem to have the main objective of showing that future money growth will not be necessary to finance the deficit and thereby make the stated monetary deceleration program more credible. Whatever one thinks about the effects of such proposals, it seems clear that there are substantial advantages to achieving credibility.

Serious consideration might also be given to other ways of increasing forecasting accuracy. There are two potential barriers to the use of rational expectations in practice, which in principle could be overcome. First, the costs of using sophisticated forecasting procedures are unlikely to generate sufficient benefits for an individual firm or worker, even though, as shown above, the social benefits are large. Second, the use

14. "Shadow Open Market Committee, Policy Statements and Position Papers," unpublished report, University of Rochester, 1981.

of rational expectations requires some consensus on how inflation is generated and the dynamics of this process. Without such a consensus firms may not think that other firms are using rational forecasts.[15] Unfortunately, the current lack of consensus among economists makes such a possibility seem dubious. It is possible that the kind of macro model formulated in Okun's book, but augmented with more optimal (rational) forecasting on the part of firms and workers, might form the basis of such a consensus. Such models have received, and continue to receive, extensive attention by microeconomists in the literature on implicit contracts, and are very similar to the staggered contract models with rational expectations that are already close to being formulated for detailed structural econometric work.

Concluding Remarks

This paper has argued that many of the macro inefficiencies—such as costly monetary disinflation—generated by the long-term contract models in Okun's book are due to the rigid extrapolative forecasting clauses in these contracts rather than to the restrictions the contracts place on wage and employment variation. The practical importance of this argument for actual disinflation policy depends on the accuracy of the rational expectations assumption. The results suggest that methods be investigated under which public policy encourages the use of efficient forecasting, such as making macroeconomic policy more credible. The development of theoretical and econometric models along the lines suggested in Okun's book, but augmented when appropriate with rational expectations techniques, appears to be a necessary part of any such effort.

Comment by Robert E. Hall

ONE OF the many things Arthur Okun drummed into my head was that the inertia of wages was not necessarily related to expectations. In a way, Taylor's paper makes the same point. If inertia comes from some other source, the current emphasis on the credibility of anti-inflation policy

15. See Edmund S. Phelps, "The Trouble with Rational Expectations and the Problem with Inflation Stabilization," working paper (Columbia University, 1980).

may be misplaced. Until inertia is better understood, we should be cautious in advocating aggressive anti-inflation policies.

Taylor begins by reminding us of a central implication of rational expectations. Suppose a fully credible anti-inflation policy is announced sufficiently far in advance that all wage-price contracts and other arrangements with allocative significance can respond to the announcement before it takes effect. Then no real effects should follow—the policy should operate only on prices and wages.

Taylor then cites Okun's two major objections to this proposition. First, the full forecasts it presupposes are too expensive, especially if you count as part of the expense the effort to convince individual workers that the forecasts are correct. Second, the full disinflationary response requires that each economic agent believe that everyone else is fully rational.

It seems to me that Taylor, following Okun and numerous other authors on this subject, takes a lot for granted about the form of labor contracts and other aspects of wage determination.

First, contracts are viewed as setting wages that have an allocational role. Once the wage is determined through the operation of the contract, firms set the level of employment by equating the marginal revenue product of labor to the wage. The polar opposite view thinks of employment as very long term and current wages as nothing more than installment payments on a long-term obligation. Although I think the evidence favors a considerable short-term allocative role for wages, the point deserves much more investigation and debate than it usually receives in this kind of discussion.

Second, according to Taylor, a major goal of contracts is to stabilize wages relative to wages earned by other workers. Preserving wage relationships takes precedence over keeping wages low enough to provide employment for all the workers covered by an agreement. I am not persuaded that the evidence requires us to invoke a noneconomic role for outside wages. The economic links across sectors in the labor market can be strong. Wages in alternative employment determine the opportunity cost of workers' time. One of the puzzles of U.S. labor markets, in fact, is the evident lack of formal indexation to wage indexes.

Third, everything in the Okun-Taylor line of thought depends on the inability to make contingent contracts. Management and labor cannot make wages respond to events as they occur. Instead, they have to rely on forecasts made at contract time. Rational expectations would not matter under fully contingent contracts. The absence of contingencies in labor contracts other than cost-of-living indexing remains a mystery, though a good deal of thinking about this has been done recently. Information limitations and moral hazard block many attractive procedures. Contract contingencies can interfere with unrelated aspects of the employment relationship—for example, making wages contingent on outside wage offers gives workers incentives to train themselves for other jobs even when their comparative advantage will remain in their current jobs.

Taylor's discussion assumes a fairly brief contract period. But many aspects of the employment contract must last as long as the employment itself, which is often many decades. Annual or triennial wage discussions may take place in such a constrained setting that they cannot respond effectively to new economic conditions. If so, the contract period is really much longer and the response of wages to demand much more sluggish than Taylor indicates.

At the end of the paper, Taylor suggests that the social costs of wage mistakes far exceeds the private costs. Except for the usual distortions from unemployment insurance and income taxes, it is not clear to me what creates the externalities he has in mind. The major costs of underemployment fall precisely on the underemployed.

Taylor's paper is a helpful review of some important and unsettled issues. As unemployment rises in Britain and the United States to levels unprecedented since the depression, we are reminded of how central these issues are.

Comment by George L. Perry

JOHN TAYLOR'S treatment of rational expectations in wage and price determination can be divided into two parts. First, how the world works: is rational expectations a useful way to describe the behavioral process in this area of economic decisionmaking? And second, how the world could be made better: would encouraging the use of rational expectations in this process improve macroeconomic performance?

On how the world works, Taylor is formally agnostic. He suggests that under one general technique for trying to explore that question— vector autoregression—one will never get a clear verdict because the rational expectations will always be approximated by a simple extrapolation of the most recently observed wage (or price) increases. Because such a simple extrapolation is a plausible rule for a world in which expectations, as such, are not normally important to wage setting, the rational forward-looking model cannot be distinguished from alternatives. Indeed, the rational expectations rules in Taylor's equations 11 to 13 look just like a sluggish wage norm formulation.

When I tried my hand at distinguishing between forward- and backward-looking behavior using data from long-term labor contracts, I found that wage setting was better explained by backward-looking catch-up behavior than by a *good* forecast of the future. Logically, that does not rule out forecasts as a factor in wage setting. But it does imply that, if they are a factor, the forecasts are made by extrapolating the past rather than by some superior technique that provides better forecasts of the future.

The proposition that wage setting does not seem to involve good forecasts has relevance for whether forecasts are important in the process at all. Although some formal properties of rational expectations macro models require only that expectations be unbiased and efficient, in practice they should also be good forecasts by some standard. If they are not, nobody will attach any importance to them. This observation supports Okun's argument that simple, backward-looking wage setting is optimal under the implicit contracts sealed by the invisible handshake.

As I interpret his paper, Taylor leans toward the position that rational expectations have not been important in wage setting, for he devotes himself to considering how they might be made important, thus improving macro performance. I believe his simple model, which is appropriate and valuable in highlighting the difference between inertial and expectational views of wage setting, becomes deceptively simple when applied to this second task.

Taylor illustrates the improvement available in macro performance by allowing rational expectations to guide wage setting according to his equation 3. He then assumes that policymakers, in period t, convince the world that wages set in $t + 1$ will be set at the same level as in $t - 1$. Sure enough, the wages set in t are then also set at the level of those set in $t - 1$, and disinflation is painlessly achieved. But surely the assumption begs all the interesting questions.

What do the wage setters expect policy to control? The money supply, fiscal policy, nominal GNP, and unemployment are all more plausible answers than the wage level. The variables most easily controlled are the furthest from the wage level in most macroeconomic models, and the connection between them and wages is the weakest. Thus the first problem is how to convince today's wage setters that wages will be low tomorrow.

On top of this basic difficulty, the proximate aims in wage setting are almost surely very different from those Taylor describes. If one alters the form of his equation 3 so that current wage setting is dominated by the desire to match prevailing *rates of increase* in wages and attempts to align wage *levels* are only secondary, the disinflation process looks much different. If wage setting has one component that applies to relative wage levels and is affected by unemployment and another component that is governed by the prevailing norm for rates of wage increase, then even if rational expectations could affect the first component, as Taylor indicates, it would have little effect on the total actual wage change.

This formulation is not artificial. Most wages are set at least annually and keeping up with the prevailing rate of wage inflation involves little risk of serious error in that length of time. These wages are fixed for too short a period to make expectations in contract theory a crucial part of the wage model. Wages set in three-year cycles—a period over which a forecast error would make a much bigger difference—are in fact conditional contracts with escalators that minimize the need to forecast inflation.

Let me now put aside these reservations about the process and stick to Taylor's premise that expectations are truly a central element in wage setting. He emphasizes that increasing credibility is the best hope for changing the wage-setting relation in the appropriate way. Although it has not mattered in the past, one can make the promise of disinflation matter and get wage setters to take notice in the future. Economic relations will shift, and the credibility hypothesis is a plausible story about how a predictable shift in the inflation relation might be engineered.

Taylor makes no excessive claims or optimistic forecasts for this strategy, but he does argue that it should be tried because there is nothing to lose and possibly a lot to gain. Then, as concrete examples of his strategy, he cites recent efforts to enhance credibility by (1) putting the jobs of the Federal Open Market Committee on the line, (2) adopting a gold standard, and (3) committing fiscal policy to a balanced budget.

Some of these proposals are worse than others. But as examples of the sorts of "innocuous" things we might do to give Taylor's model a fair chance, they make one long for the 1970s as an example of the good old days. And while I am aware of their many imperfections, I am puzzled that, in this imperfect world, Taylor does not mention tax-based incomes policy or other forms of incomes policy as a useful aid to credible disinflation. Although practical objections to them have stressed worries that imply backward-looking behavior—there is no fair time to institute such policies because new wage-setting agreements need to catch up to what has happened elsewhere in the economy—Taylor's model seems to cry out for such policies because they would help fix expectations about future wage changes.

In more than one view of the world, including both the credibility variant on rational expectations and more backward-looking explanations for inertia, a plausible hypothesis about how the inflation relation has shifted in recent years can include the success of stabilization policy in the postwar period, particularly before the supply shocks of the 1970s came to dominate economic performance. The credibility hypothesis must attempt to persuade wage setters that the pursuit of real stabilization is being abandoned in favor of a different goal. Maybe that would be a useful one-shot policy, aimed at helping us down from the present inflation plateau. But why would it be of any lasting value in shifting the inflation relation unless we *maintained* the expectation that real stabilization and high employment were no longer objectives of policy. To credibly maintain that expectation, policy would have to deliver on it. But why would we want to? Why should we favor, in general, inflation goals rather than goals for output?

Of course, some new classical models maintain that the problem of choosing between stabilizing prices and quantities does not exist. But within the more reasonable confines of Taylor's paper, it does. And a recent paper by Charles L. Schultze shows that the cyclical division of GNP into real and price changes has not altered much under all the different peacetime policy regimes of this century.[16] It appears to take extreme and extended periods of cyclical boom or bust to change that division. This adds evidence to the proposition that, rather than relying on the single-minded pursuit of price stability to achieve both output and inflation objectives, we should be looking elsewhere for improvements in macroeconomic performance.

16. "Some Macro Foundations for Micro Theory," *Brookings Papers on Economic Activity, 2:1981,* pp. 521–76.

Product Markets

ROBERT J. GORDON

A Century of Evidence
on Wage and Price Stickiness
in the United States,
the United Kingdom, and Japan

In dealing with suppliers, says Gale Frank, purchasing manager for Aro Corp., "the worst problem in purchasing today is the attitude that the supplier has a right to automatically pass along cost increases. We're trying to combat that."
— *Wall Street Journal,* January 28, 1981

MACROECONOMIC RESEARCH needs to be reoriented away from a search for the theoretical underpinnings of wage and price stickiness, and toward an explanation of the enormous differences in the degree of stickiness observed over time and across countries. I thus begin by criticizing Arthur Okun's book for contributing a theory of *universal* wage and price stickiness and for providing no explanation at all of historical and cross-country *differences* in behavior. The paper then provides a new empirical characterization of price and wage changes over the last century in the United States, the United Kingdom, and Japan in order to demonstrate the wide variety of historical responses that have occurred. Finally, it lays out a series of issues that must be treated in theoretical models if this historical experience is to be adequately explained.

Wage and Price Stickiness

Economists have been obsessed with sticky wages for almost fifty years, an occupational disease that can be traced back to Keynes's

I am grateful to George Kahn, Stephen King, and Joan Robinson for their assistance.

decision in the *General Theory* to embed stickiness in his labor market's rigid nominal wage. An initial generation of Keynesian models joined rigid nominal wages to a traditional classical treatment of the product market that retained perfect competition and price flexibility, as in the *General Theory*. This competitive product market assumption appeared in most postwar macroeconomics textbooks, in Milton Friedman's verbal treatment that gave rise to the Friedman-Lucas supply function, and in the extensive new literature on labor-market contracts for firms that are price takers in product markets and wage setters in labor markets.[1]

Early in the postwar years, however, "mainline" macroeconomics diverged from the competitive product market assumption by shifting to a stress on "full-cost pricing" that made the price level mimic the sticky wage level, with little if any role for a flexible price response to changes in aggregate demand. This view of the wage adjustment process as a slowly crawling tortoise and the price level as the slowly crawling shadow beneath the tortoise led several prominent economists to develop the "fix-price" model of macroeconomic behavior, in which output is viewed as a residual that reflects the interaction of variable nominal demand growth with sluggish wage and price adjustment.[2] At the same time, frustrated with the failure of mainline macroeconomists to provide an adequate theoretical explanation of stickiness, the "new classical macroeconomists" in the 1970s reverted to the market-clearing paradigm, in which there was no distinction between wages and prices—both could move rapidly enough to clear markets and to allow agents to remain on voluntary (or "notional") supply curves. Neoclassical agents were pushed off their voluntary schedules not by the effective demand constraints of the mainline models, but only by expectational errors having a duration roughly equal to the publication lag of the St. Louis Federal Reserve Bank weekly financial statistics.

1. Milton Friedman, "The Role of Monetary Policy," *American Economic Review*, vol. 58 (March 1968), pp. 1–17; Robert E. Lucas, Jr., "Some International Evidence on Output-Inflation Tradeoffs," *American Economic Review*, vol. 63 (June 1973), pp. 326–34; and Martin Neil Baily, "Wages and Employment under Uncertain Demand," *Review of Economic Studies*, vol. 41 (January 1974), pp. 37–50.

2. The best exposition remains that of Robert J. Barro and Herschel I. Grossman, *Money, Employment, and Inflation* (Cambridge University Press, 1976), especially chapter 2.

Unanswered Questions in Okun's Analysis

Arthur Okun's last book can be viewed as an attempt to provide the missing theory needed to explain the mainline assumption of macroeconomic wage and price stickiness.[3] While initially dazzled by Okun's common sense, insight, and expository skill, however, I have become convinced that this great man wrote a book that is more satisfactory as a description of *micro*economic behavior than as a contribution to the *macro*economic debate on the causes of output fluctuations.[4] The problem is that Okun treated the postwar U.S. economy in isolation from its own past history and from the development of labor- and product-market institutions in other industrialized nations. The book contains no reference to any event in U.S. history earlier than the post-Korean era, except for one reference to World War II price controls and another to the implausibility of the search model as an explanation of workers' behavior during the Great Depression. The book's index contains only a single reference to another country, and that, to the United Kingdom, involves incomes policy rather than cross-country differences in macroeconomic behavior. These omissions are serious, for neither Okun's "career" long-term attachments model of the labor market nor his cost-plus "customer" model of the product market can explain historical and cross-country differences in behavior. Each model emerges from reasoning on the situation of a universal *homo economicus* floating free in time and space.

Historical and cross-country differences raise questions that must be addressed by any reasonably complete theory of price adjustment and inflation. Okun, with his sluggish wages and sticky prices, seems to be the source for the view that in the current year output responds by 90 percent and prices by only 10 percent of a change in nominal gross national product.[5] Yet in the United States during World War I and its aftermath, the division was much closer to 10 and 90 than to 90 and 10

3. Arthur M. Okun, *Prices and Quantities: A Macroeconomic Analysis* (Brookings Institution, 1981).
4. My overall assessment thus coincides with that of Edmund S. Phelps, "Okun's Macro-Micro System: A Review Article," *Journal of Economic Literature,* vol. 19 (September 1981), pp. 1065–73.
5. Arthur M. Okun, "Efficient Disinflationary Policies," *American Economic Review,* vol. 68 (May 1978, *Papers and Proceedings, 1977*), pp. 348–52.

(see below). In the hyperinflations that Sargent has proposed as a counterexample to current mainline thinking, the division was more or less 0 and 100 within the current *month*.[6] What factors explain the ability of customer markets to shift from sluggish to speedy price adjustment in these cases, and could those factors recur? Similarly, postwar wages have responded more sluggishly in the United States to nominal GNP changes than in most other countries, yet long-term career attachments between workers and firms are as important, if not more so, in Japan, Germany, and elsewhere as in the United States.

Okun's labor and product markets not only lack a historical or cultural dimension, but they also provide almost no room for interaction between agents and policymakers. Wage behavior in Germany in 1973–74 or Japan in 1979–80 may be hard to explain in isolation from the expectations of workers and firms about the likely actions of monetary policymakers; reverse causation is relevant as well, if the different "propensity to accommodate" apparent on the part of, say, the British versus the German Central bank can be traced to their different expectations about the likely behavior of individual wage and price decisions in response to their own monetary initiatives.

Comparative Macroeconomic History as a Stimulus for New Answers

In three previous papers I have suggested economic and noneconomic factors that might help partially to explain historical and cross-country differences in macroeconomic behavior. The first began as a critique of those monetarists whose explanation of inflation consisted of little more than a time-series chart showing a high historical correlation between prices and money, without any explanation of why the rate of monetary expansion had differed across time and between countries. Although my analysis involved wartime finance, fixity of exchange rates, and the political independence of central banks, its main point was that central banks were less likely to "supply inflation" in response to fiscal or supply-shock pressures if wage- and price-setting institutions allowed a rapid and complete response of prices to monetary restriction.[7] This

6. Thomas J. Sargent, "The Ends of Four Big Inflations," conference paper 90 (National Bureau of Economic Research, 1981).

7. Robert J. Gordon, "The Demand for and Supply of Inflation," *Journal of Law and Economics,* vol. 18 (December 1975), pp. 807–36.

then required an explanation of differences in those institutions. The second paper suggested that shifts in the degree of price flexibility over time might be fruitfully explained by embedding Friedman's and Lucas's distinction between local and aggregate information in a model of price setting by monopolists.[8] The most recent exercise documented the unusual sluggishness of U.S. postwar nominal wage adjustment compared to that in Britain and Japan, attributed this difference to the form of labor-market contracts, and suggested that contract form and length were related in part to cultural attitudes toward social and class conflict.[9]

The core of this paper, contained in the second part, consists of an empirical analysis of historical shifts in the degree of price and wage flexibility in the United States, the United Kingdom, and Japan. These results develop a set of puzzles that form a research agenda for macroeconomic theory. The third part develops a few ideas to explain historical and cross-country differences in labor-market behavior. A central issue in any macroeconomic discussion of labor markets is the extent of the contingencies, if any, to which labor-market contracts are indexed; the forces working against full indexation of labor markets are the same as those that prevent firms from fully insulating their own real outcomes from nominal shocks. The fourth part investigates the economic forces that distinguish auction markets from customer markets where prices are set and addresses the most difficult issue, the determinants of shifts in the speed of adjustment by firms that have access to aggregate information.

The paper does not develop mathematical theorems or firm solutions to tractable, narrowly defined problems. Instead, it contains conjectures and suggestions about a broad area in which microeconomics and macroeconomics overlap. Although some of the themes developed here echo those of my recent treatment of the product market in the *Journal of Economic Literature*,[10] this paper differs by including a more extensive empirical treatment of parameter shifts across time and countries, by forswearing any systematic survey of related papers and ideas, and by attempting to include some specific suggestions about the problems that must be faced in developing formal models of product-market behavior.

8. Robert J. Gordon, "Output Fluctuations and Gradual Price Adjustment," *Journal of Economic Literature,* vol. 19 (June 1981), pp. 493–530.
9. Robert J. Gordon, "Why U.S. Wage and Employment Behaviour Differs from That in Britain and Japan," *Economic Journal,* vol. 92 (March 1982), pp. 13–44.
10. "Output Fluctuations."

Empirical Evidence on Price and Wage Responsiveness

This section presents estimates of simple reduced-form equations that describe the response of price and wage changes to demand disturbances and supply shocks. A single equation, using an identical specification, is estimated from annual data for the United States, the United Kingdom, and Japan over a period beginning in the late nineteenth century and extending to 1980. The main purpose of the econometric work is to characterize shifts in the responsiveness of wages and prices to changes in aggregate demand over this long historical period. The results provide the basis for my claim that wages and prices are less sticky and inertia-bound in postwar U.K. and Japanese data than in the postwar United States, and that inertia in U.S. wage and price behavior is purely a postwar phenomenon.

The Basic Specification

In the notation used here, upper-case letters designate logs of levels, and lower-case letters designate rates of change. The basic hypothesis to be tested emerges from separate equations for changes in wages (w_t) and prices (p_t), in both of which the explanatory variables include the level and change in real aggregate demand and a vector of supply shift terms. In both equations the demand effect is proxied by the level and change in the "output ratio," that is, the ratio of actual real GNP to "natural" (or "potential") real GNP ($\hat{Q}_t = Q_t - Q_t^*$). In the postwar United States this output ratio concept has a high negative correlation, through Okun's Law, with the demographically adjusted unemployment rate that George Perry introduced into the U.S. Phillips curve literature a decade ago.[11]

The rate of wage change, then, is written as:

$$(1) \qquad w_t = a_1(a_0 + p_{t-1}) + a_2\hat{Q}_t + a_3\,\Delta\hat{Q}_t + a_4 z_{wt} + u_{wt},$$

where z_{wt} is a vector of supply shift variables relevant for wage behavior, and u_{wt} is an error term. Here $a_1 = 1$ would be consistent with a vertical long-run Phillips curve, and in this case a_0 could be interpreted as the

---

11. George L. Perry, "Changing Labor Markets and Inflation," *Brookings Papers on Economic Activity, 3:1970,* pp. 411–41.

equilibrium growth rate of the real wage when the log output ratio is zero and supply shocks are absent ($z_{wt} = 0$). The parallel price markup equation is:

$$(2) \qquad p_t = b_1(w_t - b_0) + b_2\hat{Q}_t + b_3 \Delta\hat{Q}_t + b_4 z_{pt} + u_{pt},$$

where z_{pt} is a vector of supply shift variables relevant for price behavior, and u_{pt} is an error term. The constant term b_0 can be interpreted as the rate of productivity growth relevant for price-setting behavior, for example, "standard productivity," so that $w_t - b_0$ is the growth in "standard unit labor cost."

When the wage-change equation, 1, is substituted for w_t in equation 2, and when coefficients are relabeled, the following reduced-form price-change equation is obtained:

$$(3) \qquad p_t = c_0 + c_1 p_{t-1} + c_2\hat{Q}_t + c_3 \Delta\hat{Q}_t + c_4 z_t + u_t,$$

where

$$c_0 = b_1(a_1 a_0 - b_0)$$
$$c_1 = b_1 a_1$$
$$c_2 = b_2 + b_1 a_2$$
$$c_3 = b_3 + b_1 a_3$$
$$c_4 z_t = b_4 z_{pt} + b_1 a_4 z_{wt}$$
$$u_t = u_{pt} + b_1 u_{wt}.$$

Several simplifications are introduced into equations 1 and 2 in order to allow this simple version of 3 to emerge. First, lagged wages are excluded from both 1 and 2, and thus do not appear in 3. Second, only a single lagged value of price change is entered (p_{t-1}), rather than a polynomial in the lag operator, as in my more detailed studies of quarterly U.S. data. Next, the growth in the equilibrium real wage and in standard productivity are introduced as constants rather than variables, allowing estimation to proceed without the introduction of data on productivity change. Two obvious advantages of combining 1 and 2 into 3 are evident immediately—no data on wages need be collected, and no attempt need be made in advance to decide which supply shifts (tax changes, programs of government intervention) are relevant for wage-setting as opposed to price-setting behavior.[12]

12. The specification in equation 3 has been tested for postwar U.S. quarterly data, with Perry's weighted unemployment rate instead of the output ratio, in my "Inflation,

It is possible to derive an alternative version of equation 3 by defining "adjusted nominal GNP growth" as the excess of the growth rate of nominal GNP over that of natural real GNP ($\hat{y}_t = y_t - q_t^*$). We can substitute the identity

(4) $\hat{Q}_t \equiv \hat{Q}_{t-1} + \hat{y}_t - p_t$

into 3 and, after simplifying, obtain:

(5) $p_t = \dfrac{1}{1 + c_2 + c_3} [c_0 + c_1 p_{t-1} + (c_2 + c_3)\hat{y}_t + c_2\hat{Q}_{t-1} + c_4 z_t + u_t]$.

In this framework the significance of the estimated coefficient on the lagged output ratio indicates the presence of an output "level effect," while the difference between the coefficient on adjusted nominal GNP growth and the lagged output ratio indicates the relative size of the "rate of change effect." [13] If the coefficients on lagged price change and on adjusted nominal GNP change sum to unity, then the "accelerationist" hypothesis is validated, in the sense that a positive output ratio ($\hat{Q}_{t-1} > 0$) or an adverse supply shift ($z_t > 0$) causes an acceleration of the inflation rate relative to its past value. [14]

Questions may be raised about the appearance of nominal GNP change in equation 5, an equation explaining price change. Nominal GNP change is indeed an endogenous variable, although no more so than the current unemployment rate that has traditionally been used in Phillips curve studies. The choice, then, between specifications 3 and 5 comes down to whether nominal or real GNP is "more exogenous." The advantage of using equation 5 for estimation becomes clear in considering

Flexible Exchange Rates, and the Natural Rate of Unemployment," in Martin Neil Baily, ed., *Workers, Jobs, and Inflation* (Brookings Institution, 1982), pp. 88–157. That paper is the source of the estimates of postwar natural real GNP used to generate the postwar annual output ratio series used in this paper; it also tests and accepts the restrictions assumed in equation 3 that lagged wage changes are absent; and finally, it allows changes in standard productivity behavior.

13. The specification written as equation 5 was first estimated in Robert J. Gordon, "A Consistent Characterization of a Near-Century of Price Behavior," *American Economic Review*, vol. 70 (May 1980, *Papers and Proceedings, 1979*), pp. 243–49. The same approach was subsequently used with quarterly data to test the Lucas-Sargent-Wallace policy ineffectiveness proposition in my "Price Inertia and Policy Ineffectiveness in the United States, 1890–1980," *Journal of Political Economy*, vol. 90 (December 1982).

14. While a sum of coefficients of unity is consistent with the accelerationist hypothesis, a sum of coefficients below unity does not necessarily conflict with that hypothesis; this important point was originally made in Thomas J. Sargent, "A Note on the 'Accelerationist' Controversy," *Journal of Money, Credit and Banking*, vol. 3 (August 1971), pp. 721–25.

a period like 1915–22, when prices responded extremely rapidly to changes in nominal GNP, with little residual effect on real GNP. The exogenous event in this instance was an upsurge in money-financed nominal spending. In a world of complete and contemporaneous price responsiveness to serially correlated nominal GNP movements, as in some models in the tradition of the "new classical economics," an investigator who forced all of the price adjustment to be explained by real variables and lagged price change, as in equation 3, would find his results plagued by positive serial correlation and an upward bias in the coefficient on lagged price change.

Another alternative to equation 3, which would involve replacing nominal GNP change by the change in a monetary aggregate, has the quite different disadvantage that the resulting coefficient on money mixes up aggregate demand and aggregate supply effects; that is, it reflects the combined influence of the response of velocity to monetary changes and the response of prices to nominal GNP changes. The most obvious source of bias in the coefficient on nominal GNP change, stemming from the simultaneous increase in prices and in nominal GNP that would occur if supply shocks were accompanied by an accommodating monetary policy, can be mitigated by careful attention to the specification of the supply-shift variables (z_t).

The tables presented below include not only estimates of equation 5 with price change as the dependent variable, but also estimates of the same specification with wage change as the dependent variable. A reduced-form wage-change equation containing the same variables as 5 can be derived by solving equation 2 for w_t, substituting out $\hat{Q}_t$ using identity 4, and, finally, substituting equation 5 for p_t. Differences in the coefficients on the same variables in the wage-change and price-change equations provide evidence on the response of the real wage to demand and supply disturbances. Since wage changes and nominal GNP changes are measured independently and are not linked by a simple identity, the coefficient on nominal GNP change in the wage-change equation is less subject to simultaneous equations bias and may provide a more reliable estimate of the "rate of change effect" of aggregate demand.

Estimates of Price and Wage Equations for the United States

In this paper the estimates of equation 5 attempt to capture the impact for the United States of seven supply shifts. Six of these are dummy variables to capture the impact of separate episodes of government

Table 1. *Equations Explaining Annual Changes in Prices, Wage Rates, and the Real Wage in the United States, 1892–1980*

Description	GNP deflator (1)	Hourly wage rate (2)	Real product wage (3)
1. Adjusted nominal GNP ($\hat{y}$)			
a. Entire period	0.34***	0.32***	−0.02
b. Extra effect, 1892–1914	−0.05	0.14*	0.19*
c. Extra effect, 1915–22	0.54***	0.51***	−0.02
d. Extra effect, 1942–49	0.18***	0.25***	0.07
2. Lagged adjusted nominal GNP ($\hat{y}_{t-1}$)	0.09**	0.19***	0.10
3. Lagged real GNP ratio ($\hat{Q}_{t-1}$)			
a. Entire period	0.18***	0.01	−0.16*
b. Extra effect, 1892–1914	−0.01	0.30**	0.31**
c. Extra effect, 1929–41	−0.16***	−0.04**	0.12*
4. Lagged "net" price change ($\bar{p}_{t-1}$)[a]			
a. Entire period	0.05	0.12	0.07
b. Extra effect, 1950–80	0.40***	0.31**	−0.08
5. Supply shifts[b]			
a. World War I controls, 1915–22	−8.72***	−1.36	7.36***
b. NIRA, 1933–36	7.66***	18.78***	11.04**
c. Wagner Act, 1936–37	1.61	11.54**	9.94**
d. World War II controls, 1943–47	−19.00***	−10.97***	8.01***
e. Korean War controls, 1950–52	−2.44**	−1.74	0.70
f. Nixon controls, 1972–75	4.77***	−1.12	3.65*
g. Relative price of food and energy, 1947–80[c]	0.55*	−0.46	−1.01*
6. Constant term	0.61**	1.82***	1.20***
Summary statistic			
R^2	0.92	0.88	0.47
Standard error	1.66	2.42	2.80

Sources: See the appendix to this chapter.
* Statistically significant at the 10 percent level.
** Statistically significant at the 5 percent level.
*** Statistically significant at the 1 percent level.
a. Lagged price changes are computed by netting out the influence of the supply shift variables. Thus if D_{it} is the level of dummy variable i, and d_i is its coefficient, the net lagged price change is calculated as

$$\bar{p}_{t-1} = p_{t-1} - \sum_{i=1}^{6} d_i D_{i,t-1} - d_0 p_{t-1}^{FE},$$

where d_0 is the coefficient on the relative food-energy price variable (p_t^{FE}).
b. All dummy variables, except for the Wagner Act, are defined to sum to unity over the period when a program of government intervention was in effect, and to −1 during the period of its termination. The NIRA, World War II, and Nixon era dummy variables are defined exactly as in Gordon, "Consistent Characterization," p. 246. The World War I, Wagner Act, and Korean War dummy variables are new:

World War I		NIRA		Wagner Act		World War II		Korean War		Nixon era	
1918	1.0	1933	0.4	1936	0.5	1943	0.5	1950	−0.5	1972	0.5
1919	−0.5	1934	0.6	1937	0.5	1944	0.4	1951	−0.5	1973	0.5
1920	−0.5	1935	−0.4			1945	0.1	1952	1.0	1974	−0.3
		1936	−0.6			1946	−0.6			1975	−0.7
						1947	−0.4				

Footnotes continued on p. 95.

intervention in the price- and wage-setting process, and the seventh is the annual change in the relative price of food and energy. Except for the "Wagner Act" variable, the dummy variables are not of the usual "0, 1" form. In my previous research on the Nixon controls and the National Recovery Act, I found that both programs not only shifted the price level during their official period of impact, but caused a shift in the opposite direction after their termination as well.[15] The five dummy variables listed in table 1, lines 5a, 5b, 5d, 5e, and 5f, are defined to sum to 1.0 during the period of a program's impact, and to -1.0 after its termination, thus constraining the impact and rebound efforts to have exactly the same absolute value. The resulting coefficients on those dummy variables indicate the cumulative displacement of the price level during the period of the program's impact. This method implies that, because these five dummy variables sum to zero, collectively they do not explain *any* of the elevenfold increase in the GNP deflator that occurred between 1892 and 1980. The sixth dummy variable, representing the impact of the 1935 Wagner Act on unionization in 1936–37, is of the usual "0, 1" form and measures the permanent increase in the real wage achieved by unionization.[16]

One obvious way of providing information on parameter shifts would be to estimate separate versions of equation 5 for each major subperiod within the available data set. Most previous investigators have followed this approach and have concentrated on "normal" peacetime periods, often omitting the years of the Great Depression and World War II. An alternative method involves estimating a single equation for the entire

15. The most recent evaluation of controls is contained in Jon Frye and Robert J. Gordon, "Government Intervention in the Inflation Process: The Econometrics of 'Self-Inflicted Wounds,' " *American Economic Review,* vol. 71 (May 1981, *Papers and Proceedings, 1980*), pp. 288–94. Econometric estimates of equation 3 for the interwar period are presented in Robert J. Gordon and James A. Wilcox, "Monetarist Interpretations of the Great Depression: An Evaluation and Critique," in Karl Brunner, ed., *The Great Depression Revisited* (Martinus Nijhoff, 1981), pp. 49–107; see especially p. 88.

16. The dummy variables are defined in note b to table 1. The odd timing of the Korean War variable reflects my verdict that the Korean War controls did no more than consolidate the unwinding of the speculative commodity boom of 1950–51. This interpretation is supported by the fact that the variable is significant in the price equation but not in the wage equation.

Footnotes to table 1, continued.

c. The variable used to represent changes in the relative price of food and energy is the difference between the annual rates of change of the deflators for, respectively, personal consumption expenditures and personal consumption expenditures net of expenditures on food and energy. This variable is available only for 1947–80 and is set equal to zero before 1947.

period for which data are available, and then searching for parameter shifts. If additional variables are defined as the product of the individual economic variables of interest ($\hat{y}_t$, $\hat{Q}_{t-1}$, and so forth) and "0, 1" dummy variables for each subperiod, then the t-ratios on the additional variables provide estimates of the statistical significance of parameter shifts.

In developing the equations displayed in table 1, I followed this search procedure in an attempt to locate parameter shifts in both the price and wage equations during the following subperiods: 1892–1914, 1915–22, 1929–41, 1942–49, 1950–53, 1954–66, and 1967–80. Only six shifts could be located; as shown in the table, all six of these are statistically significant in the wage equation, of which four are also significant in the price equation.

In the equation for price change in column 1, the elasticity of changes in the GNP deflator to current changes in nominal GNP is stable at about one-third throughout the sample period, except for significant upward shifts during World War I (0.34 + 0.54 = 0.88) and during World War II (0.34 + 0.18 = 0.52). Once the effect of price controls is taken into account by the method outlined above, it appears that the first-year division of nominal GNP change between output and prices ranged from roughly 50-50 to 10-90 in the two wars, considerably above the peacetime division of 66-34, and far from Okun's estimate of 90-10.

The other variables listed in rows 2 through 4 are all lagged one year. The coefficient on lagged nominal GNP change is quite stable. There is a significant impact of the lagged output ratio—the traditional Phillips curve "level effect"—except during the depression years, 1929–41, when the "level effect" was zero.

Only a small and insignificant "inertia effect" of lagged price change is evident until 1950, when the coefficient exhibits a significant jump from 0.05 to 0.45. I have previously suggested two explanations for this shift:

it seems quite consistent with a change in attitude in the first postwar decade toward recognition of a fundamental change in the stabilizing role of government policy (initiatives based more on the automatic stabilizers and new institutions like FDIC than on countercyclical policy). The shift also emphasizes the crucial role of three-year staggered-wage contracts, a unique American institution that dates back to the first postwar decade.[17]

17. "A Consistent Characterization," p. 249.

Unfortunately I can provide no easy explanation for the disappearance of the Phillips curve "level effect" during the depression; this result both describes and results from the mysterious absence of downward price pressure emanating from the huge, decade-long real output gap. It may suggest an asymmetric price response, with more downward than upward rigidity, but careful testing does not confirm any such asymmetry.

The supply-shift coefficients indicate that World War II price controls cumulatively held down the price level by almost 20 percent, and World War I price controls by almost 10 percent, while the National Industrial Recovery Act (NIRA) boosted prices by 8 percent.[18] The effects of the Korean War and Nixon episodes were more modest, but nonetheless large in relation to the small year-to-year variance of price change during the postwar era. The Wagner Act had no significant impact on price changes. The effect of food and energy prices is a marginally significant 0.55. Taken as a whole, the price-change equation in column 1 has important implications for current macroeconomic debates. If the sum of coefficients on nominal rate-of-change variables ($\hat{y}_t$, $\hat{y}_{t-1}$, and p_{t-1}) were unity, the equation would be consistent with the "accelerationist hypothesis" that a permanent acceleration in nominal GNP growth leads to a permanent acceleration in inflation with no residual impact on real output. For the 1950–80 period the relevant sum of coefficients is 0.89 (0.33 + 0.10 + 0.05 + 0.41), which is not far from unity, and this sum becomes 0.97 when the constant is omitted. Another important implication is contained in the finding that the coefficients are stable for the 1950–80 period, which leads me to question the unsupported conjectures of Robert Lucas, William Fellner, and others that a credible return by monetary policymakers to the regime of the 1950s would lead to substantial shifts in parameters.[19]

An equation explaining annual changes in average hourly earnings is presented in column 2. All the right-hand variables are identical to those

---

18. On World War I controls, see Frank W. Taussig, "Price-Fixing as Seen by a Price-Fixer," *Quarterly Journal of Economics*, vol. 33 (February 1919), pp. 205–41.

19. The major parameter shift evident in a more detailed study of quarterly postwar data is a shortening after 1966 in the mean lag of the distribution of weights on past inflation, which I interpret as being due to the growing importance of cost-of-living escalators. A return to a low-inflation regime might well cause cost-of-living escalators to become less important, but this would not reduce the output cost of the transition to that regime.

in column 1. The wage equation exhibits few differences from the price equation in the coefficients on nominal GNP change (rows 1a–d and 2) and lagged price change (rows 4a and b). The nominal GNP responsiveness coefficients in the wage equation exhibit the same overall value of roughly one-third, with the same large and significant upward shift in World War I and World War II. Further, the coefficients on lagged price change are similar, while lagged nominal GNP change seems to be somewhat more important in the wage equation.

Perhaps the most surprising result, however, is that the pattern of wage response to the output ratio is completely different. While the output ratio has no effect on either the wage equation or the price equation in the interval between 1929 and 1941, the wage equation differs from the price equation in that the output ratio had no effect on wage change over the "entire period" (row 3a). I would have guessed on the basis of postwar U.S. evidence that the "rate-of-change" effect was relatively more important in the price-change equation, and the "level" effect of the output ratio was more important in the wage-change equation. In fact, the opposite appears to be true.

Finally, both the rate-of-change and level effects of aggregate demand on wages appear to have been substantially more important in 1892–1914 than thereafter (rows 1b and 3b). This would seem to be the sole evidence in this paper that, at least for the United States, the first-year responsiveness of wages has become "stickier." Prices, on the other hand, have exhibited no important peacetime change in behavior except for (a) the mysterious disappearance of the "level effect" in the 1930s, and (b) the emergence of inertia beginning in 1950.

The difference between the coefficients in the wage and price equations, respectively, indicates the effect of the demand, inertia, and supply variables on changes in the real product wage. These real-wage responses are shown separately in column 3, where an equation for the annual change in the real wage has been estimated in order to provide measures of statistical significance of the coefficients. Perhaps the most important finding is that *changes* in the real wage behave countercyclically; this relationship is different from Keynes's assumption in the *General Theory* that there is a negative relation between the *level* of the real product wage and the level of output. To validate Keynes's relation, we should find a significant negative impact of the *change* of real aggregate demand on the change in the real wage, whereas in fact this coefficient is positive. Equation 5 can be used to recover the reduced-form parameters as follows:

	Price equation	Wage equation	Implied real-wage response
Output "level effect" (c_2)	0.32	0.02	−0.30
"Rate-of-change effect" (c_3)	0.43	1.02	0.58
"Inertia coefficient" (c_1)			
Before 1950	0.09	0.24	0.15
After 1950	0.79	0.88	0.09

The other important finding in column 3 is that several of the supply-shift variables have a significant impact on changes in the real wage. Controls in World War I, World War II, and the Nixon era, as well as the NIRA, all raised the real wage temporarily (recall that these are dummies of the 1, −1 form), while the Wagner Act appears to have raised the real wage permanently. These coefficients, indicating that government intervention has rather consistently operated to shift the distribution of income toward workers, may help to explain why controls continue to be popular in public opinion polls. The coefficient in row 5g indicates a unit-elastic negative response of the real wage to the relative price of food and energy, achieved in part through a positive response of the price level, and in part through a negative response of the nominal wage rate.

Estimated Price and Wage Equations for the United Kingdom

The specification of the U.K. price, wage, and real-wage equations in table 2 differs from the U.S. equations in only two respects. First, the lagged change in adjusted nominal GNP ($\hat{y}_{t-1}$) is insignificant, and so does not appear in table 2. Second, there are obvious differences in the particular programs of government intervention that require the introduction of dummy variables. Three periods of freeze or restraint are included, and in each case the dummy variable is of the "1, −1" form. The choice of timing for the "rebound" or "unwinding" effect of the control programs is based on the same iterative method used in my research for the United States; residuals from a first iteration were used

Table 2. *Equations Explaining Annual Changes in Prices, Wage Rates, and the Real Wage in the United Kingdom, 1875–1938 and 1955–80*

Description	GNP deflator (1)	Hourly wage rate (2)	Real product wage (3)
1. Adjusted nominal GNP ($\hat{y}_t$)			
a. Entire period	0.45***	0.41***	−0.04
b. Extra effect, 1914–23	0.13	−0.16*	−0.28**
c. Extra effect, 1955–80	−0.13	0.17*	0.30**
2. Lagged real GNP ratio ($\hat{Q}_{t-1}$)			
a. Entire period	0.24***	0.17***	−0.07
b. Extra effect, 1914–23	0.45**	0.67***	0.23
c. Extra effect, 1924–38	−0.10	−0.25**	−0.14
d. Extra effect, 1955–80	0.89***	0.86***	−0.03
3. Lagged price change (p_{t-1})[a]			
a. Entire period	0.11**	0.35***	0.24***
b. Extra effect, 1955–80	0.45***	0.05	−0.36***
4. Supply shifts[b]			
a. Late 1960s intervention (1967–72)	−1.72	−5.05**	−3.33
b. Early 1970s intervention (1973–75)	−5.39***	−3.12**	2.26*
c. Social contract (1977–80)	−0.67	−10.33***	−9.65***
d. Foreign exchange rate[c]	−0.08**	−0.16***	0.09***
5. Constant term			
a. Entire period	−0.18	0.16	0.34
b. Extra effect, 1955–80	1.60**	1.91***	0.31
Summary statistic			
R^2	0.93	0.94	0.54
Standard error	1.91	1.95	2.07

Sources: See the appendix to this chapter.

*, **, ***, and a. Same as table 1.

b. All dummy variables are defined to sum to unity over the period when a program of government intervention was in effect, and to −1 during the period of its termination. The variables are defined as follows:

Late 1960s intervention		Early 1970s intervention		Social contract	
1967	0.33	1973	1.0	1977	1.0
1968	0.33	1975	−1.0	1978	−0.6
1969	0.33			1979	−0.2
1970	−0.33			1980	−0.2
1971	−0.33				
1972	−0.33				

c. The foreign exchange rate, included in percentage change form, is the pound-dollar rate for 1900–70 and the effective exchange rate of the pound for 1971–80. See the appendix.

to determine the length of time required for the control effect to wear off.

The U.K. price-change equation in column 1 displays a number of similarities to the corresponding U.S equation and a few interesting differences. The similarities begin with the stable coefficient on nominal GNP change $(\hat{y}_t)$, with a U.K. coefficient in the current year of 0.45, compared to U.S. coefficients in the current and first lagged year summing to 0.43. The "entire period" coefficient on the lagged output ratio, as well as the shift toward increased inertia in the postwar period, seems to be consistent with U.S. behavior. The major differences are the absence of a significant upward shift on the $\hat{y}_t$ coefficient for the United Kingdom during World War I, and the enormous upward shift in the U.K. output ratio coefficient in the postwar years (row 2d).

It is in the wage equation that U.K. behavior contrasts dramatically with that of the United States. First, nominal GNP changes had a substantially larger impact on wage changes in postwar Britain than in the postwar United States. My more detailed analysis of wage responsiveness, based on bivariate Granger causality tests for quarterly data, reached the same conclusion.[20] In table 2 the contrast shows up not just in the higher U.K. nominal GNP coefficient (row 1a plus row 1c), but even more strongly in the large upward shift in the U.K. postwar coefficient on the output ratio (row 2d). Another contrast is in the inertia effect, which shifted upward substantially in U.S. data in the postwar years, but which shows no upward postwar shift in Britain from its "entire period" coefficient of 0.35. Overall, the U.K. results are consistent with the long-run neutrality of nominal GNP changes in the postwar period; the relevant sums of coefficients on the nominal GNP and lagged price variables are 0.88 in the price equation (0.45 − 0.13 + 0.11 + 0.45) and 0.98 in the wage equation (0.41 + 0.17 + 0.35 + 0.05).

The supply-shift variables also introduce an interesting contrast with the United States in that the "late 1960s" and "social contract" interventions reduced the real wage temporarily, unlike the U.S. intervention programs that consistently increased the real wage. And another interesting contrast is the peculiar response of the real wage to exchange rate changes—a devaluation (treated as a negative change in the exchange rate) increases U.K. wage change more than price change, leading to an increase in the real wage. Exchange rate effects for the United States,

20. "Why U.S. Wage and Employment Behaviour Differs," p. 22.

though important in quarterly data for the 1970s, do not have a significant impact on the annual data and thus are omitted from table 1.[21] In the opposite direction, changes in the relative price of food and energy, though important in the U.S. equations, did not make a significant contribution in the equations for the United Kingdom and Japan, and are thus omitted from tables 2 and 3.

Estimated Price and Wage Equations for Japan

The equations for Japan in table 3 have fewer variables than those for the United States and Britain, both because fewer significant parameter shifts were identified and because changes in the relative price of food and energy and in the exchange rate produced no significant impact. The price-change equation for Japan in column 1 suggests substantially greater price flexibility than in either the United States or the United Kingdom, with large and significant "entire period" coefficients of price change on both current nominal GNP change and on the lagged output ratio. The upward shift in price responsiveness during World War I, which was reflected in a higher coefficient on nominal GNP change for the United States, is reflected here in a higher coefficient on the lagged output ratio for Japan (row 2c). There is no evidence of price inertia in the price equation in the entire period or in any subperiod.

Japan, unlike Britain and the United States, exhibits virtually no responsiveness of prices (or wages) to changes in nominal GNP or to the lagged output ratio before 1914 (rows 1b and 2b). This fact, together with the high standard errors in these equations compared to those for the United States and the United Kingdom, suggests to me that there may be substantial measurement errors in the early Japanese data. When we control for this low responsiveness before 1914, as in table 3, there seems little doubt that the price deflator in peacetime periods after World War I was considerably more flexible and less inertia-bound in Japan than in the other two countries.

There are two differences between the wage and price equations for Japan, and these show up as significant coefficients in the real wage equation in column 3. First, the rate-of-change effect in the wage equation is negative, reflecting the fact that an expansion in the economy is associated with a decline in the real wage. Second, lagged prices seem to have a somewhat larger impact in the wage equation than in the price

21. In my "Inflation, Flexible Exchange Rates, and the Natural Rate of Unemployment" I find significant exchange rate effects in quarterly U.S. data.

Table 3. *Equations Explaining Annual Changes in Prices, Wage Rates, and the Real Wage in Japan, 1892–1940 and 1961–80*

Description	GNP deflator (1)	Hourly wage rate (2)	Real product wage (3)
1. Adjusted nominal GNP ($\hat{y}_t$)			
a. Entire period	0.77***	0.37***	−0.40***
b. Extra effect, 1892–1913	−0.53***	−0.31***	0.21**
2. Lagged real GNP ratio ($\hat{Q}_{t-1}$)			
a. Entire period	0.64***	0.77***	0.13
b. Extra effect, 1892–1913	−0.52***	−0.75***	−0.22
c. Extra effect, 1914–22	1.46***	2.10**	0.63
3. Lagged price change (p_{t-1})[a]			
a. Entire period	0.05	0.22***	0.17*
b. Extra effect, 1914–22	−0.03	0.38***	0.40**
4. Constant term			
a. Entire period	2.06***	3.66***	1.60***
b. Extra effect, 1961–73	−1.78*	5.52***	7.30***
Summary statistic			
R^2	0.81	0.84	0.47
Standard error	3.34	3.58	4.46

Sources: See the appendix.
*, **, ***, and a. Same as table 1.

equation. The extremely high significance level of the constant shift term for 1961–73 in the wage and real wage equations demonstrates the importance of allowing every parameter to change, including the constant. The implication, of course, is that the explosive productivity growth enjoyed by the Japanese economy was a temporary phenomenon, since after 1973 real wage growth returned approximately to the average rates experienced before 1940.

Comparison with Okun's Theoretical Framework

The characterization of historical price and wage behavior in the three tables differs substantially from Okun's algebraic theory, as presented in his equations 7′ and 8′ on page 259 (renumbered here for convenience):

$$(6) \qquad w_t = (1 - s)w_{t-1} + sy_t,$$

and

$$(7) \qquad p_t^C = (1 - s)p_{t-1}^C + sy_{t-1},$$

where the superscript C on price change refers to nonauction or "customer" market sector. Otherwise, Okun and I use the same notation.

To simplify the discussion, I first compare equations 6 and 7 with the results for the United States obtained in table 1, since this was the nation that most concerned Okun, and subsequently comment on the relation of equations 6 and 7 to the results for Britain and Japan. At least four important differences between Okun's framework and my description of U.S. data are immediately apparent. First, the wage equation, 6, embodies Okun's basic theme—that the inflation process is propelled by "wage-wage" inertia. In contrast, the wage equation in table 1 reflects my long-standing empirical finding that postwar wage changes in the United States exhibit feedback from lagged product prices, not lagged wage rates.[22] When a single lagged wage-change term is added to the equation in column 2, its coefficient is 0.05 with a t-ratio of 0.4. Additional shift terms for 1929–41 and 1950–80 are also insignificant.

The second difference is that Okun's model allows only a "rate-of-change effect" in the influence of aggregate demand on wage and price change, whereas the equations in table 1 also include the traditional Phillips curve "level effect." Third, Okun obtains a relationship between price change and lagged nominal GNP change in equation 7 by assuming that $p_t^C = w_{t-1}$. This specification is strongly rejected by the U.S. data; when current and lagged wage changes are added to the price equation, their coefficients range from 0.05 to 0.08, with t-ratios below unity, and with no evidence of significant structural shift parameters. This finding is directly relevant to my subsequent discussion of the product market, since the U.S. results in table 1, column 1, indicate that there is a strong contemporaneous effect of nominal GNP change, with an added impact of the lagged level of real GNP, which implies that product prices are not simply set as a markup over labor cost. Finally, there is no room in Okun's model for the major parameter shifts that occurred during the two wars, nor is there any explanation of the shift from zero to positive inertia in the inflation process after World War II.

The results for the United Kingdom and Japan compound the conflict between Okun's analysis and the facts presented in the tables. In those two countries, wages are far from sticky, and at least for the postwar

---

22. I emphasized the role of product prices as far back as "Inflation in Recession and Recovery," *Brookings Papers on Economic Activity, 1:1971,* pp. 105–58. A contest between lagged product prices and lagged wages in my "Inflation, Flexible Exchange Rates, and the Natural Rate of Unemployment," yields a coefficient on lagged wages that is both insignificant and of the incorrect sign.

years, the main impact of aggregate demand on wage behavior works through the output ratio variable that is omitted from equations 6 and 7. There is no evidence at all of wage-wage inertia in the postwar results for Britain and Japan, relatively little feedback from lagged prices to wages, and no evidence of Okun's mechanical unit-elastic markup relation between current changes in customer market prices and lagged changes in wage rates. Yet all of the features involved in Okun's theory— the "toll" that produces career labor markets and the information lags that generate the shopping model of customer markets—are shared by all three countries and most historical eras.

Limitations of the Results

Numerous questions may be raised about the results displayed in table 1. There are good reasons to think that the coefficient on current nominal GNP change is biased upward. When the U.S. equation is reestimated for the postwar years with the fixed-weight deflator rather than the implicit deflator as dependent variable, the coefficient on nominal GNP change drops from 0.34 to about 0.20, indicating that part of the current-year nominal GNP impact may be a spurious weighting effect. Table 1 retains the implicit deflator throughout, simply because the fixed-weight deflator is not available for the prewar years, and a shift in the concept used as dependent variable would prevent any analysis of historical shifts in coefficients. Similarly, the U.S. wage-rate series used in columns 2 and 3 is average hourly earnings, not the postwar index that adjusts for changes in overtime and interindustry employment shifts. Thus part of the response of wages to current nominal GNP changes in table 1 represents a change in overtime and in the employment mix, not a change in actual wage rates. Again, comparability prevents a postwar shift in indexes.

The possibility that the demand responsiveness coefficients may be biased upward in the results for the United States, and possibly for the United Kingdom and Japan as well, limits the usefulness of the empirical results for the analysis of hypothetical future policy changes. The point of the analysis is to use relatively homogeneous data sources across time and to identify shifts in parameters; we are interested in the fact that U.S. prices were more flexible during 1915–22 than before or after, for instance, not in the precise quantitative values of the responsiveness parameters. The results are intended to pose a challenge for theorists, not to be used as they stand for short-term forecasting. A better job of identifying the crucial parameters for short intervals, such as 1954–80, can be performed with quarterly data and a more complex specification.[23]

Wages, Contracts, and the Mystery of the Missing Escalator

Okun's book contains many insights about microeconomic behavior in labor and product markets but lacks a theoretical explanation for some of the phenomena described in the preceding empirical analysis. The rest of this paper contains some conjectures and speculations about the lines that theorists might fruitfully pursue for labor and product markets.

Explaining Cross-Country Differences in Nominal Wage Flexibility

The preceding section provided evidence that wage changes in the three countries have not been characterized by wage-wage inertia and that nominal aggregate demand influences wage changes through three channels—(1) current changes in nominal spending, (2) the output ratio, and (3) the feedback from lagged product prices, which may represent the combined impact of labor demand on the value of labor's marginal product and of cost-of-living-adjustment escalation on previously negotiated union wages.[24]

Postwar wage adjustments in Britain and Japan have been more responsive to aggregate demand and less characterized by inertia than in the United States. If the U.S. institution of three-year overlapping wage contracts is cited as an explanation of some or all of this difference in behavior, then why contract form and length differ among countries that *all* share long-term labor-market attachments must be explained. The fact that Japan can simultaneously achieve lifetime employment (at least for males under fifty-five in large firms) and relatively flexible nominal wages presents a powerful challenge to proponents of the "career-labor-market-wage-wage-inertia" theory.[25]

---

23. This is performed in Gordon, "Inflation, Flexible Exchange Rates, and the Natural Rate of Unemployment."

24. Although omitted from table 1 in order to simplify the presentation, the difference between changes in the CPI and those in the GNP deflator makes a small and significant contribution in the U.S. wage equation, particularly in the 1967–80 subperiod.

25. In light of Robert Hall's recent evidence on the importance of lifetime jobs in the

My explanation of differences in contract form and length is based on the simple idea, developed by Jo Anna Gray, Ronald Dye, and others, that the choice of contract length, like most economic choices, involves a balancing of costs and benefits.[26] Long contracts allow more time for the amortization of negotiation and strike costs, while short contracts allow agents to adjust to unanticipated nominal and real events quickly. This balancing act tends to lead to a long contract duration in a society such as the United States, with its history of labor strife (particularly between 1935 and 1941 and between 1946 and 1948), and a short contract duration in Japan, with its tradition of avoiding conflict, on-the-job social equality, and the nonoccupational nature of attitudes toward hierarchy.[27]

But both short and long contracts may be fully indexed to a nominal variable like consumer prices, nominal GNP, or a monetary aggregate. The literature on contracts, in fact, views short contracts as a viable substitute for long-contracts-with-indexing when low negotiation costs allow short contracts to evolve as the dominant form. Thus a central issue in the origin of macroeconomic fluctuations is the lack of full indexation of wages and the product prices of individual firms.

The Missing Escalator[28]

What range of possible contingencies will be written into contracts? Asymmetric information mitigates against contracts contingent on "local" variables specific to the firm, such as firm sales, product price, or worker productivity. Any informational advantage on the part of the employer leads to a moral hazard problem—that the firm has an incentive to understate the realization of the variable on which the wage is contingent in order to minimize wage cost. Contracts are thus more likely to be contingent on aggregate nominal variables like the consumer price index or the money supply. But as Gray has shown, indexation to

---

United States, it is interesting to find that, in 1966, 56 percent of males aged thirty-five to thirty-nine had more than ten years seniority in Japan, against only 34 percent of the same group in the United States. See Robert E. Cole, "Permanent Employment in Japan: Facts and Fantasies," *Industrial and Labor Relations Review,* vol. 26 (October 1972), pp. 615–30.

26. Jo Anna Gray, "On Indexation and Contract Length," *Journal of Political Economy,* vol. 86 (February 1978), pp. 1–18; and Ronald Dye, "Optimal Contract Length," working paper (Carnegie-Mellon University, October 1979).

27. These generalizations are supported by citations and additional arguments in Gordon, "Why U.S. Wage and Employment Behaviour Differs," part 4.

28. This section overlaps part of section III.2 in ibid., pp. 30–33.

a consumer price index rigidifies real wage growth over the life of the contract. While this is an optimal outcome if all disturbances are nominal and the growth of productivity is perfectly predictable, full consumer-price indexation imposes an efficiency loss when an unpredictable supply shock (such as those caused by OPEC) changes the equilibrium real wage.

Since full indexation to the consumer price index has the fatal defect that it rigidifies the real wage, an appealing alternative is indexation to nominal GNP, for this allows the real wage to adjust automatically to unexpected changes in productivity growth (the advantages and disadvantages of indexation to a nominal monetary aggregate are treated below). Adopting the notation in the first part of this paper, with changes in nominal GNP, prices, actual real GNP, and equilibrium real GNP designated, respectively, as y, p, q, and q^*, gives the identity:

$$(8) \qquad\qquad y - q^* \equiv p + q - q^*.$$

Assume for convenience that equilibrium labor input is constant, so labor productivity growth in equilibrium is the same as equilibrium real GNP growth (q^*). Then indexation of the wage rate to nominal GNP ($w = y$) implies, when substituted into equation 5:

$$(9) \qquad\qquad w - p = q^* + (q - q^*).$$

Thus growth in the real wage ($w - p$) automatically reflects equilibrium productivity growth (q^*) as long as there are no fluctuations in real output relative to its equilibrium value ($q - q^* = 0$).

No matter how superficially attractive, nominal GNP indexing of wage contracts has never been observed. This occurs, I suggest, because four sets of barriers prevent agents from making the comfortable assumption that real business cycles have been vanquished ($q - q^* = 0$) and therefore in equation 9 that the growth of the real wage mimics the growth of productivity. The barriers are preset prices and wages, foreign trade, information imperfections and delays, and velocity shifts.

1. *Preset prices and wages.* Firms have a legitimate reason to fear that nominal GNP fluctuations will, at least initially, take the form of real GNP fluctuations. First, in many markets it is efficient for prices to be preset rather than established in auction markets, to save on the time and transportation costs that centralized auctions impose. Second, prices that are preset for even a short interval imply that firms will initially experience a nominal fluctuation as a real event—a decline in real purchases at the price initially preset. Their expectation that the real

demand shock will soon be eliminated depends on the speed with which the costs of inputs purchased from other firms mimic the movement in nominal demand. If information on the nominal shock is imperfect, firms may, at least at first, interpret it as local rather than aggregate in nature and may believe that there is no reason for their input costs to move in proportion to the demand shift. Once it is admitted that individual product prices, and hence the aggregate price level, may adjust gradually to changes in nominal GNP, workers will fear the consequences of nominal-indexed wage contracts. Consider a 20 percent decline in nominal GNP, accompanied initially by only a 10 percent decline in the aggregate price level. Workers under a wage contract indexed to nominal GNP would experience a decline in their real wage of 10 percent. Eventually prices would adjust fully in proportion to the nominal GNP change, but workers, particularly if risk averse, would object to the instability of real wages implied by nominal-GNP indexation in a world of gradual price adjustment.

The preceding paragraph is unconventional in that it deduces nominal wage stickiness from price stickiness, while it is more common to do the reverse. But in fact the argument works both ways. If nominal wages do not adjust instantly, firms face nominal marginal costs that are less than unit elastic with respect to nominal GNP change. The problem is properly treated as dynamic rather than static, in which several sources of resistance to full nominal indexation interact and reinforce each other.

2. *Foreign trade*. When firms observe an increase or decrease in their real sales at the initially preset price, their choice of a new price depends on a guess about the fraction of the demand shift representing a nominal aggregate shock, as opposed to a real aggregate or real local shock, and on a guess about the extent to which suppliers of inputs recognize the aggregate component of the shock. As economists in Britain, Japan, and other open economies know, the perceived stickiness of marginal cost is a rational response when agents realize that a substantial fraction of their inputs is imported from other countries, where suppliers may have been unaffected by an aggregate nominal demand shock of national rather than international origin. Full insulation of real sales from a perceived nominal *national* disturbance would require that each agent (a) assume his national suppliers immediately perceive the same shock and (b) ignore the fact that suppliers of imports are unaffected by a national demand shock. Both of these surely strain credulity.

3. *Information imperfections and delays*. Before the postwar development of monetary aggregates and national income accounts, timely

measures of nominal aggregates did not exist, as good a reason as any to explain why nominal aggregate indexation has never occurred. Even today, nominal GNP indexation would require a two-month average delay in the United States (data for the second quarter, centered on May 15, become available in the third week of July). Lags are considerably longer in some other countries. Wage contracts indexed to nominal GNP thus cannot prevent a short-run reduction in hours worked in situations when nominal GNP growth suddenly decelerates, as in the United States in the second quarter of 1980 and the second quarter of 1981. Profit-maximizing firms naturally resist the implications of nominal GNP indexation that, because of information lags in situations of temporary fluctuations of nominal GNP growth, they reduce prices just when the economy is recovering and raise prices just when it is collapsing.

4. *Velocity shifts.* Information on monetary aggregates is available fairly promptly, but indexation to a particular monetary aggregate cannot insulate real variables even if information is contemporaneous. Stochastic disturbances in commodity and money demand functions, which may be serially correlated, lead to serially correlated fluctuations in the velocity of money. A price-setting agent who chose to index his product price to the money supply, Ml, in the United States would find that a slump in real sales occurred in any week or month in which velocity grew more slowly than the average written into the indexation formula.

Contractual arrangements cannot obviate fluctuations of hours worked in response to fluctuations in real supply or in nominal demand. Both firms and workers are unwilling to accept the risk implied by a contract that is fully indexed to nominal spending or money. If it is impossible to eliminate fluctuations in nominal demand, labor-market contracts should be of relatively short duration. Frequent contract renewals can partially substitute for the absence of nominal GNP indexation, by allowing the latest information on both real and nominal shocks to be incorporated into wage-setting and price-setting decisions.

Indexation and Product-Market Adjustment

The preceding discussion, which emphasized the obstacles to full indexation of labor contracts, would appear to apply with much more force to product markets. Yearly, monthly, and even daily adjustments in relative prices must be accomplished by the price system if it is to perform its traditional job of efficient resource allocation. Thus long-term product contracts that index the nominal price to an aggregate index while maintaining fixed relative product prices are rarely observed. Because in most historical eras the variance of relative prices has been greater than that of the aggregate price level, agents have relied on short contracts to perform required adjustments in relative prices, and have been able to eschew formal indexation to aggregate variables, knowing that soon a contract revision will allow incorporation of any relevant aggregate information.

The cost-benefit approach to explaining contract length would also point out that, while there are much greater disturbances in product markets that would warrant a short contract, there are also much lower negotiation costs. While strikes are a frequent event in labor markets, there are no "strikes" by suppliers who are unwilling to provide intermediate goods. If a final goods producer is unwilling to accede to a supplier's price "demand," the supplier will either make a price concession or take his goods elsewhere, depending on his expectations about future demand. Other reasons there are no supplier strikes may be legal institutions that prevent supplier collusion but encourage worker collusion, and the fact that most suppliers produce multiple products while most workers do not.

The absence of complete indexation of product prices to nominal demand disturbances opens the way to output fluctuations. This would not matter if all product prices were set in auction markets, with supply and demand equated continually. Nor would it matter if firms could "see through" the fog of information on nominal aggregate demand provided every day by the newspaper and could be certain that each supplier and customer would "see through" to the same true state of affairs. Thus the operational tasks for product-market theorists are to explain, first, why prices for all products are not set in auction markets, and then, why firms do not and cannot insulate the real economy from nominal disturbances. Okun's book makes a good start on these two questions, but there is more to be said on each one.

The Response of Prices to Demand Shocks When Prices Are Preset

Why Prices Are Preset

My analysis of product market behavior rests firmly on the same foundation as Okun's; the prices of at least some products must be preset for a finite period of time. When combined with the shopping model that Okun formulated, the need to form expectations about the costs of goods provided by suppliers (a factor I have stressed), and the lack of complete indexation, the assumption that prices are preset can explain the sluggish adjustment that is sometimes observed in product markets. While some commentators find that the need for presetting prices is too obvious a phenomenon to warrant serious attention, two arguments persuade me that there is a need for a careful analysis. First, a whole tradition has developed in macroeconomics in the last decade that is based on the behavior of "yeoman barbers" who, like "yeoman farmers," are price takers receiving signals from some distant auction market and who produce a service. However attractive for its tractability, this analytical approach impedes understanding by providing no explanation of price tags and by ignoring the consequence of decentralization in breaking the link between common information and firm behavior.

Heterogeneity is crucial for the theory of price adjustment because it explains the coexistence of auction markets and price-setting markets. In describing auction markets, Okun states on page 134: "Those commodities traded on auction markets have a large number of producers and of potential buyers; they are homogeneous or readily gradable; and typically they are storable at relatively low cost." My explanation of price setting differs from Okun's only in placing more emphasis on heterogeneity of time and space in product markets and less on the homogeneity of the product itself. Retail transactions are characterized by a large number of customers making brief individual visits to different locations, in contrast to the Board of Trade, where each trader remains at his post throughout the day. Unlike the empty supermarket, the essence of a spot-auction market is its liquidity, which can only be achieved if many buyers and sellers are present at the same time. When price tags are preset rather than continually changed, as in an auction, goods and services can be made available at conveniently dispersed locations and with a purchase time that is at the discretion of the buyer.

How might a theorist go about building a model to explain the prevalence of price-setting practices? Overlooking for the moment markets involving manufacturers and wholesalers, he might begin by adopting Gary Becker's treatment of consumption goods as a combination of marketed items and time.[29] For an analysis of markets, the crucial

29. Gary S. Becker, "A Theory of the Allocation of Time," *Economic Journal,* vol. 75 (September 1965), pp. 493–517.

contribution of time is not in the need for time in actual consumption, as when watching television, but rather in the requirement for time to make purchases. On this issue, I like Alan Blinder's reflection on why, when workers go to get stationery from the office supply cabinet, "do they not just take what they need for the next day (or hour or minute)? It is not because there is a large transportation cost or because there is book-keeping to do. Rather, it is because each trip to the cabinet occupies some of the workers' time—valuable time that they could spend on something else."[30] Although Blinder was interested in managerial costs of adjusting inventories by retail firms, time is just as relevant in the shopping decisions of their customers. Our theorist might do well to begin with an explicit model of the resource costs of the shopping process, including both time and distance. The feature that distinguishes retail markets from centralized auction markets is that the ratio of the value of shopping time to the value of the average transaction is relatively large. Furthermore, the fact that people and their furniture do take up space, even when crammed together as in Manhattan, means that a costly trip is required to buy anything.

Space and time may be convincing as factors requiring decentralization of retail markets, with the resulting loss of liquidity that is an essential prerequisite for an auction market. But these considerations should be less important in sales by manufacturers to wholesalers and by wholesalers to retailers. Here the contrast between the vegetable market and the auto parts market is instructive. Heterogeneity of product must be the key element that explains the existence of price setting, for how else are we to explain the central role in most wholesale firms and purchasing departments of the printed catalog detailing the myriads of products available? The market for a rear trunk lid for a 1969 Plymouth four-door sedan delivered on a Wednesday in 1981 in Evanston, Illinois, is a rather thin one, lacking the liquidity and central location necessary for an auction to take place. Preset prices in a catalog allow transaction times and locations to be freely chosen and thus increase economic efficiency. In the case of the 1969 Plymouth trunk lid, printed prices help the Evanston body shop and the automobile insurance adjuster located ten miles away to base their allocative decisions on the same information.

Some theorists might insist that the parts catalog should be indexed to some nominal aggregate number, so that prices can be marked up

30. Alan S. Blinder, "Retail Inventory Behavior and Business Fluctuations," *Brookings Papers on Economic Activity, 2:1981*, p. 454.

each day or month by a fixed parameter that is announced in the newspaper. Recent visitors claim that they have seen this done in Tel Aviv restaurants. But to search so far for an example of this practice is to identify the phenomenon that prevents it from becoming widespread, and this is the low historical variance of aggregate nominal indexes as compared to relative prices. Phillip Cagan's charts document the wide dispersion of price changes in recessions for wholesale price index commodity categories; presumably the dispersion of price changes for individual products is even greater.[31] Because relative prices change all the time, fixed-parameter indexation does not obviate the reprinting of catalogs. And if catalogs must be reprinted (and this is done separately, page by page, in the wholesale business), why should firms bother with indexing except in extraordinary macroeconomic conditions?

Specialists in industrial organization may be surprised to learn that such elementary phenomena as price-setting practices are still under discussion by macroeconomists. Industrial organization, at least as I learned it,[32] would collapse as a subdiscipline if it were stripped of product heterogeneity and preset prices. Product heterogeneity, which is ruled out in the new classical "yeoman barber" models, is central to an understanding not only of price setting, but also of the basic economic concepts of the industry, the firm, and the product. Classic definitions of industries rest on distinctions that revolve around the similarity of products or production processes. The existence of the firm has been explained as a way of economizing on transactions costs when heterogeneous labor, capital, and materials must be brought together to produce a given range of products. And anyone involved in antitrust cases knows that the ability of firms to preset prices is assumed from the beginning, while some of the arguments depend on the definition of product classes or individual products within a vast sea of heterogeneity.

Modeling the Demand Responsiveness of Prices as a Varying Parameter

The shopping model and kinked demand curve that play the central role in Okun's chapter on product markets constitute only the beginning

31. Phillip Cagan, "Changes in the Recession Behavior of Wholesale Prices in the 1920's and Post-World War II," *Explorations in Economic Research,* vol. 2 (Winter 1975), pp. 54–104.
32. From Carl Kaysen, with frequent interruptions by Frank Fisher, at Harvard in 1960–61.

of an adequate analysis. Okun has no explanation for a varying responsiveness of prices to changes in nominal aggregate demand, as has occurred in Latin America and Israel and in various hyperinflations. When provoked, business firms are capable of changing prices very fast. A step forward can be made when we allow the firm to become like Janus, simultaneously looking forward in the input-output table toward its customers and backward toward its suppliers. The one-sided forward-looking nature of Okun's analysis is symbolized by his figure 4-2 on page 177, which has the demand curve shifting along a constant cost curve. For macroeconomic analysis the central question is, what factors can be invented to provide a rigorous explanation of the fact that, in the face of public information on nominal aggregate demand, the demand and cost curves of a firm do not generally move in proportion?

The principal ingredients in an explanation are, first, a distinction between aggregate and local shocks and, second, a multiplicity of pieces of available information about nominal aggregate demand that creates ambiguity about the exact value of current changes. A third ingredient is decentralization combined with imperfect information. The one-good yeoman barber model misses the main point if, through the usual methods of solving models with rational expectations, every agent can casually assume that everyone else is just like him. John Anderson called Reaganomics "economics with mirrors." Yet homogeneous one-good structures are really "models with mirrors," in which agents look around and see only themselves.

In thinking about the sources of gradual price adjustment in a recession, in which agents have a lot of current information about nominal aggregate demand (information that is dispersed around an ever-changing mean), it has always seemed to me that the fundamental source of stickiness involves input costs. For a moment let's ignore labor input and concentrate on materials. Our Janus-like firm must pay for materials, and this limits its flexibility in lowering its product price if it perceives a drop in nominal demand. In 1980 Chrysler could have offered rebates of 50 percent instead of 10 percent if only the cost of steel and other materials had cooperatively dropped by 50 percent in the second quarter of 1980. But our firm looks back into the murky recesses of the input-output table and sees only risk. If the steel firm does not cut prices because it perceives a sticky price of coal or oil, then a unilateral 50 percent cut in the price of Chrysler autos would lead to bankruptcy even faster than would occur with a smaller price cut.

In contrast to models with mirrors, the essence of the price adjustment problem comes closer to models of public goods, with their prisoner's dilemmas and free-rider problems. Each agent must realize its fundamental vulnerability in the absence of a central coordinating authority, because an initial move to cut prices—if followed by competitors but not by suppliers—may lead to bankruptcy. The problem is the same in labor markets. No single agent will be willing to agree to a unilateral wage cut when he knows that the cost of his market basket depends on the wages of everyone else.

One reaction to the cost-based story points to an alleged "sunk" nature of input costs. If Chrysler has already bought the steel, the fact that the steel was constructed at the higher cost level of an earlier period is irrelevant. Only demand considerations should govern the price. In the extreme, this view must regard all costs as fixed over the length of time during which prices are preset, and it thus ignores the numerous day-by-day adjustments to input quantity that a firm can achieve. More basically, it ignores the speculative element involved in holding inventories. The firm may choose to hold the steel rather than convert it into autos at distress-sale prices if it believes that conditions will improve in the next period. This "reluctance to produce" might be interpreted as voluntary underproduction in a model with mirrors. But it translates in fact into sticky final-goods prices and is just enough to create the wedge between effective and notional demand curves that Barro and Grossman and Malinvaud need to carry out their "fix-price" analyses.[33]

This makes it clear that a formal model of the problem of sunk costs must specify carefully the kinds of precommitments that firms must make covering input prices and quantities. And it must specify the timing of a firm's output and price decisions in relation to the availability of information about nominal demand. Since real-world firms with preset prices must initially learn of a demand surprise through real events—the nonappearance of expected customers and the unexpected buildup of inventories—the model must require firms to set the price before they learn the news. Without costless communication to every supplier and every supplier's supplier (both here and abroad), the firm is likely to respond in the next period with an adjustment that takes the form partly of lower production and partly of lower selling prices. With nothing special on the front page of the daily newspaper, the adjustment may be

---

33. See Barro and Grossman, *Money, Employment, and Inflation;* and Edmond Malinvaud, *The Theory of Unemployment Reconsidered* (Basil Blackwell, 1977).

weighted toward production, but if headlines scream that a wartime enemy has surrendered, the adjustment may be weighted toward prices.

I suspect that some progress may be possible in building models of a Janus-like firm by careful specification of the sequential learning process. Imagine that a firm presets its output price and purchases materials one week at a time. At the end of the first week it receives initial information about its local demand shock, in the form of a buildup or reduction in inventories (or unfilled orders) compared to its initial plan. At the same time it may receive a new price list from one or more suppliers and can begin to form an inference about the state of aggregate demand. News about the state of aggregate demand is not received as a neat package, but rather as bits of information arriving week after week. Our firm might not learn until the end of the second week of the *Business Week* index for the first week, and not until the end of the third week of the unemployment rate and index of industrial production for the first week. Because all of these information sources about both local and aggregate demand are noisy, several weeks are likely to be observed before major changes in plans are made. Sluggish price adjustment may emerge from this process under normal peacetime conditions if firms wait for price cuts by suppliers before feeling that it is safe to cut prices substantially in response to a perceived dip in aggregate demand, while suppliers wait to cut prices until their assessment of the current aggregate demand situation is confirmed by a reduction in orders from final goods producers. The more rapid adjustment of prices during wartime may stem from the role of dramatic political and military news in cutting through the normal drawn-out sequential learning process.

Conclusion

The historical experience of the last century reveals a number of different patterns of price and wage adjustment. In the postwar United States prices and wages responded modestly to the level and change in aggregate demand, with a substantial role for inertia. In other times and places, however, prices and wages responded in greater degree to the change and level of aggregate demand and were less influenced by inertia. Prices and wages were particularly flexible in the United States during World War I and its aftermath, in Japan after 1914, and in postwar Britain.

Some of these changes in behavior seem to have plausible explanations. For instance, the theoretical ideas sketched in the last section may have some potential for explaining the greater degree of price responsiveness in the United States during World War I. The postwar inertia in the United States, as contrasted with Britain and Japan, seems consistent with the interpretation that the unique U.S. institution of three-year staggered wage contracts plays a central role in price and wage dynamics.[34] Other changes in behavior are more mysterious. The "output level" impact of aggregate demand on price and wage changes seemed to disappear in the United States between 1929 and 1941, and in the United Kingdom between 1924 and 1938. This merely restates what we already knew—that high unemployment in those episodes did not lead to the expected downward adjustment in prices and wages. Should we conclude that the adjustment process is asymmetric in extreme cases?

Neither the empirical estimates nor the theoretical suggestions contained in this paper are intended as final answers. Parameters estimated from a century of annual data should not be used to make precise assessments of current policy issues, but rather should be regarded as providing some rough guidelines concerning the frequency and magnitude of parameter shifts that seem to characterize the price and wage adjustment process in different countries. Interpretation of policy mistakes in past historical episodes and estimates of the impact of future policy actions require more careful attention to shorter periods using quarterly or monthly data and indexes of price and wage changes that distinguish shifts in output and employment mix from actual changes in individual prices and wage rates. The research agenda for econometricians and theorists seems, as always, to be a full one.

Data Appendix

The key to the abbreviations is given after the listing for each country.

United States
1890–1928 (all data are from LTEG)
Nominal GNP: Series A7, linked in 1909 to series A8.
Real GNP: Series A1, linked in 1909 to series A2.

---

34. This paper, with its emphasis on the unique role of the postwar U.S. labor contracting system, reflects the influence of ideas set forth in two earlier papers: Jeffrey

GNP deflator: Nominal GNP divided by real GNP.

Wage rate: Series B70, multiplied by series B69.

Natural real GNP:1892–1953, RJGM, app. B.

1929–80

Nominal and real GNP: SCB, vol. 60 (December 1980), table 7; and SCB, vol. 61 (June 1981), tables 1.1, 1.2

GNP deflator: Nominal GNP divided by real GNP.

Natural real GNP:1954–80, RJGI, app. B.

Wage rate:1929–46, LTEG, series B70, multiplied by series B69; 1947–80, total private nonagricultural average gross hourly earnings, current dollars, ERP, table B36.

Key to abbreviations

ERP *Economic Report of the President, January 1981.*

LTEG Bureau of Economic Analysis, *Long-Term Economic Growth, 1860–1970* (Government Printing Office, 1973).

RJGI Robert J. Gordon, "Inflation, Flexible Exchange Rates, and the Natural Rate of Unemployment," in Martin Neil Baily, ed., *Workers, Jobs, and Inflation* (Brookings Institution, 1982), pp. 88–157.

RJGM Robert J. Gordon, *Macroeconomics*, 2d ed. (Little, Brown, 1981).

SCB *Survey of Current Business,* various issues.

United Kingdom

1870–1938 (all data are from F)

Nominal GNP: Table 1, col. 1.

GNP deflator at factor cost: Table 61, col. 7.

Natural real GNP: Broken exponential trend line benchmarked in 1913, 1922, 1937, and 1950.

Wage rate: Table 65, col. 1.

Foreign exchange rate: See below.

D. Sachs, "Wages, Profits, and Macroeconomic Adjustment: A Comparative Study," *Brookings Papers on Economic Activity, 2:1979,* pp. 269–319; and William H. Branson and Julio J. Rotemberg, "International Adjustment with Wage Rigidity," *European Economic Review,* vol. 13 (May 1980), pp. 309–32. Sachs does a particularly good job of calling attention to labor market institutions as an important source of differing dynamic wage behavior; see pp. 303–07.

1955–80 (from IMF, 1971 and 1981, unless otherwise specified)
   Nominal GDP: Line 99b.
   GDP deflator: Nominal GDP divided by real GDP.
   Real GDP: Line 99b. p.
   Natural real GDP: Broken exponential trend line benchmarked in 1950
      and 1970.
   Wage rate: Average monthly earnings, all industries, line 65c.
   Foreign exchange rate: 1900–70, annual average dollar exchange rate,
      BEKS, 1900–70. 1970–80, effective exchange rate, IMF, line
      amx.

Key to abbreviations
BEKS *The British Economy Key Statistics.*
F   Charles H. Feinstein, *National Income, Expenditure, and Out-*
        put of the United Kingdom, 1855–1965, Studies in the National
        Income and Expenditure of the United Kingdom, vol. 6 (Cam-
        bridge University Press, 1972).
IMF   International Monetary Fund, *International Financial Statistics,*
        1971 Supplement, vol. 24; *International Financial Statistics,*
        Yearbook 1981, vol. 34.

Japan
1870–1940
   Nominal GNP: OHK (1957), table 3, col. 1, linked in 1905 to OHKR
      (1973), table 1, col. 6.
   GNP deflator: OHK (1957), table 3, col. 1, divided by table 4, col. 1,
      linked in 1905 to OHKR (1973), table 14, col. 3.
   Real GNP: Nominal GNP divided by GNP deflator.
   Natural real GNP: Broken exponential trend benchmarked in 1855,
      1890, 1903, 1914, 1919, 1929, 1938, and 1953.
   Wage rate: OHK (1957), table 1, col. 1.

1960–80 (all data are from IMF, 1971 and 1981)
   Nominal GNP: Line 99a.
   Real GNP: Line 99a. r.
   Natural real GNP: Broken exponential trends benchmarked in 1953
      and 1971.
   GNP deflator: Nominal GNP divided by real GNP.
   Wages: Line 65.

Key to abbreviations
IMF   *International Financial Statistics,* 1971 Supplement, vol. 24;
       International Financial Statistics, Yearbook 1981, vol. 34.
OHK   Kazushi Ohkawa, *The Growth Rate of the Japanese Economy
       Since 1878* (Tokyo: Kinokuniya Bookstore Co., Ltd., 1957).
OHKR Kazushi Ohkawa and Henry Rosovsky, *Japanese Economic
       Growth: Trend Acceleration in the Twentieth Century* (Stanford
       University Press, 1973).

Comment by Barry P. Bosworth

AT THE BEGINNING of his paper Robert Gordon comments that he finds
Arthur Okun's book more satisfactory when viewed as a contribution to
microeconomics rather than to macroeconomics. I think that was Okun's
intention. The basic issue that divides us today in the theory and practice
of aggregate economic policy involves an issue of microeconomics.
Should the economy be viewed as an aggregation of relatively competitive "flex-price" markets where price fluctuations are the consequence
of changes in demand and supply—that is, prices adjust to clear the
market? In such a situation, inflation can be controlled by monetary
policy alone at relatively small cost, and efforts to stimulate employment
through the manipulation of aggregate demand are ineffective and
misguided. The alternative view discussed by Okun stresses the "fix-
price" nature of many markets in the sense that demand and supply
changes have a relatively small influence on prices. In that case the costs
of controlling inflation by restraint of demand alone will be high, the
economy converges only slowly toward any equilibrium, and fiscal and
monetary policy are important means of stabilizing employment.

    This is certainly not a new issue—it was at the heart of the dispute
between Keynes and the classical economists. But it has been brought
to the forefront by the failure to provide effective control of inflation
during the 1970s and by the efforts within the profession to integrate
microeconomics and macroeconomics. For too long, we have assumed
in much of our microeconomic analysis competitive flex-price behavior
while much of our aggregate analysis incorporates a fix-price assumption.
The fix-price adherents seemed to win the argument on empirical grounds
since the existence of sustained involuntary unemployment is contrary
to the assumption of a market-clearing price. However, the recent

contributions of the new classical economists, who explain departures from full employment on the basis of information lags and formal contracting, make clear that the fix-price adherents are losing the argument on theoretical grounds. Keynes simply asserted that such behavior existed without providing convincing arguments as to why. And in the subsequent period most macroeconomists were content to continue the assumption. But today they are challenged by a competing theory that is logically consistent in its microeconomic foundations. It is this issue that Okun addressed when he sought to advance the theory of fix-price behavior at the level of individual markets.

Despite the focus of this volume on product markets, Okun's book and Gordon's paper are directed primarily toward labor markets. This emphasis also seems correct to me, as prices are less puzzling to explain. The profit-maximizing firm should maintain a ratio of price to marginal cost that changes only with perceived changes in the price elasticity of demand for its products. Over the cycle the firm would not be expected to fundamentally alter its view of that elasticity. New competing firms do not leap into the market on the basis of cyclical market conditions, and shifts in the level of demand do not imply a change in the price elasticity. Most empirical studies find that marginal costs (or what the firm may call direct costs) for most industrial products and services are also relatively constant over a wide variation in capacity utilization. Thus the stability of prices, given costs, over the business cycle seems consistent with normal profit-maximizing behavior for firms with relatively elastic short-run supply functions.

Okun adds the consideration that in customer markets, where there are costs of shopping, concern about the future benefits of repeat business will affect the firm's current-period pricing and lead to some smoothing of prices relative to cost changes. On balance, Okun's customer markets imply some damping influence of current market conditions but do not alter the basic applicability of the neoclassical market to product market pricing. The same cannot be said for his view of labor market behavior.

The central portion of Gordon's paper, however, is empirical and addresses the issue of whether the actual economy displays a high degree of price flexibility. Okun often stated that 90 percent of a reduction in nominal demand would be reflected in lower physical output and only 10 percent in prices. Gordon's results conflict sharply with this view. He finds a very large short-term effect of demand on prices; and, at least since 1950, there is a rapid and nearly full translation of any changes in nominal demand into prices, with no lasting effect on real output. If we believe Gordon, the return of the United States to price stability is relatively simple and costless because prices will adjust quickly to a more restrictive monetary policy. While Okun sought an explanation for sticky prices, Gordon has shown that they do not exist.

Critical to Gordon's results is his use of nominal GNP as an explanatory variable. He uses a measure of nominal GNP growth in excess of the growth in real potential output, $\hat{y}$, as the primary variable; that is,

$$(1) \qquad\qquad p = f(\hat{y}, z)$$

and

$$(2) \qquad\qquad \hat{y} = y - q^*,$$

where y represents the growth in nominal output, q^* represents the growth in potential output in constant dollars, and z represents other variables in the price change equation.

We also have, as an identity,

$$(3) \qquad\qquad y \equiv p + (q - q^*),$$

where p and q represent the growth in prices and actual real output, respectively. If equation 3 is simply inserted into 2, one interpretation is that Gordon estimated an identity of p as a function of p, where the $(q - q^*)$ introduces an element of measurement error on the right-hand side that biases the coefficient toward zero. On that basis the results have no causal interpretation.

As Gordon mentions, neither real nor nominal GNP can be regarded as predetermined, and the introduction of either raises potential problems of estimation bias. It is possible, however, to transform his equation, using identity 3, into an equation with $(q - q^*)$ rather than y on the right-hand side. The overall fit of that equation, if there are no problems of spurious correlation, should be the same as with the first version. For the postwar period, Gordon's equation formulation can be approximated with readily available data, and I can report that there is an enormous change in the equation's performance depending on whether $[p + (q - q^*)]$ or $(q - q^*)$ is used on the right-hand side. I cannot settle the issue of whether nominal or real GNP is the more predetermined, but for rather obvious reasons using nominal GNP changes to explain price changes may introduce severe statistical problems. Thus the empirical conclusions are strongly affected by one's prior belief about whether real or nominal GNP is the more predetermined.

In the third section Gordon discusses the indexation of wages to prices and proposes that the use of nominal GNP rather than the CPI would yield superior results. He advances several reasons from a rational expectations perspective for the fact that such indexation has never occurred. I will mention a nonrational alternative: local bargainers have never heard of the GNP, do not understand what it is, and would not perceive it as relating to any of their concerns if they did. I am puzzled by this section of the paper and unclear about its objective. If prices and wages are as flexible as Gordon's empirical results suggest, indexation is not of major concern. Indexation to nominal GNP rather than to prices offers some advantages of adjusting to extended shocks, but it amounts to contracting for income shares rather than real wages. There are other types of economic changes for which this type of indexation is as inappropriate as indexation to prices.

I found the fourth section, which contains a discussion of some of the theoretical issues raised in modeling price behavior, interesting, but I have no substantive comments to contribute.

Comment by Steven C. Salop

PROFESSOR GORDON'S paper challenges theorists to devise proper and workable neo-Keynesian models. The models should be simple enough to analyze easily but complete enough to capture the fundamentals of macroeconomic phenomena. They should satisfy the tests of rigor generally applied to microeconomic theory. They should have a concrete and consistent general-equilibrium structure, grounded firmly in the concepts of supply and demand. The neo-Keynesian properties should be demonstrated analytically, not assumed. In this comment, I discuss several such models.[35]

The rubric *neo-Keynesian* implies that the models generate the properties associated with Keynes's *General Theory*. On the real side, these properties include quantity adjustments with a "multiplier" property, an important role for confidence and expectations, and the possibility of low-level equilibrium (or stationary disequilibrium). Finally, the

35. Earlier versions of this comment were presented at the Federal Reserve Board, the Federal Trade Commission, and the Massachusetts Institute of Technology. I thank especially David Cass, Judith R. Gelman, Edmund S. Phelps, Joseph A. Stiglitz, and James Tobin for help with its predecessors.

acid test of any neo-Keynesian model is its ability to generate a positive role for government, especially for fiscal policy.

In his paper, Gordon follows Okun's view that a neo-Keynesian product market model might usefully "begin with an explicit model of the resource costs of the shopping process." Gordon goes on to argue that such a model is essential to a proof that prices are set in advance and changed only slowly. Such preset prices are in turn essential to the excess supply equilibrium that many neo-Keynesians emphasize. As the following analysis demonstrates, other approaches may also be productive.

Imperfect Competition and Product Market Equilibrium

I previously constructed a shopping process model of a labor market with flexible wages.[36] That model was characterized by two assumptions—imperfect information by workers and firms and transactions costs in the form of firm-specific turnover costs. These assumptions endow firms with monopsony power in the labor market by enabling them to reduce turnover at the margin by raising their relative wage rates. This generates an inefficient market equilibrium even when entry is free, real wages are fully flexible, and all parties have rational expectations. By some standards these firms can be viewed as only moderately sophisticated. In making decisions they take into account the effect of wage changes on employee turnover but ignore the (small) effect of their own decisions on competitors' subsequent decisions and on the unemployment rate.

The equilibrium of this model has a number of neo-Keynesian properties. The equilibrium unemployment rate (the "natural rate") is positive and above the efficient level. The model can generate involuntary unemployment in the sense that all firms, even the one paying the lowest wages, may have queues of excess applicants, that is, unemployed workers who would be willing and able to work at the firm's going wage

36. Steven C. Salop, "Wage Differentials in a Dynamic Theory of the Firm," *Journal of Economic Theory*, vol. 6 (August 1973), pp. 321–44; and Salop, "A Model of the Natural Rate of Unemployment," *American Economic Review*, vol. 69 (March 1979), pp. 117–25. See also Edmund S. Phelps, "Money Wage Dynamics and Labor Market Equilibrium," in Edmund S. Phelps and others, *Microeconomic Foundations of Employment and Inflation Theory* (Norton, 1970), pp. 124–66, especially the footnote on p. 124; and Arthur M. Okun, *Prices and Quantities: A Macroeconomic Analysis* (Brookings Institution, 1981), chap. 2.

rate. In spite of this excess supply, firms do not lower their wage rates enough to eliminate the unemployment.

The logic of these results is as follows. Wage reductions cause an increase in costly turnover, limiting the ability of wage reductions to eliminate unemployment. And firms do not fire their experienced workers to hire unemployed applicants for two reasons. First, because of the firm-specific turnover costs (Okun's "toll"), such an exchange would be economical only if accompanied by a wage reduction for the new workers. However, union contracts or morale problems may make such a discriminatory wage differential infeasible. Second, even if a lower wage were offered and accepted, it would not be cost-minimizing. Once hired, these new workers are identical to the old ones. Because a lower wage results in more intense on-the-job search efforts and higher quit rates by experienced workers, turnover costs rise, eliminating the possibility of cost reductions. Together, these factors limit the ability of wage reductions to lower unemployment.

Moreover, at any resulting level of unemployment, the unemployed's optimal search process is inefficient. Too many applicants queue up for the limited places at the high-wage firms. Yet these firms cannot eliminate this search inefficiency with application fees, because applicants will suspect firms of falsely advertising nonexistent job vacancies.

Finally, workers who quit to search for new jobs do not bear the burden of the turnover costs they create, and firms ignore the impact of their actions on the welfare of the unemployed. Both these effects also lead to unemployment in excess of the efficient level.

Although it is a general-equilibrium formulation,[37] the model's product market is primitive at best.[38] This incompleteness necessarily limits its use for policy analysis. However, two instruments that can be introduced into the model—turnover taxes and employment subsidies—do affect the equilibrium. As for the acid test of government having a positive role, it can be demonstrated that aggregate welfare is raised at the margin by a well-implemented policy of making the government the employer of last resort. Since the equilibrium level of unemployment is too high, entry by an additional firm would raise welfare, since it would reduce the unemployment rate.

37. The average wage rate is endogenous although the model is solved only in the case of homogeneous wage rates. Its only "mirror" is "unconscious" symmetry.

38. The product market is always in equilibrium. It is effectively characterized by perfect competition for a single homogeneous product.

I agree with Gordon's observation that a similar shopping-process model of the product market is possible.[39] It could relate customer loyalty to the turnover costs of search, experience, and other information-gathering techniques. Prices would be preset as in the labor market version.

A narrow view of product-market models seems unnecessary, however. As Gordon emphasizes, to focus solely on the economics of the shopping process ignores an important and enduring Keynesian property—the impact of effective demand on production and the feedback of production to income and effective demand. It is this feedback cycle that forms the basis of the multiplier that figures so prominently in Keynesian analysis. Indeed, these feedback effects might well be called the fundamental externality of Keynesian macroeconomics.

It appears that a complex shopping-process model is unnecessary for capturing this fundamental macroexternality. Instead, one can rely on a shopping-process model of the labor market to generate equilibrium unemployment while using imperfect competition in the product market to generate "effective demand." Because imperfectly competitive equilibria are almost always suboptimal even when prices are flexible, imperfect competition can play an important role in neo-Keynesian formulations. Because firms ignore the effects of their actions on both their rivals' profits and consumer surplus,[40] imperfect competition can be viewed as a decentralization or externality problem. This approach has been criticized on the grounds that the American economy is generally unconcentrated. However, it is now fairly well established that information imperfections lead to market power even for small firms in industries with free entry competition.[41]

It is also worth emphasizing that it is not difficult to construct a consistent model of a general-equilibrium economy that gets stuck at a

39. See also Edmund S. Phelps and Sidney G. Winter, Jr., "Optimal Price Policy under Atomistic Competition," in Phelps and others, *Microeconomic Foundations,* pp. 309–37; the paper by Calvo and Phelps in this volume; and Peter Diamond, "Aggregate Demand Management in Search Equilibrium," unpublished paper, Massachusetts Institute of Technology, 1980.

40. See Michael Spence, "Product Differentiation and Welfare," *American Economic Review,* vol. 66 (May 1976, *Papers and Proceedings, 1975*), pp. 407–14, for a good survey.

41. See Steven Salop and Joseph Stiglitz, "Bargains and Ripoffs: A Model of Monopolistically Competitive Price Dispersion," *Review of Economic Studies,* vol. 44 (October 1977), pp. 493–510. In addition, measurement of market power for this model is carried out at an industry, not aggregate, level.

low level of output. For example, consider the following primitive general-equilibrium model of imperfect competition.[42] Type A persons produce apples but desire beer. Type B persons produce beer but desire apples. All trade takes place in a market with a flexible relative exchange price. Either product can be viewed as the numéraire. However, suppose that in making his production decision each individual acts as a Cournot, rather than a perfect, competitor and takes the *quantities* of apples and beer offered on the market by others as given. Individuals are rational in the sense that they efficiently forecast rivals' production levels and their own demands.

There may be at least two equilibria in this model. First, there may be one or more standard Cournot equilibria.[43] Perhaps of more significance to neo-Keynesians, there must be a *zero-output equilibrium:* if no beer is produced for exchange, no type A individual will find it rational to produce apples for sale, nor will any type B produce beer if no apples are produced. Of course, if everyone produces, then mutually advantageous exchange occurs and welfare rises.

A focus on the dynamics of this process might reveal that initial production by only one or a few individuals begins a disequilibrium process of additional production by others that "multiplies" itself until a garden-variety, positive-output, Cournot equilibrium is achieved.[44] However, beginning at the zero-output point, initial production by any one individual is irrational, since that output cannot be sold and has no other value to its producer. Of course, a sophisticated strategy-minded firm—or the government—might begin production in the hope or expectation that others would follow once the process of demand (and supply) creation was under way.

A similar approach is taken in the more realistic neo-Keynesian model of Oliver Hart.[45] Although complex, Hart's model has much to commend it. It is a carefully constructed, general-equilibrium, Cournot model. Wages and prices are flexible. The balanced budget multiplier is positive. With the addition of a unionized labor market, the model also generates unemployment, though unionization is unnecessary to generate the multiplier result.

Thus in spite of fully flexible prices and rational expectations (in the

42. Steven C. Salop, "Rational Expectations and Multiple Equilibria: Love, Faith, Money and Underemployment," unpublished paper, Federal Reserve Board, 1977.

43. Multiple equilibria often occur in Cournot models.

44. That is, the zero-output equilibrium may be unstable.

45. Oliver Hart, "A Model of Imperfect Competition with Keynesian Features," *Quarterly Journal of Economics,* vol. 97 (February 1982), pp. 109–38.

limited sense that each Cournot player correctly predicts the level of output produced by others), a Pareto-dominated zero-output equilibrium exists.[46] A preferable equilibrium can only be achieved if one player acts in a more sophisticated, or "superrational," fashion.

Static versus Dynamic Models

While imperfect information and competition are sufficient to generate unemployment, an inefficient (low-level) equilibrium, the multiplier, and a positive role of government policy, certain neo-Keynesian features are lacking in the models discussed so far. Although decentralization has a concrete interpretation in these models, it does not seem quite right.[47] Indeed, one could argue that the decentralization language used here is nothing more than a statement of the simultaneity of a two-equation model.

To illustrate this point simply, consider a general-equilibrium version of the usual single-industry model of imperfect competition.[48] Suppose output is produced from labor alone. In this single-good economy, workers essentially exchange labor for output. A single-exchange market thus suffices. Imperfect competition involves each firm that has market power in purchasing labor in exchange for a share of the output produced from that labor.[49]

The equilibrium of this single-market model is suboptimal. However, it clearly cannot capture the type of decentralization that macroeconomists seem to believe is added by the complexity of multimarket, monetary transactions. Nor does it capture the distinction between "notional" and "effective" demand analyzed by Clower,[50] since equi-

---

46. One could object to this definition of rational expectations as too limited on the grounds that rational players can predict reactions as well as levels. Unfortunately, there are often multiple reaction function equilibria too, if any equilibrium exists at all. See John Roberts and Hugo Sonnenschein, "On the Foundations of the Theory of Monopolistic Competition," *Econometrica*, vol. 45 (January 1977), pp. 101–14, for results on the nonexistence of equilibrium.

47. This point is also made by Hart, "A Model of Imperfect Competition."

48. Assume that scale economies limit the number of firms.

49. An alternative but equivalent dual-market approach could construct the model as an imperfectly competitive labor market with a perfectly competitive product market, or vice versa. Of course, Walras's Law teaches that the addition of the second market is redundant.

50. Robert Clower, "The Keynesian Counterrevolution: A Theoretical Appraisal," in F. P. R. Brechling and F. H. Hahn, eds., *The Theory of Interest Rates* (London: Macmillan, 1965), pp. 103–25.

librium occurs at a point where effective demand equals notional demand.

The other models discussed so far share this problem because all are essentially static, single-market formulations. One way to introduce such dynamics is with an *overlapping-generations* model. Such models generate other desirable neo-Keynesian properties as well. First, they have an important role for expectations and confidence. Second, the equilibria of such models are often not Pareto-optimal. Third, embedding the product-market model in the overlapping-generations structure begins the melding of the real and financial sectors that is necessary for completeness.[51] Finally, an easy way to add true decentralization is to embed a model of imperfect competition into the overlapping-generations structure.

Decentralization in an Overlapping-Generations Economy

Consider the following simple *overlapping-generations* economy. Suppose each individual lives two periods. Assume that the preferences of the representative individual are captured by the most extreme version of the life-cycle savings hypothesis—all income is earned when young and all consumption occurs when old, irrespective of prices or income. Assume that asset markets do not exist, but that each child is endowed with equity shares at birth. Thus each individual receives dividend income when young.

If, as in a point-input–point-output model, output were to take one period to mature after labor input was applied, the economy would be fully equivalent to the simple one-sector model discussed earlier. Such synchronization of desired consumption and output maturation dates effectively eliminates all real dynamics from the model.[52] Instead, assume that output matures *immediately* and, to simplify the model, that output is not storable. This makes it essential as well as desirable to pass

51. It has recently been argued that the overlapping-generations model is also the proper approach to the asset market, since the model is truly dynamic. See Neil Wallace, "The Overlapping Generations Model of Fiat Money," in John H. Kareken and Neil Wallace, eds., *Models of Monetary Economics* (Federal Reserve Bank of Minneapolis, 1980), pp. 49–96; and David Cass and Karl Shell, "In Defense of a Basic Approach," in ibid., pp. 251–60. Wallace has developed one such model. Incidentally, I think that inside credit can have more significance than Wallace's formulation permits. For example, inside credit in the sense of private IOU's can increase production by allowing firms to purchase factors in advance of the sale of actual production.

52. This perhaps ironic effect illustrates the essential cause of the decentralization effect—the nonsynchronization of receipts and expenditures.

output "backward" in time in the sense that output produced by young workers is consumed by the retired.

The labor market is perfectly competitive, so that firms take the wage rate as given. Firms do not take into account the effect on their product demand in the next period of hiring an additional young worker in this period. (This degree of sophistication will be added later.) Managers ignore the fact that some workers might also be shareholders. That is, assume that decisions in the economy are completely decentralized.[53]

The demand firms face is the exogenous level of income earned by the retired workers in the previous period. (For concreteness, one can imagine firms making wage payments in "chits" measured in "wage-units" to young workers, leading to that nominal income being measured in "wage-units.") Firms compete without regard for the effects of this period's actions on next period's profits. If bequests of goods and chits are not permitted, all income is spent by the retired people themselves. Thus the aggregate demand curve is unitary elastic,[54] or

$$(1) \qquad p = Y/\Sigma\, x_i,$$

where p is the current price, Y is the level of income generated in the previous period, and x_i is the output of representative firm i.

This neo-Keynesian approach is in striking contrast to the demand for goods implicit in the static formulations discussed earlier. In those models, the demand for goods in the next period is derived directly from the representative individual's goods-leisure trade-off, or

$$(2) \qquad p = w U_x/U_1,$$

where p is the expected price of goods in the next period, w is the contemporaneous nominal wage, and U_x/U_1 is the marginal rate of substitution between goods and leisure, evaluated at the level of production (and employment) in the market.

To return to the overlapping-generations formulation, Y is a measure of effective demand. If the level of effective demand, the output of its competitors, and the wage rate are taken as exogenously determined, each representative "Cournot" firm maximizes profits by choosing a

53. Hart, "A Model of Imperfect Competition," induces a somewhat comparable effect with multiple Phelpsian local markets.

54. A slightly more complex version could have N products. In the simplest Cobb-Douglas formulation, consumers would allocate to each product an equal share of total income, or $Y' = Y/N$ chits. Firms in each industry would then face a demand curve like that in equation 1 with nominal income Y'. As such, the equilibrium would be unaffected by this limited extension.

production level, x_i. By observing that there is a relationship between output and employment (given by the production function) and aggregating across all firms, we have an "aggregate product demand" function. Note that this function depends on each firm's expectations of income and competitors' production levels as well as on the wage.

The corresponding supply of labor function comes from utility maximization by young individuals. Again noting the relationship between output and employment given by the production function and aggregating, we have the "aggregate product supply" function. Of course, this function is contingent on the expected price of future output as well as on the current wage rate.[55]

The real sector achieves a *stationary equilibrium* when (1) aggregate product demand equals aggregate product supply, (2) aggregate real income generated equals aggregate output produced, (3) all expectations are fulfilled, and (4) all quantities replicate every period.

Since the product-demand function in the overlapping-generations model is generally different from the demand function in the static model discussed above, the equilibria of the two economies generally diverge. More important, the overlapping-generations model shares several properties with the apple-beer example. First, a zero-output equilibrium point exists. If there is no effective demand, no output will be produced to satisfy the (nonexistent) demand, and zero income will be generated. Second, if a firm (for instance, General Motors or the government) becomes more foresighted or sophisticated about the effect of its labor hiring decision today on the demand for its output in the future and takes these future effects into account in its planning, then the stationary equilibrium will be altered.[56] In particular, such foresightedness produces a multiplier reaction throughout the economy's input-output matrix as production moves to the new equilibrium.

General Motors could take future demand effects into account in any one of a number of ways. First, it could reckon the impact of its hiring decision today on its workers' future demand for Chevrolets, as expressed by equation 2. Alternatively, GM could also take into account

55. The supply of labor function mirrors equation 2 above, where p denotes the expected price of goods in the next period.

56. Thomas C. Schelling, "Raise Profits by Raising Wages?" *Econometrica*, vol. 14 (July 1946), pp. 227–34, recognized this point in his model. See also Nicholas Kaldor, "Alternative Theories of Distribution," *Review of Economic Studies*, vol. 23, no. 2 (1956), pp. 83–100.

the effect of its workers' increased incomes on other firms' output demands and the resulting increases in demand for Chevrolets two periods hence. And so on.[57]

With a zero rate of time discount, all these income and demand-generation effects should be taken into account by the firm. However, it is doubtful that firms do so in practice. Firms that attempt the exercise must predict rivals' reactions, in contrast to the Cournot assumption. One might imagine firms making different conjectures about ultimate effects according to their confidence about the economy and their expectations of rivals' degrees of confidence. In such a world, jawboning may work.

Conclusions

A number of possible neo-Keynesian models have been explored above. The models generate unemployment and underemployment and give importance to the concepts of effective demand and the multiplier. Yet in all the models wages and prices are flexible, expectations are rational and self-fulfilled, and markets are in stationary equilibrium. Market failures occur from the usual microeconomic causes—imperfect information, imperfect competition, and transactions costs.

These models have obviously not yet been fine-tuned to the purity of the standard IS-LM/aggregate demand–aggregate supply synthesis. They are far too rough. Asset markets have been ignored. Nonetheless, these models make it clear that any number of neo-Keynesian models can be constructed to meet the challenge of the rational expectations school.[58] The attractiveness of taking up this challenge can also be expected to increase shortly. Just as the inflation of the 1970s generated interest in models of the inflationary process, the failure of supply-side economics to prevent recessions in the 1980s is likely to create renewed enthusiasm for neo-Keynesian formulations.

57. One might expect that with each increment in sophistication the size of the total effect would rise. However, this may not occur. For example, a producer of inferior goods reckons that increased incomes will lower demand. Similarly, if industry demand is inelastic, one producer may cut output rather than increase it and thereby cause a decrease in the total income generated by the industry.

58. See Robert E. Lucas, Jr., "Expectations and the Neutrality of Money," *Journal of Economic Theory*, vol. 4 (April 1972), pp. 103–24; and Lucas "An Equilibrium Model of the Business Cycle," *Journal of Political Economy*, vol. 83 (December 1975), pp. 1113–44.

GUILLERMO A. CALVO and EDMUND S. PHELPS

A Model of Non-Walrasian General Equilibrium

THE MODERNIST'S vision of the contemporary market sector is riddled with competitive imperfections, even missing markets. Nowhere is that vision more systematically exemplified than by Arthur Okun's *Prices and Quantities,* in which imperfections penetrate every corner of social life and traditional business practice is an evolutionary coping with those imperfections.[1] The satisfactory performance of this sector without remedial public action is, to say the least, open to question.

By now there are several "paradigms" of imperfect competition and absent competition with which to study certain welfare aspects of enterprise behavior and government intervention. The competitive imperfection in the non-Walrasian theories of recent years is scarcity of information about prices (and possibly quantities) among market partic-ipants. Two prototypes of that theory are the Phelps-Winter product-market model of price-setting firms and the Mortensen labor-market model of wage-setting firms.[2]

These early non-Walrasian models yielded a distinctive result on economic equilibrium: Provided the real rate of interest remains positive, the competition of atomistic forms will not wipe out all pure profit—nor close all the gap between price and marginal cost—owing to costly "frictions" in the transmission of price information. However, an extension of this partial-equilibrium result to a general-equilibrium model, if that is possible, and an examination of its welfare significance, if any, have not so far been undertaken.

1. Arthur M. Okun, *Prices and Quantities: A Macroeconomic Analysis* (Brookings Institution, 1981).
2. Edmund S. Phelps and Sidney G. Winter, Jr., "Optimal Price Policy under Atomistic Competition," in Edmund S. Phelps and others, *Microeconomic Foundations of Employment and Inflation Theory* (Norton, 1970), pp. 309–37; and Dale T. Mortensen, "A Theory of Wage and Employment Dynamics," in ibid., pp. 167–211.

This paper embeds the Phelps-Winter firm in a general-equilibrium model. The original study by Phelps and Winter was partial equilibrium in character: While not neglecting questions of the existence, uniqueness, and stability of its non-Walrasian industry equilibrium, it treated consumers' demand for products as independent of industry income, as Marshall used to do, and it took the real rate of interest and real wage rate to be exogenous. The possibility of a more general analysis, with the foregoing restrictions removed, is our subject.

Questions of the economic efficiency of the general equilibrium (or equilibria) are the objects of special attention. Is the non-Walrasian equilibrium a Pareto optimum? If not, is it nevertheless a constrained Pareto optimum, unimprovable by feasible and admissible market interventions? If not, by what methods compatible with private incentives may a Pareto improvement be engineered?

A word on specifics and novelties. We model a pure-credit economy (no money). The model posits a stationary population of perpetual households, just like the theory of saving and earning in Ramsey.[3] Presumably a theory of the bequests of dynastic families such as that developed by Barro offers a theoretical rationale for this otherwise fanciful postulate.[4] (Our analysis of the alternative hypothesis of life-cycle employment and saving, with zero bequests, could not be fitted into this paper.) We also make the unusual, though not unprecedented, postulate that capital is insufficiently productive and profitable to be accumulated; output is produced by labor alone, with constant returns. In this respect our model resembles the consumption-loan model by Samuelson.[5] Yet the former's informational friction makes a radical difference: In our non-Walrasian equilibrium, though lacking capital or other durables and without Samuelson's social security or any other market intervention, a person could retire and live on his savings—invested at positive interest in profit-making firms.

The plan of the paper is this. The first part lays out the model with its utility-maximizing firms. Careful attention is paid to the choice of a

3. Frank P. Ramsey, "A Mathematical Theory of Saving," *Economic Journal,* vol. 38 (December 1928), pp. 543–59.
4. Robert J. Barro, "Are Government Bonds Net Wealth?" *Journal of Political Economy,* vol. 82 (December 1974), pp. 1095–1117.
5. Paul A. Samuelson, "An Exact Consumption-Loan Model of Interest with or without the Social Contrivance of Money," *Journal of Political Economy,* vol. 66 (December 1958), pp. 467–82.

numéraire and to the distinction between market clearing and market equilibrium. The latter is an expectational concept for which the former concept is neither necessary nor sufficient. We then draw some implications of the model about stationary equilibria: the features of a stationary-equilibrium plan of households and of a stationary-equilibrium plan of firms.

The second part contains a general-equilibrium analysis of the model. The (expectational) non-Walrasian equilibrium here is general in the sense that *all* the expectations of *all* the individual agents are correct— everyone's expectations of the firms' average price (the price level), the price of the (homogeneous) shares, the rate of return to share-holding (saving), and other deducible expectations are borne out by events. The conditions for any such general equilibrium are reduced to two: that the firms correctly expect the going price in the (economywide) industry and that the households correctly expect their cash flow, particularly their dividends (capital gains being absent in stationary equilibria). The ensuing analysis indicates the possibility that one or more stationary equilibria exist in the model. But the perfectly competitive equilibrium of Walrasian yore is *not* an equilibrium here; it is not among our non-Walrasian stationary equilibria. Nevertheless an employment subsidy can move the (best) equilibrium *closer* to the ideal Walrasian allocation. The findings of the analysis are discussed from a policy standpoint in the concluding section of the paper.

The Dynastic Model

All families are assumed to be identical in tastes, productivity, and (though this is not essential) initial wealth. All firms are identical in costs, competitiveness, and (also not essential) their initial share of customers. There are n customers, hence n families, per firm. At first and without loss of generality, each firm has the same number of shares outstanding. There is no public or private debt, no land or capital. Hence each family's wealth amounts initially to one share.

The labor market and the share market are perfect (Walrasian). The former market is postulated to establish at every time t a uniform wage rate, w_t^h, after any payroll tax or subsidy. The household wage will serve as numéraire so that w_t^h equals 1 for all t. The wage rate to firms will be denoted w_t^f so that $1 - w_t^f$ denotes the government subsidy, if any, to firms per unit of labor employed. It will follow from our concept of equilibrium and the aforementioned similarity of firms and families that each firm sets the same price, p_t, at any moment t along a general-equilibrium path. The corresponding experience of firms is then identical, and the share market accordingly establishes a uniform share price, q_t, at any moment t along the equilibrium trajectory. The equilibrium profit (in labor units) after any profits tax is denoted π_t^h per share.

In this notation, the instantaneous rate of return at time t on shares *expressed in terms of labor time*, to be denoted r_t, satisfies

(1) $$r_t q_t - \dot{q}_t = \pi_t^h, \qquad q_t \geq 0.$$

It is assumed here that all profits are paid out in dividends to shareholders. To obtain the rate of return in terms of *goods*, $\dot{p}_t/p_t$ must be subtracted from r_t. By national income accounting, after-tax profit per family equates households' cash-flow saving to zero (more generally, to the public deficit per family); hence

(2) $$l_t + \pi_t^h - p_t c_t = 0,$$

where l_t denotes current labor-time per family and c_t is consumption per family. When firms' prices are identical and families behave alike, each consuming c_t and working l_t, this accounting relation holds ex post for every family if (as here) taxes on profits equal employment subsidies (balanced budget).

We suppose that each family plans at every time $t \geq 0$ a sequence of employment $\{l_s\}$ and consumption $\{c_s\}$, $s \geq t$, to maximize a Ramsey lifetime utility integral,

$$\int_t^\infty u(c_s, l_s) e^{-\rho(s-t)}\, ds, \rho \geq 0,$$

subject to a budget constraint. Let $\hat{p}_s$ denote the price of goods, $\hat{q}_s$ the price of shares, and $\hat{r}_s$ the rate of return that the household *expects* at t to prevail at s, $s \geq t$. Here and above, the implied index t is suppressed from the notation of expectations and plans. The budget equation constraining the household plan may be stated in terms of a wealth variable, v_s, as follows:

$$l_s + \hat{r}_s \hat{v}_s - \hat{p}_s c_s = d\hat{v}_s/ds, \qquad \hat{v}_s \equiv \hat{q}_s \hat{z}_s^h, \hat{v}_t = v_t;$$

here z_s is the number of shares each household will own, and $\hat{z}_s^h$ the number each household expects to own, by time s. The left-hand side is planned saving *including* expected capital gains. By our earlier assumption, $z_t = 1$, at least initially, at $t = 0$; if all families remain alike, as must be true on an equilibrium path, $z_t = 1$ for all $t \geq 0$. Equivalently, one may use equation 1 and the derivative relation, $dv/ds = q(dz/ds) + z(dq/ds)$, to write the budget equation in expected-cash-flow terms, where the left-hand side is now planned share purchases:

(3) $$l_s + \hat{\pi}_s^h - \hat{p}_s c_s = \hat{q}_s \cdot (dz_s/ds).$$

Hence the selected household plan, denoted (c_s^*, l_s^*, z_s^*), is utility-maximizing relative to the expected course of "prices." Note that at every t the current price charged by the family's particular goods supplier is known to the family; hence $\hat{p}_t = p_t$. Also, the current share price is known by all; hence $\hat{q}_t = q_t$. But $\dot{q}_t$, $\dot{p}_t$, r_t, and π_t^h are not known. They may nevertheless be correctly anticipated.

We are interested only in outcomes—in time paths—that keep positive the price of goods, the real wage, consumption, and employment. It happens to be a feature of our model that if the labor market is functioning thus, that market is continuously cleared: the wage continuously reconciles the planned labor supply to the quantity of labor time that firms are willing to employ. Likewise, firms' product prices instantaneously reconcile planned consumption to what firms are willing to produce. Hence employment and consumption in the present model must meet the current-time *market-clearing conditions*

(4) $$l_t = l_t^* > 0, \qquad c_t = c_t^* > 0.$$

Thus at each historical time $t \geq 0$ households realize their current intentions whether or not their plans for the future are realizable.

The achievement of market clearing, however, is neither necessary nor sufficient for the attainment of equilibrium (in the standard expectational sense). We conceive of an *equilibrium* as a path along which all events and parameters pertinent to their decisionmaking conform to the actors' expectations. The *equilibrium conditions* that pertain to household plans of time t are

(5) $$p_s = \hat{p}_s, \qquad q_s = \hat{q}_s, \qquad r_s = \hat{r}_s, \text{ for all } s \geq t.$$

It can be seen that any equilibrium path (any path satisfying 5 on top of the antecedent equations), if such a path exists, is one on which each family's plan is necessarily feasible over the future, $s \geq t$. By equations

1 and 5, we can substitute $\hat{\pi}_s^h$ for π_s^h in 2, and by 4, substitute c_s^* and l_s^* for c_s and l_s in 2 to obtain

$$(6) \qquad\qquad l_s^* + \hat{\pi}_s^h - \hat{p}_s c_s^* = 0.$$

Recalling equation 3, we recognize the left-hand side to be planned share accumulation at time s, $\hat{q}_s(dz/ds)^*$. On the two conditions 4 and 5, therefore, families do not plan infeasible share accumulation or decumulation. (Infeasible planned accumulation might be founded on $l_s^* > l_s$ or $\hat{r}_s > r_s$; decumulation on $c_s^* > c_s$ or $\hat{r}_t < r_t$.)

It is an interesting conjecture that the foregoing information (including the stationary production function) is enough to deduce that all equilibria are stationary states. (How implausible that there might be nonstationary paths along which algebraic capital gains are sometimes nonzero but precisely matched by planned saving!) If true, we are justified in restricting our attention, as we do now, to stationary equilibrium.

The Households in Stationary Equilibrium

Consider now the possibility of stationary equilibrium. For all $s \geq t$, c_s^* and l_s^* are positive constants, independent of s. On standard restrictions, households' chosen plan satisfies the first-order conditions for an interior utility-maximum:

$$(7a) \qquad \frac{1}{u_c(c_s^*, l_s^*)} \cdot \frac{d}{ds} u_c(c_s^*, l_s^*) = -\left(\hat{r}_s - \hat{p}_s^{-1}\frac{d\hat{p}_s}{ds} - \rho\right);$$

$$(7b) \qquad u_c(c_s^*, l_s^*) = -\hat{p}_s u_l(c_s^*, l_s^*), \text{ all } s \geq t.$$

(Note again that the sum of the first two terms on the right side of the Euler equation, 7a, is the expected rate of return in terms of goods; so these conditions are the well-known results of Irving Fisher and, for stationary expectations, of the aforementioned Ramsey.) It follows, from 7b essentially, that any stationary-equilibrium $\hat{p}_s$ is a positive constant, independent of s. Hence, according to 7a, $\hat{r}_s$ is also a constant, equal to ρ, a positive constant. The expected dividend per share, $\hat{\pi}_s^h$, must also be constant, just large enough to finance $\hat{p}c^* - l^*$. It can then be argued that $\hat{q}_s$ is likewise constant. (Proof: no share accumulation is planned, by 6, and since $\hat{r} = \rho$, no wealth accumulation is planned, by

"Ramsey"; therefore, households cannot be expecting any change in the price of shares.)

One could instead characterize stationarity of an equilibrium path by the constancy of $\hat{p}_s$, $\hat{r}_s$, and $\hat{q}_s$, and deduce the constancy of c_s^* and l_s^*. If $\hat{r}_s = \hat{r} \neq \rho$, there would be planned saving or dissaving which, taken with constancy of $\hat{q}_s$, would contradict 5; so $\hat{r} = \rho$ in stationary equilibrium. Then 7a and 7b yield constancy of c_s^* and l_s^*.

Let us write the corresponding labor-supply and consumption-demand functions of the family in the form $l^*(p, \hat{\pi}^h, \hat{r})$ and $c^*(p, \hat{\pi}^h, \hat{r})$, where the index s is suppressed. Then we have shown that in stationary equilibrium

(8) $$pc^*(p, \hat{\pi}^h, \rho) = l^*(p, \hat{\pi}^h, \rho) + \hat{\pi}^h,$$

since $\hat{r} = \rho$ and $\hat{p}_s = p_s = p$, a constant, for all $s \geq t$. By definition of equilibrium, p, c^*, $l^* > 0$. It is obvious that the planned constants l^* and c^* are such as to maximize

$$\int_t^\infty u(c^*, l^*)e^{-\rho(s-t)}\, ds \quad \text{subject to} \quad pc^* = l^* + \hat{\pi}^h.$$

Equations 7b and 8 together constitute the first-order conditions for the attainment of this basically static utility maximization.

The Firms in Stationary Equilibrium

We can now bring on the firms. Their decision problem under stationary expectations (the case here) is analyzed in the paper of Phelps and Winter.[6] Here we consider only the constant costs case (their pages 332–34). By suitable choice of output units, one unit of labor is required for each unit of output. The firm produces the amount demanded by its customers at its optimal price. Let θ_t be the fraction of (pure) profit at t taxed away by the government, $0 \leq \theta_t < 1$, and let $1 - w_t^f$ be the government subsidy to each unit of labor employed, at time t. Suppose that $\hat{\theta}_s = \theta_t$, $w_s^f = w_t^f$, for all $s \geq t$. Hence if p_s denotes the price planned for s and $\hat{n}_s$ the number of customers expected, the after-tax least-cost profit expected by the firm (at t) to result at $s \geq t$ may be expressed as

$$(1 - \theta_t)[(p_s - w_t^f)\, c^*(p_s, \hat{\pi}_s^h, \hat{r})]\hat{n}_s.$$

---

6. Phelps and Winter, "Optimal Price Policy."

Given its current stock of customers, n_t, each firm plans provisionally a price path $\{p_s\}$ to maximize the present discounted value of profit,

$$(1 - \theta_t) \int_t^\infty [(p_s - w_t^f)c^*(p_s, \hat{\pi}^h, \hat{r})]\hat{n}_s e^{-\hat{r}(s-t)}\, ds,$$

subject to an expected customer-flow relation,

$$(9) \qquad \frac{d\hat{n}_s}{ds} = \hat{n}_s \cdot \delta(p_s, \hat{p}^f),$$

$$\hat{n}_t = n_t, \quad \delta_p(\cdot) < 0, \quad \delta_{\hat{p}}(\cdot) > 0, \quad \delta(\hat{p}, \hat{p})$$

$$= 0, \text{ and } \delta_{pp}(\cdot) \leq 0 \text{ for all } \hat{p} \text{ and } p.$$

Here $\hat{p}^f$ denotes the firm's stationary expectations, held at t, of the other firms' identical price for all $s \geq t$. The firm assumes that, if it keeps its own price above (below) the price set by other firms, it will find itself losing (gaining) customers as information of the price disparity spreads among its (others') customers. Since, by our hypothesis, families have stationary price expectations, customers believe that their suppliers' price is permanent and that they will not find better prices elsewhere; so, by implication, the diffusion process here is by passive "word of mouth," not by active search.

It is clear that the firm's optimal price, p_t^*, is independent of its current customer size, n_t, owing to constant costs. Hence p_s^* must be independent of $\hat{n}_s$. It follows that p_s^* is constant. But according to 9, $(d\hat{n}_s/ds)\hat{n}_s^{-1}$ is a constant, $\delta(p, \hat{p}^f)$, if p_s is constant. The optimal p therefore maximizes

$$(1 - \theta_t) \int_t^\infty [(p - w_t^f)\, c^*(p, \hat{\pi}^h, \hat{r})]n_t e^{[\delta(p,\hat{p}) - \hat{r}](s-t)}\, ds$$

$$= n_t(1 - \theta_t)\frac{(p - w_t^f)\, c^*(p, \hat{\pi}^h, \hat{r})}{\hat{r} - \delta(p, \hat{p}^f)}.$$

Phelps and Winter show[7] that the optimum rate of growth of the firm—that is, $\delta(p^*, \hat{p}^f)$, if such exists (and that requires $\hat{r} > 0$)—leaves a positive and constant pure profit per customer, hence $p^* > w_t^f$. Of course, the level of the optimal price and profit will depend on $\hat{p}^f$, $\hat{r}$, and the customer demand function, $c^*(\cdot)$. For an equilibrium—a surprise-free

---

7. Ibid., p. 333.

outcome—among firms, $\delta(p^*, p) = 0$ must hold for each firm's p^* and the other firms' p.

Here we postulate that a maximizing price function exists, is unique, and is continuous; we denote it by $p^*(\hat{p}^f, \hat{\pi}^h, \hat{r}; w^f)$. Then, if for every $s \geq t$ all firms have the same $\hat{p}^f$ and $\hat{r}$, which they must in equilibrium, $p = p^*(\hat{p}^f, \hat{\pi}^h, \hat{r}; w^f)$ for all firms; hence the maximized profit per customer and per family, denoted π^{h^*}, is (recalling that $l = c$)

$$(10) \qquad \pi^{h^*} = (1 - \theta_t) [(p^* - w_t^f) c^*(p^*, \hat{\pi}^h, \hat{r})], \text{ all } s \geq t.$$

Firms will be said to be in stationary equilibrium, and hence achieve their planned paths of market share, if and only if their price expectation is correct:

$$(11) \qquad p^* = \hat{p}^f.$$

Implicitly, the firms do not have to forecast—since they can observe— their customer's current rate of demand.

General Equilibrium

For stationary equilibrium, it is necessary that $\hat{p}^f$ and $\hat{\pi}^h$ be such that p^* satisfies firms' price expectation,

$$(12) \qquad p^*(\hat{p}^f, \hat{\pi}^h, \hat{r}; w_t^f) = \hat{p}^f,$$

and simultaneously that π^{h^*} satisfy households' share-profitability expectation,

$$(13) \quad (1 - \theta_t) [p^*(\hat{p}^f, \hat{\pi}^h, \hat{r}; w_t^f) - w_t^f] c^*[\hat{p}^*(\hat{p}, \hat{\pi}^h, \hat{r}, w_t^f), \hat{\pi}^h, \hat{r}] = \hat{\pi}^h,$$

where, in both equations,

$$(14) \qquad \hat{r} = \rho.$$

Thus we have essentially two equations, upon substitution from 14, in the two expectational variables, $\hat{p}^f$ and $\hat{\pi}^h$. In what follows, we write the latter as $\hat{p}$ and $\hat{\pi}$.

These conditions are also sufficient to determine stationary equilibrium. If, given equation 14, $\hat{\pi}$ and $\hat{p} > 0$ are such that $p^*(\hat{p}, \hat{\pi}, \rho; w_t^f)$ and $c^*(\hat{p}, \hat{\pi}, \rho; w_t^f)$ cause 12 and 13 to be satisfied, a corresponding stationary equilibrium exists—for all the other equations of the model can then be satisfied as well. For example, if 13 holds (hence $0 = \pi^{h^*} - \hat{\pi}$), then, by

4 and 8, the government's budget (of employment subsidies) is balanced by profit taxes:

$$
\underset{\substack{\text{after-tax} \\ \text{profit earned}}}{} \qquad \underset{\substack{\text{dividends} \\ \text{expected}}}{}
$$

$$
0 = (1 - \theta_t)\,[p^*\,c^* - w_t^f l^*] - [p^*\,c^* - l^*]
$$

$$
\underset{\substack{\text{employment} \\ \text{subsidies}}}{} \qquad \underset{\substack{\text{profits} \\ \text{taxes}}}{}
$$

$$
= (1 - w_t^f)l^* - \theta(p^*\,c^* - w_t^f l^*).
$$

If 13 holds, therefore, it further follows, by using $l^* = c^*$, $p^* = \hat{p}$, and $\pi^{h*} = \hat{\pi}$, that

(15) $$(p^* - 1)c^*(\hat{p}, \pi^{h*}, \hat{r}) = \pi^{h*}.$$

We shall use equation 15 in place of 13 in the following analysis.

To analyze stationary equilibrium, we refer first to figure 1, panel A. The product market is in equilibrium—firms are, at any rate—at any point on PE, the curve corresponding to equation 12. Behind PE is a 45-degree-line diagram (not drawn) showing p^* as an increasing function of $\hat{p}$; an equilibrium level of $\hat{p}$ occurs at any intersection of the schedule with the 45-degree line. We focus on the lowest-price equilibrium if there are more than one; at the schedule's first intersection with the 45-degree line, its slope will be less than or equal to one because $p^*(\cdot)$ evaluated at $\hat{p} = 0$ is greater than or equal to $w_t^f > 0$. Here we restrict attention to the cases where the slope is less than one.[8] The PE drawn depicts a case in which, as $\hat{\pi}^h$ increases, $c^*(\cdot)$ shifts up *in such a way* that the p^* schedule shifts up, lifting the equilibrium level of $\hat{p}$. Other cases give no difficulty.

The factor market is in equilibrium—households are, anyway—at any point on FE^*. The equation of FE^* is 15 in the variables (p^*, π^{h*}), which must lead to the same intersections with PE as would equation 13, since p^* and $\hat{p}^f$ are equal at equilibria. As p^* is increased from its starting point of 1, π^{h*} must first increase, and may (as illustrated) reach a global maximum. Note that, assuming existence, for each p^* the corresponding π^{h*} is unique, assuming that leisure is a normal good.[9]

8. For convenience of exposition, we shall assume that the p^* function can be differentiated in the relevant range.

9. Pentti Kouri has shown that when the utility function is Cobb-Douglas and the δ function is $1 - \exp(p/\hat{p})$, all our foregoing conditions are met, with PE flat and FE^* upward sloping. In this case, of course, there is existence and uniqueness.

In panel B of figure 1 local maxima are encountered along FE^* on the way to the global maximum. With reference to this figure, it should be noted that the intersection where FE^* is negatively sloped cannot actually occur since, if there were an equilibrium there, it would imply that a firm, by lowering its price, would gain more future customers *and* more present cash flow (higher π^{h*}); hence it could not be maximizing.

Evidently there is room for nonuniqueness of equilibrium. The particular PE schedule shown corresponds to a zero subsidy, that is, $w^f = 1$. The intersections with FE^* labeled A, A', and A'' are possible (non-Walrasian) equilibria. An equilibrium at C is not possible with $w^f = 1$; it represents the Walrasian outcome (without intervention) marked by $p = 1$ and $\pi = 0$. Note that, by an argument similar to the one used to rule out the intersection with a negatively sloped FE^* in figure 1, panel B, it can be shown that the equilibrium with the lowest p must be the one with the smallest π^{h*}.

In figure 2 a diagram locates the above outcome A in the (l, c) plane in order to study the welfare aspects of non-Walrasian equilibrium. Should there exist more than one non-Walrasian equilibrium without intervention, then let A be the one giving greatest utility, $u(c^*, l^*)$. We assume that the utility contours are asymptotic to the vertical line at $l = 1$—the locus of zero-leisure allocations—so that there is positive leisure at A, that is, $l_A^* < 1$. It then follows that the allocation at A is Pareto-inoptimal in the traditional sense: Technologically possible allocations $(c, l < c)$ exist that give higher utility for every family and are therefore Pareto-superior to A; for at A, $- u_c/u_l = p_A > 1 = $ slope of production-possibility locus $(c = l)$, so a sufficiently small movement up that locus will yield a gain in every family's utility, $u(c, l)$.

Indeed, every allocation on the $c = l$ locus between A and C, like B, is Pareto-better than A. The Pareto optimum is at C, which is the perfectly competitive equilibrium when there is no intervention. In relation to that ideal allocation, the non-Walrasian equilibrium yields underemployment and underproduction.

An allocation is said to be a constrained Pareto optimum if it is infeasible to support any Pareto-superior allocation with only the institutions envisioned by the model—here, the noncooperating firms and "decentralized" families operating in the product and labor markets, and the specified fiscal instruments, w^f and θ, of the government. The question to be addressed now is whether A is a constrained Pareto optimum. We argue that it is not: If a non-Walrasian equilibrium at A

Figure 1. *Non-Walrasian Equilibria Characterized*

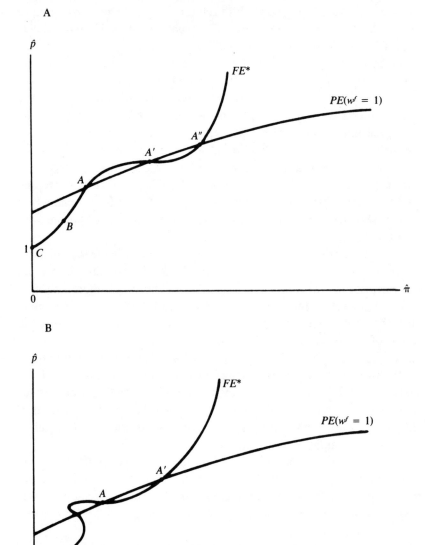

Figure 2. *Walrasian and Non-Walrasian Equilibria Compared*

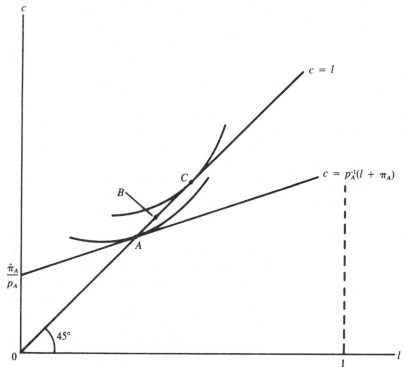

exists without intervention, there will exist *some* non-Walrasian equilibria supportable *with* intervention that lie between A and C and are therefore Pareto-superior to A.

Assuming for the moment that an equilibrium could exist at some point between A and C, like B, we first ask what fiscal setting would be implied necessary to support it. We know that $w^f \neq 1 \neq 1 - \theta$ would be required since the no-intervention setting $1 - w^f = 0 = \theta$ yields the allocation A at best, not a Pareto-better point like B.

Note to begin with that the equilibrium budget line through a point like B, $c = p_B^{-1} (l + \pi_B)$, is necessarily steeper than the one through A. If that were not so, there would be a point on the possibility locus ($c = l$) between A and C with the property that the budget line through it would have the same slope as the budget line through A; but since by hypothesis leisure is a normal good—that is, $l_\pi^*(\cdot) < 0$—such a point would have to be associated with smaller l^* than l_A^*, a contradiction. It can be shown analogously that the equilibrium budget line through a point like B is flatter than the one through C. Hence $p_C < p_B < p_A$.

Note also that the locus FE^* in figure 1 is precisely the locus of points $(\hat\pi, \hat p)$ generated by such budget lines, one for each $(c^*, l^* = c^*)$, in figure 2. Hence the points A, B, and C are all mapped onto the locus FE^*. The locus originates at C and meanders always north past A. Points like B lie on FE^* downstream from A. Notice too that the locations of A, B, and so on are invariant to the fiscal setting. Variations in w^f may shift PE, but not FE^*.

How must PE shift if its intersection with FE^* at A is to move to a lower intersection such as B? In figure 1, panel A, one can see that a *downward* shift of PE is required: A is the lowest point of intersection between the original PE and FE^* since, being the best equilibrium without intervention, it must mark the lowest equilibrium price without intervention. Although FE^* is positively sloped at A, the original PE must cross it there with algebraically smaller slope—must cross from above—else another intersection with lower $\hat p$ would be implied (since PE originates above FE^* and the latter locus is single-valued in $\hat p$). Hence a *downward* shift of PE is needed to lower its lowest intersection with FE^*.

We next observe that, on the foregoing assumptions, PE is shifted downward (upward) by a decrease (increase) of w^f. From the first-order condition for every firm's optimal p,

$$0 = [c^*(\cdot) + (p - w^f)c_p^*(\cdot)] + \frac{\delta_p(\cdot)(p - w^f)c^*(\cdot)}{\hat r - \delta(\cdot)}$$

$$\equiv F(p, \hat p, \hat\pi; w^f, \hat r),$$

and the second-order condition, $\partial F/\partial p < 0$, we calculate that

$$\frac{\partial p^*(\cdot)}{\partial w^f} = \frac{-\partial F(\cdot)/\partial w^f}{\partial F(\cdot)/\partial p} = \frac{c_p^*(\cdot) + c^*(\cdot)\delta_p(\cdot)[r - \delta(\cdot)]^{-1}}{\partial F(\cdot)/\partial p}$$

$$> 0 \text{ if } \hat p = p^*, \text{ hence } \delta(\cdot) = 0.$$

at $p^* = \hat p$. (If conversely $\partial p^*/\partial \hat p > 1$, then since $p^*(\hat p, \quad , \rho; \hat w^f) > \hat p$ at $\hat p = 0$ when $w^f = 1$, our $\hat p_A$ could not be the lowest $\hat p$ at which $p^*(\cdot) = \hat p$

when $w^f = 1$; moreover, the equilibrium at a p where $\partial p^*/\partial p > 1$ could be unstable.[10] Therefore

$$\left.\frac{d\hat{p}}{dw^f}\right|_{\hat{\pi}} = \frac{\partial p^*(\cdot)/\partial w^f}{1 - \partial p^*(\cdot)/\partial \hat{p}} > 0.$$

Hence a downward shift of *PE* requires a reduction of w^f, a subsidy.

Observe that if non-Walrasian equilibrium at a predesignated point B exists, so that there exists a subsidy $1 - w^f_B < \infty$ making $p^*(p_B, \pi_B, \rho; w^f_B) = p_B$, then the proportionate tax rate θ_B implied by budget balance, $1 - w^f = \theta(p - w^f)$, satisfies

$$0 < \theta_B = \frac{1 - w^f_B}{p_B - w^f_B} < 1,$$

since $p_B > 1 > w^f_B > -\infty$. A bounded subsidy is within taxable capacity in any equilibrium!

We suggest that there can be just two obstacles to a non-Walrasian equilibrium at a predesignated point B. One is that there is no subsidy large enough to drive $p^*(\cdot)$ down to p_B because $\partial p^*(\cdot)/\partial w^f$ vanishes as $w^f \to -\infty$. The second is that a solution $p^*(\cdot) = \hat{p}_B$ does not exist even though a solution $p^*(\cdot) = \hat{p}_A$ exists. This second obstacle will arise if the first-order or second-order conditions cannot hold at (p_B, π_B) for any w^f.

However, it is evident that, on the foregoing assumptions, an equilibrium will exist with $p^*(\cdot)$ in the neighborhood of A and with w^f in the neighborhood of 1 if, as hypothesized, an equilibrium exists at A when $w^f = 1$. A small enough reduction of w^f will leave the optimum price still in existence so that the resulting *PE* curve can be shifted down to support a new equilibrium representing a marginal Pareto improvement over A. Hence A cannot generally be a constrained Pareto optimum. And on our regularity assumptions it is never a constrained optimum.

The "Suggestiveness" of the Findings

Obviously the findings here have no literal policy implications because they are not derived from a model fit for drawing policy recommendations. Yet one can ask, if the characteristic elements of the present model

10. See Phelps and Winter, "Optimal Price Policy."

were embedded in a model presumed fit enough to carry policy advice— for example, a model with poverty, childlessness—what findings from the prototype model would recur in the super model? We will assume that the social-choice criterion in use is Paretian (more is better) and equality-preferring.

One finding that we would expect to survive extensions of the model is that of a rationale for a tax on pure profit—as a practical matter, a tax on after-interest corporate income. If that initial tax rate were zero, it might be impossible to show in any very general model that any positive tax rate (at least any nonnegligible tax rate) could make everyone better off in all generations. However, if that initial tax rate were positive yet not close to 100 percent, say, 50 percent or less, the analysis here suggests that reducing that tax rate or abolishing it would be counter-productive—the government would be throwing away virtually its only means to reduce the wedge or escape having to widen the wedge between the reward to industry and thrift and their marginal productivity.

Comment by A. Michael Spence

In view of my lack of credentials in macroeconomics, it would be presumptuous and inappropriate for me to be critical of models in macroeconomics that overlap microeconomic territory. Models are not so much right or wrong as more or less helpful in illuminating particular problems. To the extent that macroeconomists are interested in indus-tries and in labor markets, they are probably trying to answer questions different from those an industrial organization economist or a labor economist has in mind. Industrial organization economists are inter-ested, for example, in how industries differ from each other. I am reasonably sure that macroeconomists wish they were all approximately the same. Macroeconomics may be forced to take an interest in interin-dustry differences, but if there were some easier way to locate the characteristics of the average industry, I am confident that would be the chosen path.

In any case, there is no a priori reason to think that the models developed for one purpose will be useful for another. Nonetheless, I have asked myself whether there is any recent research in industrial organization that might be helpful in macroeconomics, and I offer some suggestions on where this research might be found.

I will first briefly comment on the Calvo-Phelps paper because Sidney Winter, whose comment follows, has a comparative and absolute advantage in having written a similar earlier paper with Phelps on the same subject. The Phelps-Winter paper contained an important insight, and the Calvo-Phelps paper is designed to show that the phenomenon does not go away in a general-equilibrium setting. The insight is that in most markets one of the firm's most valuable assets is its share of the market or its sales or its customer base. The current sales of an established firm are an asset that has been invested in through pricing and other decisions in the past. And usually it takes a substantial investment by other firms to diminish the size of that asset.

Share of the market is an asset for numerous reasons, including imperfect information about price and about product characteristics and investments by consumers in the use of the product. It would take me too far afield to develop the complete case for the proposition that current and past sales are an asset. But if I were asked whether inertia in the response of market shares to price differentials is a structural characteristic of markets that strongly influences the way industries set prices and evolve over time, my answer would be yes.

Calvo and Phelps establish two propositions in their paper. The intertemporal general equilibrium with the imperfect competition in product markets induced by inertia in market shares is not Pareto efficient. Furthermore, there is a subsidy to firms financed by a profits tax that will produce a Pareto improvement. I did not find either proposition surprising. But it is worth knowing that there are no general-equilibrium forces that eliminate the inefficiency.

I think it important to say that the value of the market-share asset varies considerably from industry to industry, although I cannot explain here what differing structural features of industries make this true. But if you think briefly about industrial corn starch, steel, computers, and soft drinks, you will probably be convinced of the plausibility of this proposition. An interesting question in the Calvo-Phelps framework is whether, in a world of many markets with different degrees of power to raise margins, there is a policy that does not differentially subsidize industries but that produces a Pareto improvement.

I comment briefly here on one aspect of Robert Gordon's paper, because it clarified a distinction that I had not made so clearly before. Gordon discusses evidence of inertia in the setting of wages and prices, as found in time series data. He asks two questions. The first concerns what features of industrial structure cause the price component of wage-price and price-price inertia, or its absence. I interpret this question in the following way. Industries pass cost increases through with different degrees of ease and speed, and they respond to slack demand in different ways. It is possible to imagine how the industrial sector will behave on average. Gordon is asking about the average. He speculates particularly on the internal structural characteristics of labor and product markets that give rise to upwardly mobile prices and wages. But he has a second question, in many ways more uncomfortable, based on an empirical finding. Price momentum, he argues, has been greater in the postwar period. So the question might be, why has the "average" industry changed? Is the mix of industries different? But that is unlikely to have been the cause; the mix cannot have changed that much. Also, it seems unlikely that such a change could result from changes in the internal competitive structure of industries, which could not have occurred so quickly. But internal competitive structure is only one kind of determinant of industry responses. Industries also respond to pressures from the external environment: regulation, macroeconomic policy, foreign competition. This line of thinking points to the external environment as a principal determinant of the shift. And it may be that understanding this environment has a higher payoff for understanding the inflationary process than does attention to the details of industrial labor or product markets. Or to put the matter negatively, if the purported explanation of price inertia in the face of slack demand is industrial structure, then a reasonably rapid shift in the industrial sector's pricing behavior is puzzling because the industrial structure does not change that fast.

I assume there were changes in macroeconomic policy and the expectations it creates over the relevant period. It is true that in the period immediately after World War II and for perhaps the ensuing twenty years, foreign competition was, from a U.S. standpoint, almost negligible because of the destruction of European economies. This is of course no longer true; the appearance of foreign competition has caused dislocation and confusion in certain U.S. industries.

In this context, it is useful to refer to the distinguished work of Professor Simon, and of others who have developed the competitive implications of Simon's insights concerning organizational behavior. I should mention particularly the work in the past decade by Nelson and Winter. Firms adapt to the competitive environment in which they operate. If the rules of the game change, they search for functionally useful responses. There is a kind of inertia built into this process. The inertia will be less and the responses faster to the extent that firms engage in sophisticated strategic and competitive planning, but the inertia will not disappear. In econometric terms, the coefficients will change to new ones that are perhaps consistent with a new set of rational expectations, but not too fast.

It seems to me that a generalized shortfall of demand with respect to capacity is not likely to produce a rapid change in pricing behavior in most concentrated industries, unless the shortfall is very large. Thus the use of a recession as a technique for changing the growth rates of prices hardly makes me optimistic. What does produce a very rapid response at the industry level is the entry of new competition with a different (lower) cost structure. It is therefore not surprising that industries with high entry barriers that either are not subject to or are protected from foreign competition are the most recalcitrant in the face of attempts to limit price and wage and salary increases. It would take me more time than I have here to defend these claims. But they are consistent with the cross-industry empirical evidence and the case studies of which I am aware.

I mention entry barriers and foreign competition not as practical solutions to inflation. Entry barriers are not easily lowered (except those that are the result of regulations), and not all industries are subject to foreign competition. My aim is rather to suggest that a relatively simple four-way cross-classification of industries, based on high or low entry barriers and the presence or absence of significant foreign competition, is likely to capture or explain a fair amount of the cross-industry variance in the sensitivity of margins to demand conditions. That may help with the problem of estimating average price behavior across the entire industrial sector without requiring the researcher to have detailed knowledge of individual industries.

I change direction slightly to make one or two observations about matters that have troubled me. In many of the industries that I have looked at, real prices have declined over a fairly long period (a decade or longer). In some cases, real costs have declined comparably, but in many others, real margins have declined. There are numerous reasons for these declines. One is that firms have not adjusted upward their target rates of return on investment in response to inflation. They have responded, but with a lag. The capacity to finance out of retained earnings plus relatively low-cost (after-tax) debt means that financing investment does not force the issue. Of course, stock price performance will reflect the lower real rates of return, but that is not the problem here. A subtler but equally real problem is that, in a volatile inflationary environment, a firm investing in assets with a twenty-year life is legitimately uncertain about what the appropriate real rate-of-return criterion should be, because it does not know, or does not believe it knows, what real rates will be required in the future.

It may be that these observations at the industry level represent a biased microeconomic sample. But the perception at the industry level of pressure on margins in real terms is pervasive enough to suggest to me that a thorough reexamination of the relations between price and wage indexes and factor shares might be useful.

My final thought concerns labor markets that receive a substantial amount of attention in efforts to construct the microeconomic foundations of a macroeconomic model. It is difficult to quarrel with the idea that labor markets are important. After all, part of the problem is that they do not clear in the normal sense. (I realize there is currently some debate about that.) But the point is that labor markets are somewhat segmented along industry lines, although the segmentation is obviously not complete or perfect. Engineers move among industries in response to salary differences, for example. But there are also queues of people wishing to enter some industries. To the extent that labor markets are segmented by industry, it seems to me that the determinants of wages and wage changes cannot reasonably be discussed without bringing in the structural characteristics of the relevant industries. The parameters within which negotiations take place are surely different (1) in an industry with high entry barriers, a low industry demand elasticity, and an industrywide wage-setting process, and (2) in an industry with low entry barriers, a high demand elasticity, and access to an as yet unorganized labor pool. These are extreme cases, cited only to suggest that from a microeconomic perspective at least part of wage and price setting has to do with capturing rents, the existence of which can be traced back to the structural characteristics of industries. It is of course imaginable that labor markets would be segmented only by job type, skill, and so forth, and that within segments they would be reasonably competitive and cross industry boundaries. Some labor markets look like that, but many do not. For cases where industry boundaries intrude—and they seem to me to be substantial in number and size—labor and product markets probably should not be separated in attempts to analyze the setting of wages and prices. I therefore find myself uncomfortable both with models that focus exclusively on either labor or product markets, assuming the other group is competitive, and with statements to the effect that all the action is in labor markets and that that is where efforts should be concentrated.

Comment by Sidney G. Winter

IN THE WORLD of Phelps-Winter firms, it takes actual price concessions, maintained over a period of time, to move customers from one firm to another. The absence of instantaneous customer response to tiny price discrepancies means that firms enjoy a degree of dynamic market power. In equilibrium, a firm charges a price in excess of its marginal cost and serves a constant clientele; by lowering its price for a period of time an individual firm could increase its clientele, and because price exceeds marginal cost, additional customers could be served profitably. However, such an action would involve an immediate sacrifice of revenue from existing customers for the sake of a gradual increase in the stock of customers. At the equilibrium position, further investment of this sort would not yield the going rate of return.

The Calvo-Phelps paper places this model of firm behavior in a general-equilibrium setting. There is a single primary good, labor, and firms employ labor to produce a single consumption good. In this context, the equilibrium markup that firms charge over marginal cost implies a distortion of the consumption-leisure margin. It is shown that a corrective wage subsidy, financed by a tax on pure profit, can bring about a Pareto improvement.

Given the analogy with the case of simple monopoly in a static model, this result is not particularly surprising. The analogy does not suggest, however, the scope of the difficulties that the authors have overcome in constructing an appropriate general equilibrium model for the analysis. Because the chief imperfection relates to a dynamic mechanism, a suitable model must represent the actors as planning their behavior in a dynamic environment. Thus the families in the model are infinite-horizon optimizers of integrals of discounted utility flows, subject to wealth constraints, while firms are present-value maximizers. Although the analysis is ultimately confined to stationary equilibria, it is notably clear and complete in its exposition of the logic of the equilibrium position, and the authors are punctilious in their adherence to an "expectations realized" concept of equilibrium.

The friction that impedes customer flow was loosely rationalized by Phelps and Winter as reflecting a process of slow diffusion of price information accomplished through random encounters among customers. While this explanation seems to me to provide adequate motivation for a "positive economics" exercise in the analysis of firm behavior, it may require reexamination when attention turns, as here, to normative issues. The assumption that there is no scope for consumer choice in the diffusion of price information seems too strong, and one might want to inquire into the costs and incentives that affect the information process.

For example, it seems quite conceivable that there might be important differences in the role of informational considerations between the stationary equilibrium situation and the adjustment phase. In stationary equilibrium, only the market power *consequence* of the information imperfections plays a role. A Pareto improvement can, as Calvo and Phelps show, be achieved by a corrective intervention aimed at the market power. But when stationary equilibrium does not prevail, and specifically when marginal production costs differ among firms, the informational imperfection has another, more direct efficiency implication—it affects the rate at which average production cost for total output declines as a result of the reallocation of production among firms. It seems clear that in these circumstances an appropriate policy intervention might well include a component aimed directly at the information problem rather than dealing exclusively with its market power consequence. (Of course, under the Calvo-Phelps assumptions of identical firms with constant costs, this issue does not arise, even when the system is not in stationary equilibrium.)

A related point concerns the interpretation of the corrective wage subsidy and profits tax. The analysis offered is confined to comparative statics. If the intervention described is conceived as impinging at a particular time on an economy actually operating at the uncorrected stationary equilibrium position, then its desirability would not be clearly compelling to the forward-looking families of the model economy. It would become so only if they could be assured that the transition to the new equilibrium would be virtually instantaneous, unflawed by the appearance of mutually inconsistent expectations. Without that assurance, the model as it stands is not up to the task of supporting a policy recommendation for the economy it describes.

This leads, in turn, to the question of whether the paper should be understood to have a macroeconomic moral. Perhaps because of sensitivity to the sorts of questions just raised, the authors confine themselves to remarking on the model's "rationale for a tax on pure profit" (presumably the rationale for the related wage subsidy is equally strong). But the model could also be seen as a step toward an analysis of a monetary economy in which, perhaps, stimulative aggregate demand policy would have an immediate favorable effect on real output by virtue of the lagged adjustment of the price expectations held by firms—and in which the output stimulus might be a good thing if the initial position corresponded to the underemployed stationary equilibrium of the present model. Of course, pursuit of that analysis would require elaboration of the treatment of expectation formation and behavior when the economy was not in stationary equilibrium.

Asset Markets

BENJAMIN M. FRIEDMAN

The Roles of Money and Credit in Macroeconomic Analysis

ALTHOUGH Arthur Okun devoted most of *Prices and Quantities* to analysis of the economy's product and labor markets, he was too broadly based and too perceptive as a macroeconomist to ignore the financial markets. From his own theoretical and empirical work, as well as from his close observation of economic developments, Okun clearly understood that what happens in the financial markets importantly influences the nonfinancial economy.

Economists have traditionally incorporated financial prices (usually measured inversely by yields) in macroeconomic analysis. Moreover, because the prices of (yields on) so many financial instruments are either rigidly fixed or almost perfectly flexible, so that the less tractable intermediate case of imperfect flexibility that Okun emphasized in examining the product and labor markets has appeared less relevant to financial markets, economists have typically done this in a fairly straightforward way. By contrast, the role of financial quantities in macroeconomic analysis remains much less developed.

In thinking about the relationships between nonfinancial economic activity and quantity measures of what is happening in the financial markets, most economists and economic policymakers focus primarily, if not exclusively, on money. At the theoretical level, the implicit assumption underlying most current macroeconomic analysis is that the money stock is both necessary and sufficient to represent the relevant information contained in financial quantities. Almost every macroeco-

I am grateful to Richard Clarida and Angelo Melino for research assistance; to them as well as to Phillip Cagan, James S. Duesenberry, John Lintner, Robert Litterman, Robert J. Shiller, Christopher A. Sims, Lawrence H. Summers, and Stephen P. Taylor for helpful discussions and comments on an earlier draft; and to the National Science Foundation and the Alfred P. Sloan Foundation for research support.

nomic model, no matter how simplified, includes the money stock among the variables it represents explicitly, and few such models include any financial quantities other than money. At the applied policy level, the formulation of monetary policy in most of the industrialized Western countries takes place in terms of target rates of monetary growth. The most prominent exception to the pervasive emphasis on money in macroeconomic analysis is that the large macroeconometric models often do include nonmoney financial quantities, but even here such variables are usually only peripheral.[1]

This single-minded devotion to the money stock raises issues that go beyond mere questions of definition. Any specific monetary aggregate is, after all, a collection of certain of the public's financial assets. Although it would strain the meaning of the word "money" to include in it such items as equity claims and long-term debt instruments, as long as the focus of analysis is exclusively on the public's assets the question of which ones to include is, in the end, a matter of definition.[2] The more fundamental issue stems from the underlying reality that any balance sheet has two sides. Except in the trivial sense that the entirety of the public's assets equals the entirety of its liabilities plus net worth, the distinction between assets and liabilities—between money and credit— is not definitional. Merely redefining ways of adding up the various items on the asset side of the public's balance sheet is not sufficient if there is also valuable information contained on the liability side.

What accounts for the current preoccupation with money to the exclusion of other financial quantities? Is there something about money that is special in an a priori sense, or is the reason instead an empirical presumption that, for reasons unexplained, variations in money some- how correspond more closely to the variations in the nonfinancial aggregates that are the primary object of macroeconomic inquiry?

Apart from government-issued base money, which is usually not the definition that people have in mind either in economic analysis or in discussions of monetary policy,[3] there is nothing special about money in

1. An exception in this regard is the role of the quantity of home mortgage lending in determining residential construction (and hence the level of income generally) in the MIT-Penn-SSRC model. See Frank de Leeuw and Edward M. Gramlich, "The Channels of Monetary Policy: A Further Report on the Federal Reserve–M.I.T. Model," *Journal of Finance*, vol. 24 (May 1969), pp. 265–90.

2. Indeed, one strand of literature seeks to define "money" simply as the asset aggregate that bears the closest empirical relationship to economic activity.

3. An exception is the work of Brunner and Meltzer, who have always emphasized the role of the monetary base. See, for example, Karl Brunner and Allan H. Meltzer, "Money,

an a priori sense. In the simplest abstraction of an economy with no privately issued financial instruments, base money is the only financial asset, and there are no liabilities. In modern economies, however, most money is not base money but bank money, and privately issued financial instruments constitute the great majority of all such instruments issued, held, and traded. For given growth in base money (if that is what the relevant authority does in fact control), the behavior of the banking system and that of the nonbank public together determine the growth of both bank money and bank credit, and do so jointly with the determination of nonbank financial assets and liabilities as well as nonfinancial economic activity. Economic theory provides no a priori reason at all to expect a role for the nonbank public's money holdings but not for its credit liabilities.

The reason for emphasizing money in macroeconomic analysis must instead be a set of presumptions about the empirical relationships connecting money and the behavior of key measures of nonfinancial economic activity, including especially income and prices. Indeed, during the last two decades a vast literature has developed that documents money-income and money-price relationships in a variety of forms corresponding to variations in the underlying theoretical framework and for a large number of different countries and different time periods.

Now more recent work has shown that, at least for the United States during the period since the 1951 Treasury–Federal Reserve accord, the relationship between economic activity and the public's outstanding credit liabilities exhibits the same degree of regularity and stability as does the relationship between economic activity and the public's holdings of money balances. Moreover, still incomplete analysis suggests that the approximately equal regularity of the credit-income and money-income relationships holds for other countries as well, including Canada, Germany, Japan, and the United Kingdom.[4]

The object of this paper is to present the empirical case for a redirection of emphasis in macroeconomic research, as well as in the formulation of monetary policy, away from the sole focus on money among financial

Debt, and Economic Activity," *Journal of Political Economy*, vol. 80 (September–October 1972), pp. 951–77.

4. I refer here to my own current research, which will be the basis of a forthcoming paper encompassing all four of these countries, as well as to work by Islam on Germany and Japan. Shafiqul Islam, "Monetary and Credit Aggregates as Intermediate Targets: Empirical Evidence from Three Industrial Countries" (Federal Reserve Bank of New York, 1981).

quantities. The goal is not to show that the money stock contains no information that is useful in these two contexts or even to suggest that some nonmoney quantity dominates the money stock in these contexts and therefore should replace it as the fulcrum of analysis. The point is simply that the available empirical evidence does not warrant an exclusive focus on any one financial quantity. Moreover, if for some reason there is a need to focus on just one financial quantity, the evidence provides no reason to conclude that this should be a monetary aggregate rather than a credit aggregate.

The first section reviews the evidence documenting the approximately equal regularity and stability of the relationships between money and income and between credit and income in the United States. Merely finding empirical regularities settles few interesting questions, however. Indeed, it is difficult to think of a familiar economic hypothesis that is contradicted by the finding of a close relationship between credit and income. It could always be the case, of course, that the operative chain of causation ran from money to income and thence from income to credit, so that the public's decisions about credit liabilities remained a peripheral aspect of economic behavior, one that macroeconomic analysis could safely ignore in the interest of simplification.

The second section examines evidence bearing on the interaction of money, credit, and economic activity, drawn from statistical investigations that are prior to structural economic model building.[5] Here too the results provide no justification for a special emphasis on money to the exclusion of credit in macroeconomic analysis. At the same time, the results do go beyond merely indicating parallel roles for money and credit. In the determination of real income especially, what apparently matters is neither money nor credit alone but rather their interrelationship.

The third section considers what kind of structural economic model would be consistent with this set of empirical observations. This line of investigation inevitably leads to the role of financial prices (in other words, interest rates), in addition to financial quantities, in determining nonfinancial economic behavior. Here the evidence indicates a signifi-

5. The concept of these analyses being prior to structural model building is in the sense of Arnold Zellner and Franz Palm, "Time Series Analysis and Simultaneous Equation Econometric Models," *Journal of Econometrics,* vol. 2 (May 1974), pp. 17–54; and Thomas J. Sargent, "A Classical Macroeconometric Model for the United States," *Journal of Political Economy,* vol. 84 (April 1976), pp. 207–37.

cant, but still less than complete, connection between the relationship of income to credit documented in the first and second sections and the familiar relationship of income to interest rates documented in a precise way in other recent work. Because the interest rate is the price of credit in terms of money, this analysis leads naturally to the idea of a three-market model—including the markets for goods and services, for money, and for credit—as an appropriate framework for structural analysis.

The final section brings together the major conclusions reached in the paper and then explores their implications for monetary policy. In the absence of evidence supporting a special role for money in macroeconomic behavior, there is little support for the intermediate target procedure as currently implemented with monetary aggregates as the sole intermediate targets. One alternative, of course, would be to abandon intermediate targets altogether and focus directly on the ultimate nonfinancial objectives of monetary policy. Alternatively, a two-target framework combining one monetary aggregate and one credit aggregate offers some advantages over the current emphasis on monetary aggregates alone in that it would at least facilitate the formal incorporation into the monetary policy structure of information from both sides of the public's balance sheet.

The Relative Stability of the Money-Income and Credit-Income Relationships

Results based on a variety of methodological approaches consistently indicate that the aggregate outstanding indebtedness of all nonfinancial borrowers in the United States bears as close and as stable a relationship to U.S. nonfinancial economic activity as do the more familiar asset aggregates like the money stock (however defined) or the monetary base.[6] Moreover, in contrast to the familiar asset aggregates, among which there seems little basis for choice from this perspective, total

6. This section draws heavily on my earlier papers: Benjamin M. Friedman, "The Relative Stability of Money and Credit 'Velocities' in the United States: Evidence and Some Speculations," working paper 645 (National Bureau of Economic Research, 1981); and Friedman, "Debt and Economic Activity in the United States," in Benjamin M. Friedman, ed., *The Changing Roles of Debt and Equity in Financing U.S. Capital Formation* (University of Chicago Press, 1982). See especially the former for the full set of results.

Figure 1. *Outstanding Debt of U.S. Nonfinancial Borrowers*

Percent of GNP[a]

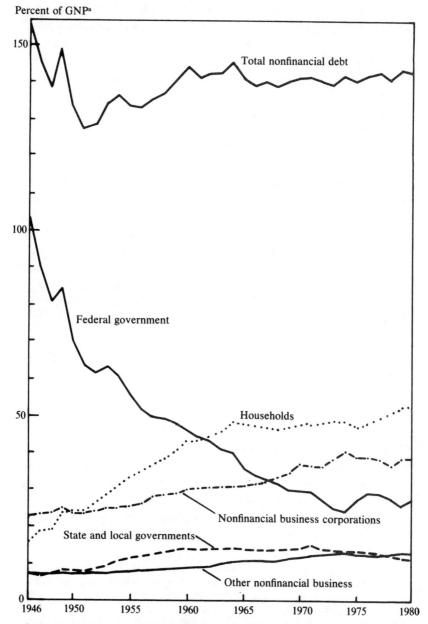

Source: Board of Governors of the Federal Reserve System, Flow of Funds Accounts.
a. Year-end credit market debt totals as percentages of fourth-quarter gross national product, seasonally adjusted, at annual rate.

nonfinancial debt appears to be unique in this regard among major liability aggregates.

Figure 1 displays data for 1946–80 showing the year-end credit market indebtedness as a percentage of fourth-quarter gross national product for the aggregate of all U.S. nonfinancial borrowers and for five different categories of borrowers that together make up the total.[7] These data are "net" in the sense that they net out financial intermediation. For example, the data include such items as a household's mortgage issued to a bank or a corporation's bonds sold to an insurance company, but they exclude any liability issued in turn by the bank or the insurance company to finance that lending activity. The data also exclude debt issued by separate financial subsidiaries of nonfinancial corporations, as well as by federally sponsored credit agencies and mortgage pools. The data are "gross," however, in the sense that they include all of the outstanding credit market liabilities of an individual household or firm, not just any excess of liabilities over either financial or total assets, and also in the sense that they include one household's borrowing from another or one firm's borrowing from another.

The strong stability of the total nonfinancial debt ratio as shown in the figure is in sharp contrast to the variation of the individual sector components. The nonfinancial economy's reliance on debt, scaled in relation to economic activity, has shown almost no trend and little variation since World War II. After falling from 155.6 percent of gross national product in 1946 to 126.6 percent in 1951 and then rising to 143.9 percent in 1960, the total has remained within a few percentage points of that level ever since (the 1980 level was 142.9 percent).[8] Otherwise it has exhibited a slight cyclicality, typically rising a percentage point or two in recession years (when gross national product, in the denominator, is weak).

The individual components of this total, however, have varied in sharply different directions both secularly and cyclically. In brief, the secular postwar rise in private debt has largely mirrored a substantial decline (relative to economic activity) in federal government debt, while

7. In part because of the capital export controls in effect during 1964–74, foreign obligors accounted for only a small fraction of borrowing in U.S. markets throughout this period. Including foreign borrowers would make little difference to the analysis that follows.

8. With the exception of the depression years and (less so) World War II, the stability goes back at least to 1921, when the ratio stood at 141.9 percent. See Friedman, "Relative Stability of Money and Credit."

Table 1. *Comparative Stability Tests for Liability and Asset Aggregates*

| | Coefficient of variation, 1953–78 | | | | Regression results (quarterly data) | | | |
| | Annual data | | Quarterly data | | 1953–78 | | 1970–78 | |
Variable[a]	Raw (1)	Detrended (2)	Raw (3)	Detrended (4)	$\bar{R}^2$ (5)	Standard error (6)	$\bar{R}^2$ (7)	Standard error (8)
Liability aggregates								
Total nonfinancial debt[a]	2.5	1.8	2.0	1.9	0.38	0.091	0.20	0.090
Nonfederal debt[b]	11.9	4.1	12.3	4.1	0.36	0.092	0.21	0.089
Private nonfinancial debt[c]	12.4	3.5	12.6	3.5	0.38	0.090	0.18	0.091
Total debt[d]	5.2	1.6	5.4	1.8	0.40	0.089	0.32	0.083
Bank credit[e]	6.8	3.2	6.8	3.2	0.28	0.097	0.18	0.091
Asset aggregates								
Monetary base[f]	16.5	5.1	16.8	5.2	0.32	0.095	0.02	0.099
Money stock[g]								
M1	22.3	3.6	22.0	3.6	0.42	0.088	0.20	0.090
M2	4.3	2.9	4.4	2.8	0.38	0.091	0.08	0.096
M3	3.4[h]	1.9[h]	3.5[h]	1.8[h]	0.38[h]	0.077[h]	0.11	0.095
Total net assets[i]	1.5	1.4	1.6	1.5	0.46	0.085	0.30	0.084

a. Total credit market liabilities of all U.S. nonfinancial sectors.
b. Total nonfinancial debt *less* credit market liabilities of the federal government.
c. Nonfederal debt *less* credit market liabilities of state and local governments.
d. Total nonfinancial debt *plus* credit market debt of U.S. financial intermediaries.
e. Commercial bank loans and investments.
f. Bank reserves *plus* currency outside banks.
g. M1 = currency outside banks *plus* demand deposits; M2 = M1 *plus* savings and small time deposits at commercial banks; M3 = M2 *plus* savings and small time deposits at thrift institutions.
h. Based on data for 1960–78.
i. Total holdings of credit market instruments by U.S. nonfinancial holders.

bulges in federal debt issuance during recessions have mostly had their counterpart in the abatement of private borrowing. Households have almost continually increased their reliance on debt in relation to their nonfinancial activity throughout this period. Both corporations and unincorporated businesses have also issued steadily more debt on a relative basis, except for temporary retrenchments during recession years. State and local governments steadily increased their relative debt-issuing activity during the 1950s and 1960s but just as steadily reduced it during the 1970s. Except for 1975–76 and 1980, the federal government has reduced its debt ratio in every year since 1953, although this relative shrinkage of the federal debt has been slower in years when recession has temporarily inflated the budget deficit (and again depressed gross national product in the denominator).

The first four columns of table 1 summarize the stability of the ratios to gross national product of ten financial aggregates—five liability groupings, including the "total nonfinancial debt" measure plotted in figure 1, and five asset groupings—by showing the coefficient of variation (standard deviation normalized by mean) for each ratio computed from both annual and quarterly U.S. data over the 1953–78 sample period (except for the M3 money stock, for which data were not available until 1959). In each case the table shows the coefficient of variation computed from raw data and from detrended data.

As columns 1 and 3 show, the comparison for data including time trends indicates that among the ten aggregates total net assets and total nonfinancial debt are (in that order) the most stable, and the M1 money stock and the monetary base (in that order) are the least stable. Whether a particular relationship exhibits a time trend, however, has little to do with its "stability" in the usual economic sense. The corresponding comparison for detrended data, shown in columns 2 and 4, again indicates that total net assets is the most stable aggregate in relation to gross national product, with total debt and total nonfinancial debt, respectively, a close second and third. The monetary base exhibits the least stability on a detrended basis, with private nonfinancial liabilities and the M1 money stock close behind. Orderings based on annual data are essentially the same as those based on quarterly data.

Simple ratios of precisely contemporaneous observations may well fail to capture the relevant concept of "stability" in the relationship among variables that move over time with some general lead or lag pattern between them. The remaining columns of table 1 present the respective coefficients of determination and standard errors of ten estimated regression equations, in each case relating the growth of nominal gross national product to a moving average of the growth of one of the ten financial aggregates listed in the table, plus a moving average of a fiscal policy measure. The equations are estimated in the familiar form:

$$(1) \qquad \Delta Y_t = \alpha + \sum_{i=0}^{4} \beta_i \Delta F_{t-i} + \sum_{i=0}^{4} \gamma_i \Delta E_{t-i},$$

where Y is gross national product, F is any of the five liability aggregates or five asset aggregates, and E is federal government expenditures calculated on a high employment basis, all expressed in natural logarithms, and α, β_i, and γ_i are scalar coefficients, with β_i and γ_i constrained to lie along respective fourth-order polynomials with the implied $\beta_{-1} = \beta_5 = \gamma_{-1} = \gamma_5 = 0$.

Columns 5 and 6 show the results of estimating equations of the form 1 based on quarterly data for the same 1953–78 sample period that was used in comparing the simple ratios. Total net assets performs best in this test, with a standard error of 0.85 per quarter in "explaining" the historical growth of gross national product, while bank credit (standard error 0.97) performs worst. Total nonfinancial debt is about in the middle. Because there is evidence of a significant break in most of these regressions at around 1970, however—probably associated with the Federal Reserve System's change to a monetary target strategy or the elimination of the Regulation Q interest ceiling from large certificates of deposit, both of which occurred in 1970—columns 7 and 8 also show the respective results for analogous regression equations based on data for 1970–78 only.[9] For this shorter period the relative performance of total nonfinancial debt is somewhat better, equaling that of the M1 money stock.

In part because of the extent to which regressions of the form 1 have been discredited by a variety of criticisms, researchers examining the money-income (or, here, credit-income) relationship have increasingly turned to methods that allow for a richer dynamic interaction between money and income by relating the variation of income not to the entirety

---

9. Except for the equation for M3, which is based on a shorter sample period because of limited data availability, the F-statistic for a break at 1970 is significant at the 10 percent level for all of these equations and at the 5 percent level for all but two (total debt and total net assets).

of the variation of money but only to the part of it that cannot already be deduced either from the past history of money itself or from the joint past history of both money and income.[10] In this context a key indication of the stability of the relationship to income of any financial aggregate is the behavior of that relationship following just such an "innovation," or unanticipated movement, in the aggregate (or in income). A more general representation of equation 1 that is consistent with this interpretation (but that omits the fiscal variable so as to keep the order of the system small) is the vector autoregression

$$(2) \qquad \begin{bmatrix} Y_t \\ F_t \end{bmatrix} = \begin{bmatrix} \alpha_1 \\ \alpha_2 \end{bmatrix} + \begin{bmatrix} B_{11} & B_{12} \\ B_{21} & B_{22} \end{bmatrix} \begin{bmatrix} Y_{t-1} \\ F_{t-1} \end{bmatrix} + \begin{bmatrix} \mu_{1t} \\ \mu_{2t} \end{bmatrix},$$

where Y and F are again as in equation 1, the μ_i are disturbances, the α_i are fixed scalar coefficients to be estimated, and the B_{ij} are fixed-coefficient lag operator polynomials to be estimated.

Solution of the autoregression 2, once it is estimated, yields a moving-average representation of the form

$$(3) \qquad \begin{bmatrix} Y_t \\ F_t \end{bmatrix} = \begin{bmatrix} \xi_1 \\ \xi_2 \end{bmatrix} + \begin{bmatrix} \Theta_{11} & \Theta_{12} \\ \Theta_{21} & \Theta_{22} \end{bmatrix} \begin{bmatrix} \mu_{1t} \\ \mu_{2t} \end{bmatrix},$$

where the ξ_i and Θ_{ij} are, respectively, fixed scalar coefficients and fixed-coefficient lag operator polynomials derived from recursive substitution of the α_i and B_{ij} from autoregression 2 to express both Y and F as functions of the current values and past histories of both μ_1 and μ_2, and the normalization convention imposed in estimating 2 constrains the zero-lag elements of the four polynomials in 3 to $\Theta_{11} = \Theta_{22} = 1$ and $\Theta_{12} = \Theta_{21} = 0$ (so that μ_1 is "the Y disturbance" and μ_2 "the F disturbance").

---

10. Among the most important criticisms of the St. Louis approach have been Stephen M. Goldfeld and Alan S. Blinder, "Some Implications of Endogenous Stabilization Policy," *Brookings Papers on Economic Activity, 3:1972*, pp. 585–640; Thomas J. Sargent, "The Observational Equivalence of Natural and Unnatural Rate Theories of Macroeconomics," *Journal of Political Economy*, vol. 84 (June 1976), pp. 631–40; and Franco Modigliani and Albert Ando, "Impacts of Fiscal Actions on Aggregate Income and the Monetarist Controversy: Theory and Evidence," in Jerome L. Stein, ed., *Monetarism* (Amsterdam: North-Holland, 1976). The methodology underlying the tests described below is derived largely from Granger and Sims, especially Sims. C. W. J. Granger, "Investigating Causal Relations by Econometric Models and Cross-Spectral Methods," *Econometrica*, vol. 37 (July 1969), pp. 424–38; and Christopher A. Sims, "Money, Income and Causality," *American Economic Review*, vol. 62 (September 1972), pp. 540–52.

Table 2. *Dynamic Responses of Liability and Asset Ratios*
Percent

	Liability aggregates[a]			Asset aggregates[a]		
Quarter	Total nonfinancial debt	Private nonfinancial debt	Total debt	Monetary base	M1	M2
Simulations of bivariate system (Y,F)[b]						
1	1.00	1.00	1.00	1.00	1.00	1.00
4	0.07	2.17	0.93	−0.23	0.19	0.64
8	0.36	2.66	1.36	−0.37	0.43	−0.14
12	0.32	2.02	0.84	−0.38	0.15	−0.30
16	0.18	0.92	0.32	−0.43	0.13	0.14
20	0.12	0.82	0.23	−0.42	−0.11	−0.07
Simulations of trivariate system (X,P,F)[c]						
1	1.00	1.00	1.00	1.00	1.00	1.00
4	−0.34	1.51	0.60	−0.01	−0.30	0.55
8	0.09	1.50	1.00	−0.14	0.03	−0.17
12	0.05	0.79	0.31	−0.12	0.30	−0.08
16	−0.03	0.30	−0.01	−0.17	−0.10	0.26
20	−0.01	0.45	0.11	−0.08	−0.11	0.06

a. See table 1 for definition.
b. Values shown are responses of F/Y to a 1 percent innovation in F.
c. Values shown are responses of $F/(X \cdot P)$ to a 1 percent innovation in F.

The orthogonalization of 3 that extracts the independent part of μ_2 (say, ϵ_2) as "the F innovation" is then just

$$(4) \qquad \begin{bmatrix} Y_t \\ F_t \end{bmatrix} = \begin{bmatrix} \xi_1 \\ \xi_2 \end{bmatrix} + \begin{bmatrix} \Phi_{11} & \Phi_{12} \\ \Phi_{21} & \Phi_{22} \end{bmatrix} \begin{bmatrix} \epsilon_{1t} \\ \epsilon_{2t} \end{bmatrix},$$

where the Φ_{ij} and the ϵ_i follow from the Θ_{ij} and the μ_i, respectively, and the ϵ_i are now independent.[11]

The upper half of table 2 summarizes simulations of 4, estimated in the form of equation 2, using quarterly data for nominal gross national

11. The orthogonalization procedure is

$$\begin{bmatrix} \Phi_{11} & \Phi_{12} \\ \Phi_{21} & \Phi_{22} \end{bmatrix} = \begin{bmatrix} \Theta_{11} & \Theta_{12} \\ \Theta_{21} & \Theta_{22} \end{bmatrix} \begin{bmatrix} 1 & 0 \\ \lambda & 1 \end{bmatrix}$$

$$\begin{bmatrix} \epsilon_{1t} \\ \epsilon_{2t} \end{bmatrix} = \begin{bmatrix} 1 & 0 \\ -\lambda & 1 \end{bmatrix} \begin{bmatrix} \mu_{1t} \\ \mu_{2t} \end{bmatrix}$$

for $\lambda = \text{cov}(\mu_1, \mu_2)/\text{var}(\mu_1)$. This orthogonalization is equivalent to placing F last in the pairwise causal ordering of Y and F. The alternative ordering placing F first, which follows from transposing the λ (or $-\lambda$) and the zero elements, gives results that are close to those reported below. See Friedman, "Relative Stability of Money and Credit."

product and three each of the liability and asset aggregates from table 1, with eight quarters of lags on each variable in each equation. For convenience the table reports the response of F/Y rather than the individual responses of F and Y separately. Each column in the table presents values, for the initial quarter and then for the final quarter in each of the first five years, indicating the time path followed by F/Y (for the definition of F indicated) in response to a 1 percent innovation in F.

What stands out in these results is the contrast between the time paths for the three asset aggregate ratios, each of which declines rapidly albeit irregularly after such an innovation, and those for the three liability aggregate ratios. The total nonfinancial debt ratio declines rapidly too, indicating about the same stability in this respect as any of the asset aggregates do; but both the (narrower) private nonfinancial debt ratio and the (broader) total debt ratio show pronounced instability, with overshooting lasting up to three years beyond the initial innovation in F.[12]

A further aspect of the tendency in recent research to avoid simple nominal income regressions of the form 1 has been a reluctance to ignore the distinction between the real and price components of nominal income variation. The lower half of table 2 summarizes simulations that are analogous to those shown in the upper half but based on the moving-average representation solved out from the trivariate vector autoregression

$$
(5) \quad \begin{bmatrix} X_t \\ P_t \\ F_t \end{bmatrix} = \begin{bmatrix} \alpha_1 \\ \alpha_2 \\ \alpha_3 \end{bmatrix} + \begin{bmatrix} B_{11} & B_{12} & B_{13} \\ B_{21} & B_{22} & B_{23} \\ B_{31} & B_{32} & B_{33} \end{bmatrix} \begin{bmatrix} X_{t-1} \\ P_{t-1} \\ F_{t-1} \end{bmatrix} + \begin{bmatrix} \mu_1 \\ \mu_2 \\ \mu_3 \end{bmatrix},
$$

where X is real gross national product and P is the price deflator (both in natural logarithms). Once again the results show a fairly rapid return of the $F/(X \cdot P)$ ratio after an innovation in any of the three asset aggregates and also in total nonfinancial debt, but a slower and less stable return after an innovation in either private nonfinancial debt or total debt.

Among the various liability measures considered, therefore, these results suggest that there is indeed something unique about total nonfinancial debt. It is as if the M1 money stock ratio were sharply unstable, but adding commercial bank time and saving deposits to form the M2 money stock ratio yielded stability, and further adding thrift institution

---

12. Analogous simulations for the M3 money stock, net financial assets, and nonfederal debt all support this contrast. Bank credit also appears to be stable, however.

deposits to form the M3 money stock ratio destroyed that stability—none of which appears to happen. Hence not only does the total nonfinancial debt ratio exhibit just as much stability as any of the five asset ratios in these dynamic tests, but it does so uniquely among the various liability aggregates tested.

In sum, the evidence provided by a variety of methodologies shows that at least one aggregate measure of outstanding credit liabilities in the United States—total nonfinancial debt—consistently exhibits just as much stability in relation to U.S. economic activity as do the more familiar asset aggregates. Indeed, the credit-to-income relationship measured in this way can appear to be more stable than any particular money-to-income relationship, depending on the specific measure of money and the specific test used. Regardless of whether the credit-income relationship is "as stable as" or "more stable than" that for money, however, like the money-income relationship it is potentially important for understanding economic behavior. Nevertheless, although the money-income relationship has long been the focus of attention, the credit-income relationship has to date stimulated little investigation.

Money, Credit, Income, and Prices

The finding of a regular empirical relationship between the outstanding debt of nonfinancial borrowers and the economy's nonfinancial activity is suggestive, but it is not necessarily of direct importance for either economic model building or economic policymaking. For example, what if the explanation for this observed phenomenon was simply that people always adjusted their borrowing to stay in line with their incomes, while their real spending and saving decisions remained predetermined with respect to their activity in the credit market? The total nonfinancial debt variable in that case would be interesting from the standpoint of an investigation of the credit market per se, but there would be little sacrifice to economic analysis in omitting it from a model primarily intended to deliver insights into the determination of nonfinancial behavior itself.

Alternatively, what if the observed stability of the credit-to-income relationship reflected the outcome of a process in which people made decisions about their spending and borrowing behavior jointly? Such a process could emerge if spending and saving decisions were sensitive to the expected yield levels that cleared the credit market, for example, or if the credit market did not clear and people's ability to spend was constrained by their ability to borrow. In that case a model that failed to account for whatever joint decision process connected spending behavior and borrowing behavior would be inadequate, even if understanding the determination of nonfinancial activity constituted the sole objective of the analysis.

The same arguments apply, of course, to the role of money (or other asset aggregates) in economic analysis. Nevertheless, although few models of macroeconomic behavior include an explicit representation of the credit market, almost all include at least a money demand function and an equilibrium condition for the money market, and many go on to treat the supply of money in some detail as well. Were it not for evidence like that summarized in the preceding section, it would perhaps be possible to rationalize this disparity on empirical grounds—although, even so, the distinction between making money an integral or a peripheral part of the analysis would again depend on whether or not the money market played a role in determining nonfinancial economic activity.

In light of the evidence summarized above showing that there is little to distinguish the respective stability of the money-income and credit-income relationships on empirical grounds, however, the rationalization for including the money market but excluding the credit market in macroeconomic analysis must hinge on a presumption that money is central to nonfinancial decisions while credit is not—in other words, that people jointly determine how much to spend and save and how much money to hold, but only secondarily determine how much to borrow.

Is there evidence to support this distinction? Just what constitutes evidence in this context depends in large part on what it means for two actions to be jointly determined or, alternatively, for one to be predetermined with respect to another. "Causality" is a concept with a precise meaning in logic (indeed, several precise meanings), but there is little prospect of using time-series evidence to settle directly questions of economic causality.[13] "Exogeneity" is a concept with a precise meaning in econometrics, and time-series evidence is better suited to bear on questions of econometric exogeneity. In recent years the literature on

13. See, for example, James Tobin, "Money and Income: Post Hoc Ergo Propter Hoc," *Quarterly Journal of Economics*, vol. 84 (May 1970), pp. 301–17; and Arnold Zellner, "Causality and Econometrics," in Karl Brunner and Allan H. Meltzer, eds., *Three Aspects of Policy and Policymaking: Knowledge, Data and Institutions,* Carnegie-Rochester Conference Series on Public Policy, vol. 10 (North-Holland, 1979), pp. 9–54.

this subject has therefore moved away from asserting that one variable "causes" another to the formulation that the one "is exogenous with respect to" the other. Even so, as the development of this literature during the past decade has amply shown, whether one variable is or is not predetermined with respect to another, even in the narrower sense of econometric exogeneity, depends on (among other considerations) what, if any, third or further variables the analysis incorporates. [14]

Perhaps the best way of formulating the question at hand so as to convey the actual meaning of the tests developed for such purposes by Granger and Sims [15] is to ask whether one variable "incrementally predicts" or "incrementally explains" another. Because the basis of such tests consists of regression equations relating one variable to lagged values of another, the issue is really whether the lagged variation of the right-hand-side variable predicts (in beyond-sample analysis) or explains (in within-sample analysis) the variation of the left-hand-side variable. The relevant prediction or explanation is not absolute but incremental, however, in that the lagged values of the specific right-hand-side variable that is the focus of the inquiry are not the equation's only regressors. Hence the question these tests address is, more accurately, whether the lagged values of that specific right-hand-side variable make an incremental contribution to the equation's predictive or explanatory capacity besides that already provided at least by lagged values of the left-hand-side variable itself and perhaps by lagged values of still other variables as well.

In these terms, one rationale for focusing on the money market but not the credit market in macroeconomic analysis would be a presumption that money incrementally explains real economic behavior in a way that credit does not. Table 3 summarizes evidence testing this proposition, drawn from two of the trivariate vector autoregression systems estimated as in 5, above. The upper half of the table presents statistics for the estimation of the trivariate system consisting of real gross national product, the price deflator, and the M1 money stock (hereafter called

14. The contrast between the results of Sims, "Money, Income and Causality," and the results of Yash P. Mehra, "Is Money Exogenous in Money-Demand Equations?" *Journal of Political Economy*, vol. 86 (April 1978), pt. 1, pp. 211–28, and Christopher A. Sims, "Comparison of Interwar and Postwar Business Cycles: Monetarism Reconsidered," *American Economic Review*, vol. 70 (May 1980, *Papers and Proceedings, 1979*), pp. 250–57, which is discussed below, is a striking example of this phenomenon.

15. Granger, "Investigating Causal Relations"; and Sims, "Money, Income and Causality."

Table 3. *Estimation Results for Systems Including Either Money or Credit*[a]

Equation	$\bar{R}^2$	Standard error	F(X)	F(P)	F(M)	F(C)
Estimation of trivariate system (X,P,M)						
X	0.9987	0.0088	319.97*	2.33**	1.39	. . .
P	0.9998	0.0031	1.05	215.36*	3.30*	. . .
M	0.9998	0.0040	2.72**	2.70**	338.34*	. . .
Estimation of trivariate system (X,P,C)						
X	0.9986	0.0090	20.45*	1.95***	. . .	1.07
P	0.9998	0.0033	1.49	346.09*	. . .	2.23**
C	0.9999	0.0027	2.81*	2.40**	. . .	196.09*

* Significant at the 1 percent level.
** Significant at the 5 percent level.
*** Significant at the 10 percent level.
a. The symbols are defined as follows: X = gross national product in constant prices; P = gross national product price deflator; M = money stock (demand deposits plus currency); C = total nonfinancial debt.

simply "money"). The lower half of the table presents analogous statistics for the estimation of the trivariate system consisting of real gross national product, the price deflator, and total nonfinancial debt (hereafter called simply "credit"). Once again all variables are in natural logarithms, and each of the lag operator polynomials includes eight quarterly values. For each estimated equation the table shows the coefficient of multiple determination and the standard error, and, for each lag operator polynomial, the F-statistic for the test of the null hypothesis that the polynomial's coefficients are all equal to zero.

The results presented in table 3 provide no basis whatever for distinguishing money from credit along lines that would warrant including the money market but excluding the credit market in macroeconomic models. The evidence indicates that neither money nor credit incrementally explains real income, given the explanatory power already contained in lagged values of real income and prices. By contrast, both money and credit do incrementally explain prices, this time given the explanatory power already contained in lagged values of prices (and of real income, which does not significantly contribute). Finally, both money and credit are incrementally explained by real income and by prices, even given the explanatory power of one another as well as of lagged values of money or credit, respectively.

Hence the evidence does not support the proposition that money holdings and nonfinancial behavior are jointly determined in some sense in which credit borrowings and nonfinancial behavior are not, nor does

Table 4. *Estimation Results for System Including Both Money and Credit*[a]

Equation	$\bar{R}^2$	Standard error	F(X)	F(P)	F(M)	F(C)
X	0.9988	0.0083	10.77*	2.42**	2.47**	2.14**
P	0.9998	0.0032	0.28	59.83*	1.35	0.55
M	0.9998	0.0040	2.50**	2.67**	107.11*	0.92
C	0.9999	0.0026	1.01	1.71	1.95***	161.10*

a. See table 3 for definitions of variable symbols and significance levels indicated by asterisks.

it support the proposition that money is prior to nonfinancial behavior while credit is not. Indeed, the results reject at the 1 percent level the proposition that money is predetermined with respect to either income or prices. By contrast, a test of the proposition that money is predetermined with respect to nominal income (that is, that nominal income does not incrementally explain money), as in Sims,[16] would impose on the analysis the constraint that the respective coefficients of lagged real income and lagged prices must be identical in the equation explaining money—a constraint that the data decisively reject.[17]

Although the finding that real income and prices incrementally explain both money and credit is not surprising (at least not to me), the apparent absence of any effect of either money or credit on real income is somewhat surprising. Because prices apparently do incrementally explain real income (albeit weakly in the second system) while both money and credit incrementally explain prices, this result is not evidence for any straightforward classical neutrality proposition. Even so, it would be surprising if prices were a sufficient statistic for whatever information financial quantities conveyed about decisions on real spending, output, and income.

Table 4 helps to resolve this puzzle by presenting statistics, analogous to those in table 3, for the estimation of the four-variable vector autoregression system, including both money and credit in addition to real gross national product and the price deflator. Apart from the expansion to include all four variables, the system summarized in table 4 is identical to those represented by autoregression 5 above.

16. Sims, "Money, Income and Causality."

17. The F-statistic for this additional constraint is 2.22, which is significant at the 5 percent level. Moreover, results for the bivariate system that imposes this constraint also reject at the 1 percent level (F-statistic 2.89) the proposition that nominal income does not incrementally explain money.

The contrast between the results for the four-variable system and the corresponding results for the two trivariate systems once again illustrates that whether or not one variable incrementally explains another depends crucially on the base from which the increment is measured—and not always in the direction that a larger information base makes the relevant increment harder to detect. Although neither money nor credit incrementally explains real income in the absence of the other, both do so in the presence of one another. In intuitive terms, what appears to matter for the explanation of real income is neither money nor credit but instead the interrelation of the two. Moreover, even in the presence of both money and credit, prices still also incrementally explain real income. Hence the effect on income represented by the price variable is at least in part independent of the effect of financial quantities; prices are not a sufficient statistic for the relevant information contained in financial quantities, nor do money and credit jointly constitute a sufficient statistic for the relevant information contained in prices.

The other results presented in table 4 are less striking but interesting nonetheless. Although money and credit each incrementally explain prices in the absence of the other, neither does so in the presence of the other (and of lagged prices and real income). Hence both money and credit apparently convey largely the same information about the determination of prices, and neither contributes significantly beyond what is contained in the other. Credit does not incrementally explain money, nor does its presence overturn the result that both real income and prices do so. By contrast, money does incrementally explain credit (although only weakly), and in the presence of money neither real income nor prices any longer do so.

The results of vector autoregression analysis of real income, prices, money, and credit therefore provide no basis for focusing on money to the exclusion of credit in macroeconomic analysis. For explaining the variation of real income, what appears to be important is neither money nor credit separately but the relationship between the two. For explaining the variation of prices, either one will do, and the choice between them is largely arbitrary.[18] Finally, the interrelationship between money and credit themselves is apparently not so simple as to warrant including one and not the other in the analysis. Macroeconomic analysis should be sufficiently broad to include both the money market and the credit market.

18. Only at the 1 percent significance level is it true that money incrementally explains prices while credit does not.

The Market for Money and the Market for Credit

The conclusion that both the money market and the credit market should play an integral role in macroeconomic analysis immediately recalls Patinkin's classic statement of the static neoclassical monetary equilibrium framework.[19] In its full form this model includes four markets—those for goods and services, labor, money, and credit[20]—but Patinkin chose to eliminate the labor market by assuming it was always at full-employment equilibrium and to work only with the markets for goods and services, money, and credit.[21]

Figure 2 illustrates the sense in which the markets for money and credit are both fundamental in Patinkin's model. The object of the analysis here is to determine the price level P and interest rate r—in other words, the two rates of exchange spanning the three markets. An equilibrium in (r,p) space is determined by the joint intersection, as at point E_1, of the three curves representing the market-clearing (r,P) combinations for the three markets: XX for the goods and services market, MM for the money market, and CC for the credit market. A change in the underlying conditions that shifts any of the three curves must also shift at least one of the others. For example, if the introduction of checkable money market mutual funds were to reduce people's demand for "money" and thereby shift the market-clearing curve for

19. Don Patinkin, *Money, Interest and Prices: An Integration of Monetary and Value Theory,* 2d ed. (Harper and Row, 1965).

20. Patinkin referred to all debt instruments as "bonds" and, for simplicity, assumed that they were perpetuities. In reality, the instruments included in the total nonfinancial debt aggregate span the entire maturity spectrum but, at least for the United States, do not include perpetuities. What actually matters for the pricing of debt instruments is not stated maturity anyway but the duration (see, for example, Michael H. Hopewell and George G. Kaufman, "Bond Price Volatility and Term to Maturity: A Generalized Respecification," *American Economic Review,* vol. 63 [September 1973], pp. 749–53), which is always shorter for coupon-bearing instruments, especially after allowance for the probability of call (see Zvi Bodie and Benjamin M. Friedman, "Interest Rate Uncertainty and the Value of Bond Call Protection," *Journal of Political Economy,* vol. 86 [February 1978], pp. 19–43).

21. Eliminating the labor market was perhaps appropriate for Patinkin's equilibrium analysis, but as subsequent work—for example, Robert J. Barro and Herschel I. Grossman, "A General Disequilibrium Model of Income and Employment," *American Economic Review,* vol. 61 (March 1971), pp. 82–93—has shown, the labor market is apparently central to disequilibrium analysis.

Figure 2. *Patinkin's Three-Market Model*

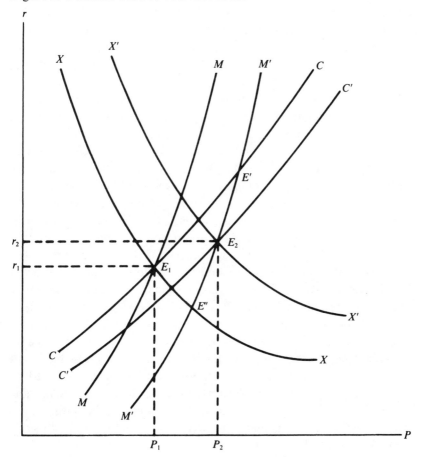

the money market from MM to $M'M'$, the logic of the budget constraints underlying the model's construction dictates that people would also either increase their demand for goods and services or decrease their demand for borrowing, or both. If only the demand for goods and services changed, the XX curve would shift so as to intersect both $M'M'$ and CC at point E'. If only the demand for borrowing changed, CC would shift so as to intersect both $M'M'$ and XX at E''. The figure as drawn shows a shift in both curves to a new equilibrium at E_2.

Two lines are sufficient to determine a point, of course, so that even in this framework it still is formally possible to eliminate one of the three markets. What remains impossible, however, is to determine the effects of a change affecting any one market without, at the very least, making a potentially refutable assumption about a corresponding change in at least one other. In the example of the money market mutual fund, shifting MM to $M'M'$ and leaving XX in place, as is analogous to the practice in the more conventional Hicks-Keynes IS-LM analysis, are the equivalent of assuming a specific shift in CC. Similarly, analyzing an increase in government spending that shifts XX to $X'X'$ by leaving MM in place is again equivalent to assuming a specific shift in CC. In either case, behavior in the credit market may or may not warrant such an assumption. The results presented in tables 3 and 4 suggest that, at least from the perspective of the determination of real income (though not of prices, as in Patinkin's full-employment model), it is not safe to assume that the credit market passively absorbs the necessary shifts in this way. Changes in the quantity of money may or may not have implications for real income, depending on what is happening to the quantity of credit.

In the context of this three-market representation of economic activity, the four-variable system summarized in table 4 uses the quantity of credit to represent the relevant aspects of behavior in the credit market, while the remaining three variables represent the quantities in the other two markets (goods and services and money) and the rate of exchange between them. To the extent that the objective is simply to include some representation of the credit market, however, the quantity of credit is not the only possible choice for this purpose. The alternative is either the rate of exchange between credit and money in a market with nominal bonds, or the rate of exchange between credit and goods in a market with indexed bonds.

Following Mehra's demonstration that including the interest rate in the analysis is sufficient to reverse Sims's earlier findings that money incrementally explains income but not vice versa,[22] Sims has estimated the analog to the system in table 4, using the rate of exchange between credit and money—that is, the nominal interest rate—to represent the role of the credit market.[23] Table 5 summarizes the results of estimating a four-variable system like that of Sims, but using the same data and details of estimation as in the work presented above.[24] The results are

22. Mehra, "Is Money Exogenous?"; and Sims, "Money, Income and Causality."

23. Sims, "Comparison of Interwar and Postwar Business Cycles."

24. Sims used monthly data, industrial production instead of real gross national product, and the wholesale price index instead of the gross national product deflator.

Table 5. *Estimation Results for System Including Money*
and an Interest Rate[a]

Equation	$\bar{R}^2$	Standard error	F(X)	F(P)	F(M)	F(r)
X	0.9989	0.0079	129.24*	0.55	1.31	2.93*
P	0.9999	0.0029	1.21	210.23*	2.16**	2.39**
M	0.9998	0.0038	2.24**	1.60	193.71*	1.55
r	0.9491	0.0090	1.13	0.58	1.71	20.30*

a. The symbol r = interest rate on four- to six-month prime commercial paper. See table 3 for definitions of other variable symbols and for significance levels indicated by asterisks.

close to those of Sims, and they offer some interesting contrasts to those in table 4. The interest rate incrementally explains real income while prices no longer do, nor does money.[25] In the absence of the credit quantity, however, money once again incrementally explains prices. Real income again incrementally explains money, but in the presence of the interest rate prices no longer do. Money does not incrementally explain the interest rate here, although it does incrementally explain the credit quantity in table 4.

Beyond the simple distinction between using the quantity variable and using the relative price variable to represent the third market, is there any relationship between the two systems summarized in tables 4 and 5? Figure 3 shows two representations of the credit market in a linear stochastic model. In each the intersection of the deterministic parts of the demand and supply curves—D_0 for borrowers and S_0 for lenders, respectively—indicates the expected equilibrium in (r,C) space. In panel A only the demand curve is stochastic, and the resulting deviations of the interest rate and credit quantity around expected equilibrium (r_0,C_0) are perfectly positively correlated. In panel B only the supply curve is stochastic, and the resulting deviations around (r_0,C_0) are perfectly negatively correlated.

Both credit demand and credit supply are presumably stochastic in reality, so that the actual correlation will be imperfect. The value of the correlation coefficient constitutes potentially useful information, however. First, the correlation's sign will indicate whether the dominant source of stochastic variation in the credit market comes from the behavior of borrowers or that of lenders. Second, and more important,

25. The finding that the nominal interest rate renders the price variable insignificant everywhere except in the price equation is not surprising since, with an eight-quarter lag, the F-test for prices is hard to distinguish from an F-test for the inflation rate.

Figure 3. *Alternative Extremes of a Stochastic Credit Market*

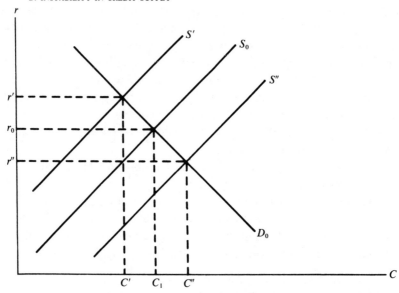

Table 6. *Correlations between Credit and Interest Rate Innovations*[a]

	Pairwise correlations	
Description	(ϵ_C, ϵ_r)	$(\Delta\epsilon_C, \Delta\epsilon_r)$
C,r ordered last	0.41	0.50
C,r ordered first	0.27	0.39

a. The variables are defined as follows: ϵ = orthogonalized innovation; C = total nonfinancial debt; r = interest rate on four- to six-month commercial paper. Results are significant at the 1 percent level.

the correlation's absolute value will indicate to what extent a univariate representation of the credit market—either the interest rate or the credit quantity—is adequate. In the extreme case in which either credit demand or credit supply is nonstochastic, so that the correlation is perfect, either variable contains all the relevant information about stochastic shifts in the credit market. At the other extreme, if credit demand and credit supply are both about equally stochastic (in independent ways), the two variables contain two separate sets of information, both of which are necessary.

Table 6 shows the pairwise correlations between the independent innovations associated with the credit quantity in the orthogonalized moving-average representation solved out from the four-variable vector autoregression system summarized in table 4 and the independent innovations associated with the interest rate in the analogous representation of the system summarized in table 5. Table 6 presents correlations between the innovations per se, as well as between their respective first differences. In addition, because the ordering assumed in the orthogonalization in general affects the computation of the innovations corresponding to particular variables, the table shows correlations for the innovations computed for credit and the interest rate ordered last in their respective systems (as in table 2 above) and also for these variables ordered first. In each case the interest rate innovations are lagged one period so that the four- to six-month span of the interest rate approximately centers on the corresponding credit quantity observation (measured as of the end of the quarter).

The correlation between the two innovations is positive regardless of the details of the computation, indicating that credit demand—that is, the behavior of borrowers—is the dominant source of stochastic variation in the credit market. None of the correlations approaches unity, however, confirming that credit supply is also importantly subject to stochastic variation. Hence it is highly unlikely that either the credit quantity or the interest rate constitutes, by itself, a sufficient representation of the credit market.

Some representation of the credit market in macroeconomic analysis is clearly better than none, and the chief contribution of the four-variable systems presented in tables 4 and 5 is that each includes one variable for this purpose: a quantity in the former and a relative price in the latter. Nevertheless, the evidence presented here suggests not only that macroeconomic analysis should explicitly incorporate the credit market, but also that it should do so with both a quantity and a relative price variable. The resulting framework would then be a fully specified three-market model, including real income, money, and credit (the quantities in all three markets) as well as the price level and the interest rate (the two rates of exchange spanning them).[26]

Implications for Monetary Policy

The evidence presented in this paper supports three conclusions about the respective roles of money and credit in macroeconomic analysis.

First, the relationship between credit and nonfinancial economic activity is just as regular and stable as is that between money and economic activity. The evidence does not warrant including the money market but excluding the credit market on grounds of the closeness, or lack thereof, of the observed empirical relationships.

Second, real income and prices are not predetermined with respect to credit, any more than they are with respect to money. The evidence does not warrant excluding either the credit market or the money market on grounds of being only peripheral to the determination of nonfinancial economic activity.

Third, the interest rate and the quantity of credit both represent aspects of behavior in the credit market that matter for nonfinancial economic activity. The evidence suggests, however, that neither variable alone is adequate to convey all of the information about the credit market that is relevant to macroeconomic analysis.

These conclusions also bear parallel implications for the choice of a framework for conducting monetary policy. The same evidence that rejects the propositions which, if true, would rationalize a special role

26. A forthcoming paper will report my analysis of such a five-variable system.

for money over credit in analysis also rejects the corollary propositions which, if true, would rationalize a special role for money over credit in the design and execution of monetary policy. Hence this evidence suggests that there is little basis for the conventional monetary policy procedures currently practiced in the United States and in most other industrialized Western economies, which revolve around specific target rates of growth for some measure(s) of the money stock with minimal attention paid to credit measures.

One way to read the evidence developed in this paper is simply as further support for the case against having any kind of intermediate target for monetary policy at all. Under the intermediate target procedure, the central bank first determines for some financial quantity a time path believed to be consistent with achieving its ultimate objectives for the nonfinancial economy, and then acts as if its objective is to control that quantity so that its subsequent growth follows the chosen path to within a predetermined range of tolerance. Hence the intermediate target, which is observable on a timely basis in the financial markets, stands as a proxy for the ultimate nonfinancial objectives of monetary policy in a world characterized by uncertainty and lags of several kinds. In practice, central banks using the intermediate target procedure have typically chosen a measure of the money stock as the intermediate target, and the main impetus for the adoption of this procedure has usually rested, at least in part, on notions of the special relationship between money and nonfinancial economic activity.

In fact, the intermediate target procedure would constitute an optimal way to conduct monetary policy only under extremely stringent conditions describing the relationship between the intermediate target and the nonfinancial objectives of monetary policy.[27] Even in the context of a simple macroeconomic model, for example, the intermediate target procedure based on the money stock as the intermediate target is optimal only if the demand for money is both perfectly stable and perfectly insensitive to interest rates.

In the wake of the much discussed collapse of previously well-accepted U.S. money demand functions during the 1970s, more evidence that the demand for money does not meet these conditions is hardly necessary. Even so, the evidence presented in this paper further strengthens the case against the intermediate target procedure by indicating the

27. See Benjamin M. Friedman, "Targets, Instruments and Indicators of Monetary Policy," *Journal of Monetary Economics*, vol. 1 (October 1975), pp. 443–73.

complexity of the relationships between money, credit, and economic activity. Indeed, the evidence shows that there is no more empirical justification for using money as the intermediate target than there is for using credit as the intermediate target. To the extent that arguments for this way of conducting monetary policy have traditionally rested on the presumption that money plays a special role, and hence that money should serve as the intermediate target, this evidence casts further doubt on the appropriateness of the entire intermediate target procedure.

Even within the more limited context of the intermediate target procedure itself, the evidence presented in this paper suggests that at the very least a two-target framework based on one monetary aggregate target and one credit aggregate target would be superior to a framework based on monetary targets only, in the usual sense of delivering a greater likelihood of achieving outcomes for key nonfinancial variables falling within any given tolerance around corresponding set objectives. (The evidence even provides some ground for believing that a three-target policy, including an interest rate in addition to money and credit, would be superior still.)

How would monetary policy function in an explicit two-target money-and-credit framework? Only with infinitesimal probability, of course, would the stated target for money and the stated target for credit ever turn out to be precisely compatible. The divergence between the two aggregates in an environment of uncertainty would indeed present a problem if the central bank were to interpret the intermediate target procedure in a strict sense. If, however, it instead regarded each intermediate target as an "information variable" that identified a limited set of incoming information to which there would be a presumption that the central bank would respond as a matter of course, there would be neither analytical nor practical difficulty in having two such targets instead of one.[28] Indeed, according to the published policy records of the Federal Open Market Committee, as well as reports to the Congress by the chairman of the Federal Reserve System, monetary policy in the United States currently uses just such a two-target framework, but with the M1 and M2 money stocks serving as the two targets.

The chief advantage of an explicit two-target framework based on

28. See ibid.; and John H. Kareken, Thomas Muench, and Neil Wallace, "Optimal Open Market Strategy: The Use of Information Variables," *American Economic Review,* vol. 63 (March 1973), pp. 156–72, for the development of the "information variable" concept in the context of intermediate targets for monetary policy.

money and credit in comparison to a two-target framework based on two separate definitions of the money stock, however, would be the incorporation of a more diverse information base in the set of signals that presumptively matter for monetary policy. Money is, after all, an asset held by the public, and each monetary aggregate is just a different way of adding up the public's assets. The combination of an M1 and an M2 target therefore relies solely on the asset side of the economy's balance sheet, although it aggregates those assets in two separate ways. A framework based on a money target and a credit target would instead establish a presumption that the central bank would respond to signals from both sides of the economy's balance sheet, and the evidence presented here indicates that both sides of the balance sheet do contain information that is relevant to the determination of nonfinancial economic activity.

In sum, the evidence presented in this paper does not support the intermediate target procedure for monetary policy, as currently implemented with some measure(s) of the money stock used as the only intermediate target(s). The evidence is instead consistent with either abandoning the intermediate target procedure altogether and addressing monetary policy directly to its nonfinancial objectives or adopting a two-target monetary policy framework based on both money and credit.

Comment by Phillip Cagan

A LONG-STANDING body of literature—partly in and partly outside the mainstream—questions the usefulness of narrow monetary aggregates (such as the present M1B) for guiding monetary policy. Since October 1979, when the Federal Reserve adopted new operating procedures that placed increased emphasis on achieving monetary targets, after a temporary setback this questioning literature revived. It has three strands. The first is the view that, while monetary aggregates can contribute to the conduct of monetary policy, they should not be used as targets. This strand is part of the once standard and still influential view that money market conditions, particularly interest rates, should play the primary role in guiding monetary policy. A second strand—related to but overshadowed by the first—is that the most reliable guides are the broad rather than the narrow monetary aggregates. A close relationship between total debt outstanding or total credit flows and GNP is cited as evidence that these broad aggregates should serve as the guides of monetary policy. Finally, a third, fairly recent, strand reflects the difficulties of defining the monetary aggregates in the face of financial innovations in the payments system. While the new M1B is an attempt to redefine transactions balances, doubts remain about whether it is sufficiently comprehensive and whether continuing market developments will not soon render it obsolete. Because of these uncertainties about the appropriate target for policy, the third strand supports the use of the monetary base—the narrowest of the monetary aggregates—as the one least subject to ambiguity and therefore the most reliable. (A fourth strand, which some of us are promoting, that regulatory reforms should protect the uniqueness and enhance the usefulness of transactions balances for control by monetary policy, has as yet little visibility.)

Benjamin Friedman's paper is an empirical analysis of policy issues and can be classified as part of the second strand—the view that the broad monetary aggregates contain useful information for the conduct of monetary policy, indeed, more reliable information than the narrow aggregates do. Total financial debt (the exact definition does not greatly matter) has grown at the same rate as GNP over most of the post–World War II period, and the ratio of this debt to GNP displays smaller variations than do the comparable ratios for narrower aggregates (even abstracting from the latter ratios' upward trends). Presumably substitutions have occurred among the components of total financial assets while a stable relationship has been maintained between the total volume of financing and aggregate expenditures. Consequently, total credit flows, which are equivalent to the change in total debt, correlate closely with changes in GNP—again, as good as or better than any of the other monetary aggregates.

As Friedman points out, the body of monetary theory does not deny that total debt or credit is related to GNP or that they might be useful guides for policy, but there is a notable lack of focus on the broad aggregates in monetary theory. There appear to be two reasons for this lack. First, no theory has been presented to imply that total debt or credit would bear an unchanging relationship to GNP. Even if the ratio of the capital stock to GNP is assumed to be stable but sources of capital financing are available outside credit markets, market sources need not be an invariant fraction of total financing. The fact that total debt has had an unchanging ratio to GNP seems to be a historical accident rather than the consequence of any fundamental economic law, despite Friedman's illuminating inquiry into why it happened. Second, monetary theory has focused on money because, historically, transactions balances were fairly well defined and important for the volume of total spending and for the determination of the price level, and because money was something that the government could and did control directly. It is the recent rapid development of new kinds of transactions balances and new forms of payment that has raised doubts about whether the traditional emphasis on money rather than on broader financial aggregates is still justified.

I have also been looking into these issues in my current research, and I can confirm Friedman's main results. It is true that broad aggregates like total debt, or even total liquid assets, show a more stable growth in relation to GNP since the early 1950s than transactions balances do— considerably or slightly more stable depending on how transactions balances are defined. The policy implication is that the Federal Reserve should make appropriate use of the information provided by broad aggregates.

This does not mean, however, that the narrow aggregates should be ignored. Friedman does not go into the policy implications of his work, but two implications seem to me worth comment. First, the Federal Reserve should consider operating with more than one target. In addition to its ultimate goals of reducing the inflation rate and producing a certain growth in nominal GNP each year, it could announce and pursue targets for total debt and M1B as being consistent with its ultimate goals. The justification for a target on more than one aggregate is that each one represents a different point in the time sequence of monetary operations. Open market operations are conducted in the monetary base, which has effects on the banking system that are reflected first in the narrow monetary aggregates, then in the broader financial aggregates, and eventually in the goals for GNP and prices. The narrow aggregates are needed to monitor the immediate effects of policy. If broader aggregates are reliable, they can help monitor the subsequent effects. To be sure, the timing sequence of monetary effects may vary, and multiple targets can disagree and provide ad hoc justifications for almost any policy that is undertaken. Before multiple targets can enjoy the public's confidence, therefore, it is necessary to be clear about their priority and how differences will be reconciled. I can see possible objections to multiple targets in practice, but not in principle.

A second consideration in evaluating the policy implications of this work is that any monetary aggregate may be a good target but not an advance indicator, or vice versa. By this I mean that an aggregate may maintain a stable long-run relationship with GNP and thus be a good target, but not provide information in advance about monetary effects on GNP. As a simple example, the Federal Reserve supplies currency elastically in response to the public's demand, which depends largely on concurrent movements in retail trade and GNP. Currency movements themselves appear to give no advance indication of future changes in GNP. Such advance indication is provided, on the other hand, by changes in the base and in transactions balances—and apparently also by changes in total debt and liquid assets.

Friedman finds not only that total debt would be a good target, but also that it provides advance information about GNP. The latter result cannot be attributed to feedback from GNP to total debt, because his analysis relates GNP to lagged values of total debt, omitting the concurrent value of debt.

He does not go on to compare the monetary aggregates for the separate information each contains. My research suggests that the information in total debt is not contained in M1B, but at the same time M1B provides advance information that is not contained in total debt. Furthermore, while the latter results pertain to the full period from the early 1950s to 1980, I find that for the shorter period since the late 1960s the advance information in M2 dominates the other aggregates, even though M2 is a poor target in the above sense. That is, changes in the growth rate of M2 reliably indicate whether monetary policy is being stimulative or restrictive, but after a lag the growth in M1B or total debt will more closely show the effects that monetary policy is having on GNP and will make a better target.

Monetary and financial relationships are in a state of flux and uncertainty. They have been changing since the late 1960s, when innovations in the payments system accelerated. High inflation combined with interest-rate ceilings and other regulatory impedimenta have fostered these flanking developments. Whether they will disappear if inflation subsides is doubtful, though the rate of new developments would no doubt slow. These developments raise questions about policy guidelines and make its conduct more uncertain. Friedman's paper opens up these questions to serious empirical analysis. The policy issues should be faced and analyzed. At the same time the analysis should not be allowed to undermine the current pursuit of an anti-inflationary policy to reduce the growth of monetary aggregates. The purpose of this analysis, in my view, is to improve the admittedly far from perfect but nonetheless crucial guide that monetary aggregates provide for monetary policy.

Comment by Robert J. Shiller

A LOT OF information about credit aggregates and macroeconomic fluctuations is presented in this intriguing paper. The approach is exploratory, the scope is wide, and the aim is to suggest models rather than to evaluate an explicit model. I think the profession generally appreciates such exploratory data analysis more than it did, say, twenty years ago. I am sure the best econometric practitioners of twenty years ago knew the importance of such preliminaries to formal model building, but they usually published only the final model and its estimation. Perhaps they were overreacting to the "measurement without theory" criticism of the apparently unproductive collection of data that preceded the computer age. But good exploratory data analysis is hardly done without theory. Rather, it proceeds with an appreciation of the competing basic or intuitive theoretical notions and with an understanding of the difficulty of converting such notions into a concrete testable model. For this paper the theoretical motivation can be found in an inchoate form in numerous public discussions of credit aggregates and monetary policy. The movement from the basic notions to the model is a creative process that can be helped along with appropriately presented evidence. I think it testifies to the greater level of development and enlightenment in the profession in recent years that there is an awareness of the importance of explicit discussion of such analysis.

Except for a brief discussion of Patinkin's model, no theoretical framework is formally laid out in Friedman's paper. What is presented is a contrast of "debt" with "money," and it is asked why it is so commonly assumed that the quantity of money is of so much more importance than that of debt. Indeed, while one can think of stock answers (money is the "medium of exchange"), it is not clear why total debt outstanding should be excluded from an econometric model, as it apparently usually is. It is worthwhile to look at these data. In an earlier paper, Friedman presented an "ultrarationality" theory and other theories, which I will refer to below.

The featured result here is that the ratio of total nonfinancial debt to gross national product has shown no trend since World War II and has apparently been fairly constant, more so than the ratio of the principal monetary aggregates to GNP. Moreover, various components of the total have shown a trend. Most notably, real federal debt has shown a steady decline since World War II, as the wartime debt was eroded by inflation. This was offset by an increase in the ratio of the other components to GNP. It should be noted that the empirical regularity is more or less summarized by the trends. There seems little tendency for short-run movements in the ratio of federal government debt to be offset by short-run movements in the opposite direction by the other debt ratios. On the contrary, the short-run movements in the debt ratios seem often to be in the same direction. This is apparently because the short-run movements are due largely to movements in the denominator (nominal GNP), which is common to all elements, while the numerators are fairly sluggish.

Because the phenomenon can be summarized in terms of trends, one might be inclined to call it a sort of coincidence. Still, one can look for explanations of why this ratio might be constant, much as the growth theorists looked for interpretations of the "constancy" of the wage share or capital–output ratio.

The "ultrarationality" theory presented elsewhere[29] asserts that total debt ratio is constant because individual debt substitutes for government debt and because individuals wish to maintain constant debt relative to wealth (which is in turn constant in relation to income). This argument might be persuasive if the decline in government debt since World War II had been due to a decline in debt-financed activities directly on behalf of a class of individual consumers who would themselves borrow to finance the activity. But it is not clear that the actual decline in real government debt, a debt incurred to finance a war, has such an interpretation. Friedman also presented other theories that were institutionally based, and these different theories together seem to represent a thorough effort to find explanations for the observed constancy.

It is worthwhile to consider the relative constancy of debt versus monetary aggregate ratios in terms of conventional macroeconomic theory, as embodied in the large macroeconometric models. These models have had as their cornerstone the variability of the money–GNP ratio. This variability, under the control of the central bank, accounts

---

29. Friedman, "Relative Stability of Money and Credit."

for their control over interest rates. The variability does not represent the variability in the *residual* in the demand-for-money equation. Moreover, since the coefficient of variation of these series is dominated by the extreme low-frequency component, it is not clear what relevance this coefficient has for short-run monetary policy. Even if this coefficient could be construed to measure the uncertainty of the error term in a demand-for-money equation, if the demand for money has a longer-run drift to it than the demand for total credit does, it does not mean that the effect of short-run policy change is any less certain.

In his 1981 paper, Friedman had an analogous plot that extended this debt–income ratio series back to 1918. In this plot, the ratio of nonfinancial debt to GNP was quite variable, covering a range of about 2.5 (in the Great Depression) to 1 (after World War I). Although, as he noted, the ratio of the total nonfinancial debt to GNP appeared to have no trend over this period, neither did the individual components. There were conspicuous co-movements in all the components, reflecting the much more volatile behavior of GNP in the prewar period. There was a tremendous increase in the ratios early in the depression, and a decline after the early 1930s, mirroring the path of nominal GNP. Indeed, there would be reason to expect instability of the ratio in the future if for any reason GNP became more volatile. If GNP drops, there is no mechanism to cause a dramatic drop in nominal indebtedness.

What is this "total financial debt" that Friedman concentrates on? It is a single statistic that summarizes a vast matrix of quantities. One could imagine an $n \times n$ matrix, where n is the total number of legal entities—individual, corporate, and governmental—in the economy. The ij^{th} element is the debt from the ith entity to the jth, positive if the entity owes money, negative if the entity is owed money. Then the sum of the elements is zero. Apparently, to arrive at total nonfinancial debt, one sums all positive elements of the matrix except for those corresponding to debt of financial intermediaries. So long as the matrix grows and shrinks uniformly through time, such a sum would unambiguously represent the size of the matrix. But if, as Friedman emphasizes, there are shifts in relative quantities, then different summary statistics could be developed by netting out or weighting elements in different ways. If one is going to attach significance to the constancy of a certain sum of elements, then one must ask the meaning of this sum. Other summary statistics might just as well be considered total credit. For example, it might seem reasonable to net out an individual's savings account against his or her mortgage debt. There are apparently substantial numbers of persons who hold both. What significance has the total debt of an individual if his or her net debt is much different? Compensating balances might also be netted out against corporate loans or corporate financial assets against their debt. I have no reason to expect that such alternative methods of summing would make important differences in the conclusions, but the very existence of such alternatives suggests that the constancy of the ratio is less interesting by itself.

Another, perhaps deeper ambiguity in definition arises because debt constitutes only certain categories of claims that legal entities have on each other. The corporate equity is very substantial relative to the total debt, and differs from corporate debt in that it represents a junior claim on profits. Certain kinds of stock, particularly preferred stock, may closely resemble debt. However, preferred stock per se is fairly small relative to total debt (in 1979 the total preferred stock listed on the New York Stock Exchange was about $20 billion, compared with $460 billion for bonds so listed). Certain kinds of debt may resemble equity. Currently, about one bond in seven of those rated by Moody's is convertible, and may therefore be regarded as equity by holders. Roughly 2 percent of all bonds rated by Moody's recently were rated Caa or lower— meaning that they are either in default or in immediate danger of becoming so and thus may be in effect equity investments. These marginal categories of stocks or bonds are apparently not important enough to suggest really substantial ambiguity in the total. It is fortunate that our institutional structure does not create too many such ambiguous liabilities. It is institutional good luck that today government bonds are not merged with lottery tickets, as they were in eighteenth century England.

In another sense, though, there is an inherent ambiguity in the definition of debt. According to the Modigliani-Miller view, if corporations change their debt–equity ratio (for example, by buying back shares with the proceeds of debt), then there should be no effect, except tax effects, on individuals' budget constraints. Debt becomes more like equity, equity more like debt, and the change in total debt is of absolutely no real significance.

Another source of ambiguity in the definition of total nonfinancial debt is this: do we want market value of debt or par value? The flow-of-funds section at the Federal Reserve has chosen to represent par value in the accounts. For some theoretical purposes, I suppose the market value might be preferable. In a world after unanticipated events have increased expected inflation rates, the present value of future coupons and principal have been effectively reduced and the par value might be considered of historical interest only. Of course, market value deviates substantially from par value when interest rates move a lot. From 1960 to 1980 the ratio of the market value to the par value of all listed bonds on the New York Stock Exchange ranged from a low of 77.8 in 1969 to a high of 100.4 in 1976.[30] The ratio of market to par value for government debt was less variable, reflecting the shorter average maturity. John Seater found that this ratio since 1946 ranged between 0.921 in 1969 and 1.03 in 1946.[31] These movements are sufficiently big to make the ratio of market value of debt to GNP considerably less stable, and possibly to reverse Friedman's conclusion. Recall that he contrasted a coefficient of variation of 1.8 percent for the total nonfinancial debt ratio to 2.9 percent for the M2 ratio and 3.6 percent for the M1 ratio.

The formal data analysis in the paper has three rather unrelated parts. The first (already alluded to) looks at plots of data and simple coefficients of variation for the ratios. The second estimates a "St. Louis" type of model. The third does innovation accounting of the kind advocated, in particular, by Sims. If these analyses are thought of as motivated by three different models, they appear quite disjointed. Here the exploratory nature of the research must be borne in mind. The St. Louis equations differ from the vector autoregressions in their exclusion of lagged dependent variables from the right-hand side. I see no a priori reason to suppose that a vector autoregression is better because it allows a "richer dynamic interaction" than a St. Louis equation. More parameters does not mean better. I suppose that the vector autoregressions are more likely to be interesting if we have in mind some efficient market models that relate the residuals in the equations to forecasting errors made by economic agents. But I do not have a model in mind that attributes any significance to the error in forecasting total nonfinancial debt. As Friedman points out, the Granger causality inferred by the autoregressions may not correspond to true causality. However, the ordering inferred does seem to be a useful way of characterizing the data.

Friedman does offer some interpretation of his regression results. He apparently feels that nothing of importance emerged from the St. Louis equation. He notes that the coefficient of determination for the total

30. *New York Stock Exchange Fact Book, 1980*, p. 71.
31. John J. Seater, "The Market Value of Outstanding Government Debt," *Journal of Monetary Economics*, vol. 8 (July 1981), pp. 85–101.

nonfinancial debt equation was neither very high nor very low relative to the $\bar{R}^2$ for money equations or to equations explaining components of total debt. Of course, this $\bar{R}^2$ is a very different quantity from the stability of the ratio emphasized earlier.

For his vector autoregressions, Friedman runs bivariate, trivariate, and four-variable systems, and with different orderings for the variables. The bivariate systems include nominal GNP and one of the financial variables. The trivariate systems add to this list the price level, and the four-variable systems add the interest rate or credit variable. The causality tests are a sort of summary statistic, which many people find noteworthy. He also emphasizes that with the bivariate and trivariate systems total nonfinancial debt has the effects of the residuals, which die out as quickly as in the corresponding simulations for money. He infers some similarity, then, between money and debt, but this is a different kind of similarity than the similar stability of their ratios, or their similarity in the St. Louis equations.

Friedman attaches particular significance to the correlation through time in the estimated residuals of the credit variable of two separate four-variable vector autoregressions. One conclusion he draws after looking at these autoregressions is that neither interest rate nor quantity of credit is adequate to convey all information relevant to macroeconomic analysis. There is a sense in which this is a correct inference. A perfect correlation between the innovation would suggest a linear dependency between the interest rate and the credit variable, so that indeed one variable would be superfluous. Of course, there is not a perfect correlation, but one variable may still be superfluous in forecasting macro variables. The logical way to test this would seem to be to test for significance one of the variables in a regression that also includes the other. The positive correlation between the two innovations may be said to carry information that demand shocks dominate supply shocks but only in a more fully specified model. It is not clear to me, from the heuristic model shown in the paper, what the definition of a demand or supply shock is. Is it the actual shift in the total demand or supply, or is it the component of this shift variable that is orthogonal to lagged data? Or is it the component that is orthogonal to other contemporaneous variables? Again, the methodology used here, exploratory in nature, is not suited to a well-defined interpretation.

In his conclusion to the paper, Friedman seems to lose confidence in the current enlightenment of the profession today, and apparently feels we expect him to present some policy conclusions based on his exploratory analysis. He says that a two-target policy framework based on one monetary aggregate target and one credit aggregate target is advisable, and that a three-target policy including an interest rate as well as money supply and credit would be superior still. As he notes in his conclusions, such advice seems inconsistent with his advice in his excellent 1975 article, in which he advocated abandoning such intermediate targets policy.[32] Actually, I interpret that paper as advocating an explicit model and objective function, so that an optimal policy emerges using optimal control theory, which simply makes each variable directly controllable by the central bank a function of all information variables. No such model is given even in the most incipient form in this paper, so no policy conclusion should be drawn on the basis of the analysis in it.

32. "Targets, Instruments and Indicators of Monetary Policy."

LAWRENCE H. SUMMERS

The Nonadjustment
of Nominal Interest Rates:
A Study of the Fisher Effect

THE IMPACT of protracted inflation on the economic system was one of Arthur Okun's central concerns. He rejected the classical paradigm in which expected inflation was neutral and had only minor effects. Instead, he emphasized the many nonneutralities associated with expected inflation in a price tag economy. He stressed the very long lags necessary for the economy to adapt to expected inflation and the infeasibility, even in the very long run, of full adaptation. As one example of his skepticism about the predictions of classical models, he devoted several pages in *Prices and Quantities* to a discussion of his doubts about the Fisher proposition that nominal interest rates should adjust so that real interest rates are unaffected by inflation.[1]

This paper studies the long-run relationship between interest rates and inflation during the last 120 years of American experience. It concludes that there is little evidence that interest rates respond to inflation in the way the classical theories suggest. Rather, the relationship between interest rates and inflation was accurately characterized by Irving Fisher himself when he wrote:

The money rate and the real rate are normally identical; that is, they will . . . be the same when the purchasing power of the dollar in terms of the cost of living is constant or stable. When the cost of living is not stable, the rate of interest takes the appreciation and depreciation into account to some extent, but only slightly and, in general, indirectly. . . . That is . . . when prices are falling, the

I am indebted to George Fenn and Robert Barsky for extremely capable research assistance and many useful discussions.
1. Arthur M. Okun, *Prices and Quantities: A Macroeconomic Analysis* (Brookings Institution, 1981), pp. 208–17.

rate of interest tends to be low, but not so low as it should be to compensate for the fall.[2]

After considering a variety of possible explanations for the anomalous behavior of interest rates, I am forced to conclude with Fisher that

men are unable or unwilling to adjust at all accurately and promptly the many interest rates to changing prices levels. . . . The erratic behavior of real interest rates is evidently a trick played on the money market by money illusion. . . . The money rate of interest and still more the real rate are attacked more by the instability of money than by those more fundamental and more normal causes connected with income impatience and opportunity.[3]

It appears to be difficult to reconcile the data with standard economic models of fully informed and rational agents.

The first section of this paper examines the theoretical relationship between rates of interest and inflation in both the short and the long run. The analysis shows that almost any relationship is possible in the short run, depending on the sources of shocks to the economy. However, theory can make strong predictions about the long-run relationship. In the absence of tax effects, interest rates should rise by about one point for each one-point increase in the expected rate of inflation. The Tobin-Mundell effect, which is often used to explain the failure of interest rates to adjust fully for expected inflation, should, for plausible estimates of the relevant parameters, be of little empirical significance. The section also demonstrates that in the presence of a tax system anything like that prevailing in the postwar United States, the real pretax interest rate should rise significantly with inflation in the long run.

The second section examines historical data on the relationship between interest rates and inflation. Most previous empirical work in this area has focused on the correlation between short-term interest rates and various measures of expected inflation. The theory developed in the first section suggests that this emphasis is misplaced. The empirical analysis here focuses on the determinant of low-frequency movements in the interest rate. The use of band spectral regression techniques makes it possible to filter out the effects of transitory shocks and concentrate on long-run factors. The results suggest that before World War II inflation had only a negligible impact on interest rates. While there is evidence of a significant response of interest rates to inflation during the postwar

2. Irving Fisher, *The Theory of Interest* (Macmillan, 1930), p. 43.
3. Ibid., pp. 415, 451.

period, there is no evidence that they have risen by as much as theory would predict when marginal tax rates were high. Furthermore, almost all of the significant association between interest rates and inflation can be traced to 1965–71. Sample periods excluding this interval reveal that inflation had only a small effect on interest rates.

Various explanations have been put forward for the failure of interest rates to respond fully to inflation. Many of them stress correlations with business cycle fluctuations. The statistical procedures used in this paper that focus on low-frequency movements filter out the effects of these shocks. A remaining possibility is that low-frequency movements in the rate of inflation are associated with other factors that also affect real interest rates. The third section examines this possibility by looking at the effect of fluctuations in the real rate of return on capital and the level of economic risk in interest rates. Although both of these variables significantly affect interest rates, their inclusion does not alter the results concerning the effect of inflation.

The relationship between inflation and stock prices is examined in the fourth section. If inflation is systematically correlated with reductions in real interest rates, it should also be associated with declines in dividend yields and earnings price ratios. This prediction is not borne out during any interval. If anything, inflation is positively related to stock yields. Joint analysis of the postwar stock and bond markets suggests that the paradoxical response of the stock market to inflation is the mirror image of the puzzling behavior of the bond market. While bond prices have been anomalously high and stock prices surprisingly low, the market value of the corporate sector has shown a fairly consistent relation to the stream of total after-tax earnings. These results provide some support for the Modigliani-Cohn hypothesis that financial markets exhibit inflation illusion.

The final section discusses some implications of the inflation-illusion hypothesis. Existing work suggesting the prevalence of inflation illusion is discussed, and several reasons for the failure of market forces to overcome this illusion are examined. An interpretation of recent economic history in terms of changing degrees of inflation illusion is then offered. Current high interest rates may reflect the market's delayed recognition of the joint impact of inflation and taxation.

An appendix to the paper documents the failure of interest rates to fully incorporate inflation premiums, using more standard techniques for modeling inflationary expectations.

Interest Rates and Inflation in a General-Equilibrium Macroeconomic Model

A simple, general-equilibrium macroeconomic model can be used to study the relationship between inflation and interest rates across long-run steady states and the short-run relation between interest rates and inflation under Keynesian and classical assumptions. It incorporates a stylized but realistic depiction of the U.S. tax system, extending previous work on taxes and interest rates[4] by considering taxes in a dynamic general-equilibrium context.

The model considered here is close to that described by Sargent.[5] It has the form:

(1a) $$C = C[Y^D, r(1 - \theta) - \pi^e] + \epsilon_1$$

(1b) $$Y^D = Y - T$$

(1c) $$I = I(q)K, I(1) = 0$$

(1d) $$G = \bar{G}$$

(1e) $$Y = C + I + G$$

(1f) $$L[r(1 - \theta), y] = \frac{m}{p} + \epsilon_2$$

(1g) $$L_s = \bar{L}$$

(1h) $$L_D = F_L^{-1}\left(\frac{w}{p}\right)$$

(1i) $$\frac{\dot{w}}{w} = \alpha\left(\frac{L_D}{L_s} - 1\right) + \pi^e$$

(1k) $$Y = F(K, L)(1 + \epsilon_3)$$

---

4. Martin Feldstein, "Inflation, Income Taxes, and the Rate of Interest: A Theoretical Analysis," *American Economic Review*, vol. 66 (December 1976), pp. 809–20; Martin Feldstein and Lawrence Summers, "Inflation, Tax Rules, and the Long-Term Interest Rate," *Brookings Papers on Economic Activity, 1:1978*, pp. 61–99; and Michael R. Darby, "The Financial and Tax Effects of Monetary Policy on Interest Rates," *Economic Inquiry*, vol. 13 (June 1975), pp. 266–76.

5. Thomas J. Sargent, *Macroeconomic Theory* (Academic Press, 1979).

(1l) $$q = \frac{F_K(1 - \tau) - \lambda\pi^e}{r(1 - \theta) - \pi^e + \beta}$$

(1m) $$\pi^e = \lambda(\pi - \pi^e).$$

Equation 1a is a standard life-cycle consumption function where consumption depends on disposable income and the real after-tax rate of return. For simplicity, real balance effects are neglected. Disposable income is defined as gross national product less taxes, where it is implicitly assumed that labor taxes, which are lump sum since labor supply is inelastic, are adjusted to offset any endogenous changes in revenues from levies on capital income.

The investment equation 1c relates the level of investment to the divergence between the after-tax marginal product of capital and the after-tax interest rate, as reflected in Tobin's q. Equivalently, investment can be thought of as depending on the ratio of the market value of the capital stock to its replacement costs. This theory, developed by Tobin in 1969, can be rigorously justified in the context of a model with adjustment costs, as shown by Abel and Hayashi.[6] The role of taxes is discussed in detail in Summers.[7]

The value of q, the market price of existing capital goods, depends on the expected present value of their stream of profits. In this paper it is assumed that investors have static expectations about the marginal product of capital, F_K, interest rates, and tax parameters. The more appealing rational expectations assumption is examined in Summers.[8] With static expectations, q is given by equation 1l. The term β reflects the risk premium required to induce investors to hold equity claims. The tax system is summarized by three parameters; τ, θ, and λ. The parameter τ represents the effective tax rate on real capital income arising from the combination of corporate, dividend, and capital gains taxes. The tax rate

6. James Tobin, "A General Equilibrium Approach to Monetary Theory," *Journal of Money, Credit and Banking*, vol. 1 (February 1969), pp. 15–29; Andrew B. Abel, "Empirical Investment Equations: An Integrative Framework," in Karl Brunner and Allan H. Meltzer, eds., *On the State of Macro-Economics*, Carnegie-Rochester Conference Series on Public Policy, vol. 12 (North-Holland, 1980), pp. 39–91; and Fumio Hayashi, "Tobin's Marginal q and Average q: A Neoclassical Interpretation," *Econometrica*, vol. 50 (January 1982), pp. 213–24.

7. Lawrence H. Summers, "Taxation and Corporate Investment: A q-Theory Approach," *Brookings Papers on Economic Activity, 1:1981*, pp. 67–127.

8. Ibid.; and Lawrence H. Summers, "Inflation and the Valuation of Corporate Equities," forthcoming.

on interest income is given by θ, and the effect of inflation on the tax system by λ, which represents the effects of historic cost discrepancies, first-in first-out (FIFO) inventory accounting, and the taxation of nominal capital gains.[9]

The remainder of the model is standard. Equation 1e provides the income expenditure identity. A normal LM curve is specified in 1f. The workings of the labor market are generated by an inelastic supply of labor (equation 1g), a neoclassical labor-demand curve holding that the real wage is equated to labor's marginal product (equation 1h), and a natural rate Phillips curve (equation 1i). The terms ϵ_2 and ϵ_3 reflect, respectively, shocks to liquidity preference and aggregate supply. Equation 1m holds that expectations about future inflation are formed adaptively.

The evolution of the economy described by equations 1a to 1m will depend on the paths of the exogenous forcing variables g and m, along with the shocks ϵ_1, ϵ_2, and ϵ_3. At any time, the money and capital stocks, along with the price level and inflationary expectation, are predetermined. The equilibrium level of output and the interest rate can then be determined from equations 1a, 1c, 1e, and 1l along the lines of familiar IS-LM analysis.

The relationship between movements in inflation and interest rates will depend on the nature of the causal shocks. It is clear from equations 1i and 1m that the only shocks that can change the level of inflation or expected inflation will be those that also affect the level of output. Such shocks will affect interest rates as well, except in the case of unlikely coincidence. Both variables are endogenous, being jointly determined by G, m, and the random shocks ϵ_1, ϵ_2, and ϵ_3. The correlation between them will depend on the sources of the shocks.

Consider first an aggregate demand shock as represented by an increase in ϵ_1 or G. The IS curve shifts right, raising interest rates and output. This leads to increasing prices and rising inflationary expectations. The resulting reduction in real money balances raises interest rates still further. This continues until output is restored to its equilibrium level. However, at this point the system is not in equilibrium because inflationary expectations are positive. Hence it overshoots, and output,

---

9. These interactions of inflation and taxes are discussed in detail in Martin Feldstein and Lawrence Summers, "Inflation and the Taxation of Capital Income in the Corporate Sector," *National Tax Journal,* vol. 32 (December 1979), pp. 445–70; and Summers, "Taxation and Corporate Investment."

interest rates, and the rate of inflation all fall. The system oscillates toward an ultimate equilibrium with no inflation, a higher price level and interest rate, and a reduced capital stock. Note that during this adjustment process there is no reason to assume that real short-term interest rates as measured on either an ex ante or an ex post basis should remain constant.

An even more dramatic example is provided by a liquidity preference shock caused by an increase in either m or ϵ_2. Initially the LM curve moves right, and nominal interest rates fall as prices start to rise. Subsequently, as prices rise reducing real money balances, the rate of inflation declines and the interest rate rises. Ultimately equilibrium is reestablished at the initial interest rate and output level, with higher prices. Again, the path involves oscillations. Note that an observer following the response of the economy to such a shock would observe a negative Fisher effect as interest rates and inflation moved inversely.

These examples could be discussed in more detail and multiplied but they are sufficient to make my point. In any reasonable short-run macroeconomic model, the rate of inflation and the short-run interest rate are determined simultaneously. The correlations between these variables will depend on the paths of the variables forcing the system. As a first approximation, demand shocks will tend to lead to a positive relation between interest rates and inflation while liquidity shocks lead to negative covariation. This suggests that there is little reason to expect any stable relation between short-term movements in interest rates and inflation. The tendency, documented below, of the association to be weak suggests the relative importance of liquidity shocks.

The preceding discussion suggests that any sort of analysis of the movements of inflation and short-term interest rates is not likely to be fruitful since both variables are endogenous. However, the model yields more explicit long-run predictions. In any long-run steady state inflation will always equal its expected value, and the capital stock will also remain constant so that the model reduces to

(2a) $C[F(K, L) - T, qK, r(1 - \theta) - \pi] + \bar{G} = F(K, L);$

(2b) $F'(K, L)(1 - \tau) - \lambda\pi = (1 - \theta)r - \pi + \beta;$

(2c) $$\pi = \frac{\dot{m}}{m}.$$

Equations 2a and 2b determine the steady state capital stock and interest rate. Differentiating yields expressions for the long-run effect of a change in the rate of expected inflation:

(3a) $$\frac{dr}{d\pi} = \frac{(1 - \lambda)(C_y F_K + C_w - F_K) - F''(K)(1 - \tau)C_r}{(1 - \theta)(C_y F_K + C_w - F_K) - F''(K)(1 - \tau)C_r}$$

and

(3b) $$\frac{dK}{d\pi} = \frac{(\theta - \lambda)C_r}{(1 - \theta)(C_y F_K + C_w - F_K) - F''(K)(1 - \tau)C_r}.$$

Consider the special case where consumption is interest inelastic so $C_r = 0$. In this case equation 3b implies that inflation has no effect on steady state capital intensity, so that 3a reduces to

(4) $$\frac{dr}{d\pi} = \frac{(1 - \lambda)}{(1 - \theta)}.$$

This condition is easily interpreted.[10] If the only nonneutrality in the tax system were the taxation of nominal interest rates, the rate of interest would rise by $1/(1 - \theta)$ for each point of inflation so as to keep the real after-tax rate of interest constant. However, inflation also increases the taxation of equity income, which drives down the required real interest rate. This accounts for the $(1 - \lambda)$ term in the numerator of equation 4. Whether increases in inflation raise or reduce the pretax real interest rate depends on the relative size of θ and λ, measures of the extra taxes imposed on debt and equity income.

It is useful to consider briefly plausible magnitudes for these parameters. The value of θ can be inferred in either of two ways. Feldstein and Summers present an explicit calculation of the average marginal tax rate faced by the holders of interest-bearing corporate assets, concluding that it is about 40 percent.[11] The somewhat lower tax rate of individuals is offset by the high rates imposed on life insurance companies and other intermediaries. The alternative method is to compare the yield on interest-bearing taxable and nontaxable assets. Long-term municipal

10. Note that this result is fundamentally different from that of Martin Feldstein, Jerry Green, and Eytan Sheshinski, "Inflation and Taxes in a Growing Economy with Debt and Equity Finance," *Journal of Political Economy*, vol. 86 (April 1978), pt. 2, pp. S53–S70. The crucial tax rate here is the marginal personal tax rate on interest income rather than the corporate rate. The difference arises because of the general-equilibrium character of the model.

11. "Inflation and the Taxation of Capital Income."

bond yields appear to be about one-third less than those of otherwise comparable corporate issues. Gordon and Malkiel arrive at a somewhat smaller estimate of the tax rate on the basis of a comparison of otherwise identical taxable and tax-free corporate bonds.[12] On balance, it seems reasonable to assume that $\theta \cong 0.33$.

The value of λ, which reflects the extra tax imposed on equity income as a result of inflation, is more difficult to estimate.[13] Its four components—attributable to historical cost depreciation, FIFO inventory accounting, taxation of nominal capital gains, and an offset of the deductibility of nominal interest at the corporate level—can be estimated from the data in Feldstein and Summers.[14] According to the figures presented there, extra taxes resulting from historic cost depreciation and inventory accounting totaled $26.1 billion in 1979; taxes on nominal capital gains were placed at $5.3 billion, and the deductibility of nominal interest reduced taxes by $15.1 billion. Assuming a 6 percent rate of inflation and a 1977 capital stock of $1,684.4 billion, this implies a value for λ of 0.14.

These parameter values imply that, if savings are interest inelastic, $dr/d\pi^e = 1.3$, significantly in excess of one. If savings are interest elastic, even this figure will understate the impact of inflation on interest rates. The real after-tax return to savings will decline, reducing the capital stock, raising the marginal product of capital, leading to further increases in real interest rates. In the limiting case where savings are infinitely elastic with respect to the real after-tax interest rate, $(dr/d\pi^e) = 1/(1 - \theta) = 1.5$. This case corresponds to the frequently assumed "infinite horizon" model of consumption decisions. Summers argues that realistically formulated life-cycle models also imply a very substantial interest elasticity of savings.[15]

The theoretically predicted value of $dr/d\pi^e$ is surprisingly insensitive

12. Roger H. Gordon and Burton G. Malkiel, "Corporation Finance," in Henry J. Aaron and Joseph A. Pechman, eds., *How Taxes Affect Economic Behavior* (Brookings Institution, 1981), pp. 131–92.

13. Note that the variable λ here includes the effect of inflation on corporate interest deductions for tax purposes. It is therefore conceptually different from the concept employed in Martin Feldstein, "Inflation, Tax Rules and the Stock Market," *Journal of Monetary Economics,* vol. 6 (July 1980), pp. 309–31. In his notation $\lambda + \tau\sigma\pi$ corresponds to my λ.

14. Feldstein and Summers, "Inflation and the Taxation of Capital Income."

15. Lawrence H. Summers, "Capital Taxation and Accumulation in a Life Cycle Growth Model," *American Economic Review,* vol. 71 (September 1981), pp. 533–44.

to the assumed interest sensitivity of savings. In terms of the loanable funds model of Feldstein and Summers,[16] this is because the supply and demand curves for funds are shifted upward by approximately equal amounts.[17]

Several features of this analysis require discussion. The formulation adopted here implies that there is no Tobin-Mundell effect. In the absence of taxes, inflation has no effect on the level of capital accumulation. This is because the consumption function does not include either real money balances or government transfers of money as an argument. This omission is of no empirical significance. Outside money holdings in the United States represent less than 2 percent of the value of the capital stock. Even if inflation increased enough to eliminate all money holding, and wealth holding was unchanged, so that the capital stock increased by an equal amount, the real interest rate would fall by only 6 basis points.

The model presented here ignores government indebtedness. This may be justified in several ways. Barro shows that if agents have operative bequest motives, government bonds will not be net worth.[18] In a 1981 article, I show that as long as there are any families that meet this condition Barro's result will continue to hold in the long run.[19] Alternatively, even if bonds are treated as net worth, the results here will continue to hold as long as they are perfect substitutes for private debt. In the special and unlikely case where bonds and outside money are perfect substitutes, their yields will differ by a fixed premium independent of the rate of inflation. This case does not seem to be very realistic. Even if the bonds and money are close but not perfect substitutes, the results here will remain valid. Note that the analytical results continue to hold even as L_r approaches negative infinity.

It is important to clarify the reason the model cannot be manipulated to yield predictions about the short-run relationship between interest rates and inflation but does have implications for the long-run relation. The model implies that in the long run the level of inflation is determined only by the rate of money growth. This is an implication of virtually all macroeconomic models. Unless the long-run rate of money growth is

16. Feldstein and Summers, "Inflation, Tax Rules, and the Long-Term Interest Rate."

17. The analysis here reaches a different conclusion from the earlier one, because it recognizes the effects of the interactions of inflation and taxation on the supply as well as the demand for loanable funds.

18. Robert J. Barro, "Are Government Bonds Net Worth?" *Journal of Political Economy*, vol. 82 (November–December 1974), pp. 1095–1117.

19. "Capital Taxation and Accumulation."

determined by the same real factors that affect output and the interest rate, inflation is in effect determined exogenously in the long run.

There does not seem to be an obvious reason for expecting a correlation between the rate of money growth and any real factors. Equation 2b implies that any systematic factor would have to involve effects either on the real marginal product of capital or on the risk premium. Both these possibilities are considered in the empirical work reported below.

Long-Term Interest Rates and Inflation

At the outset some simple averages of inflation and interest rates over a long period can be usefully examined. Table 1 records averages of the rates of inflation by decades, along with nominal and real interest rates. No clear relationship between inflation and nominal interest rates emerges. In three of the twelve decades considered, the real interest rate was actually negative. These decades were the periods with the most rapid rates of inflation. Conversely, the real interest rate is highest in the deflationary decades. The lack of a relationship is confirmed by the regression using data for the twelve decades shown at the bottom of the table. Over the long term less than one-eighth of the changes in the rate of inflation are incorporated into interest rates. Changes in the ten-year-average rates of inflation explain none of the variance in observed interest rates. A similar conclusion emerges when a test suggested by Fisher is used. The variance of the real return far exceeds that of the nominal return. If nominal rates incorporated expected inflation, they should vary, while real rates should remain fairly constant.

Breaking up the passage of time into decades may be objected to as arbitrary. Furthermore, the results may be distorted by aberrant wartime experiences. Table 2 displays average rates of inflation and interest rates over the course of business cycles, as defined by the National Bureau of Economic Research. Wartime cycles are omitted; averages are taken from trough to trough. Very similar results emerge when the averages are calculated on a peak-to-peak basis. Once again no strong relation between inflation and nominal interest rates emerges. The regression, using cyclical units as observations, suggests that interest rates fall by 11 basis points with each 1-point increase in the rate of inflation.

These results cannot be attributed to the effects of the zero floor on nominal interest rates in conjunction with deflation. If all the years in

Table 1. *Trends in Inflation and Interest Rates, by Decade, 1860–1979*[a]
Percent

Period	Average yield on commercial paper[b]	Average inflation rate[c]	Average real interest rate
1860–69	7.1	5.5	1.5
1870–79	6.5	−3.4	9.8
1880–89	5.1	−2.1	7.2
1890–99	4.6	0.3	4.2
1900–09	4.8	2.5	2.3
1910–19	7.7	8.3	−3.6
1920–29	5.1	−0.9	6.0
1930–39	1.5	−2.0	3.6
1940–49	0.9	5.5	−4.6
1950–59	2.6	2.2	0.4
1960–69	4.6	2.5	2.1
1970–79	7.2	7.4	−0.2

Regression of twelve ten-year averages
$R_t = 4.43 + 0.05\pi_t$
$\quad\ \ (0.69)\ \ (0.16)$
$\bar{R}^2 = -0.09$

Sources: Frederick MacCauley, *Some Theoretical Problems Suggested by the Movements of Interest Rates, Bond Yields and Stock Prices in the United States Since 1856* (National Bureau of Economic Research, 1938); and Bureau of Labor Statistics.

a. Computed as arithmetic averages of monthly data.

b. For the period 1860 through 1918, the data correspond to the two- to three-month rate in MacCauley. From 1919 to 1979, I used the four- to six-month commercial paper rates from the Federal Reserve.

c. For 1860 to 1918, the figures are derived from the Warren-Pearson wholesale price index. For 1919 to 1979, I used the nonseasonally adjusted consumer price index.

which prices fell are removed from the sample and cyclical averages are taken using the remaining data, very similar results emerge.

The traditional approach to the study of the relationship between interest rates and inflation involves estimation of equations of the form

(5) $$R_t = \beta_0 + \beta_1\pi_t^e + u_t,$$

where the principal empirical difficulty is the measurement of π^e. Investigators have employed a wide variety of proxies for π^e, based on autoregressive expectations, survey evidence, and rational expectations. The analysis in the preceding section suggests that the estimation of equation 5 may not be meaningful even if inflationary expectations could be properly measured. The crucial issue is the error term u_t in equation 5. Since expected inflation responds to the same underlying

Table 2. *Cyclical Averages of Inflation and Interest Rates, 1867–1975*[a]

Period (year and month)	Average yield on commercial paper	Average rate of inflation	Average real interest rate
1867:12–1870:11	8.02	− 5.52	13.54
1870:12–1879:2	6.51	− 4.53	11.04
1879:3–1885:4	5.31	− 0.00	5.32
1885:5–1888:3	4.93	0.11	4.82
1888:4–1891:4	5.13	− 0.64	5.77
1891:5–1894:5	5.12	− 6.34	11.46
1894:6–1897:5	4.19	− 1.33	5.51
1897:6–1900:11	4.02	6.28	− 2.26
1900:12–1904:7	4.77	1.49	3.28
1904:8–1908:5	5.29	1.90	3.39
1908:6–1911:12	4.25	1.32	2.93
1912:1–1914:11	5.05	1.51	3.54
1919:3–1921:6	6.72	3.98	2.75
1921:7–1924:6	4.94	− 1.13	6.07
1924:7–1927:10	4.04	0.61	3.42
1927:11–1933:2	3.84	− 5.69	9.53
1933:3–1938:5	1.02	2.04	− 1.02
1945:10–1949:9	1.15	7.30	− 6.15
1949:10–1954:4	2.06	2.58	− 0.52
1954:5–1958:3	2.79	1.89	0.90
1958:4–1961:1	3.46	1.17	2.29
1961:2–1970:10	5.01	2.91	2.10
1970:11–1975:2	6.89	6.83	0.06

Regression
$R_t = 4.66 - 0.15\pi_t$
$\quad\;\; (0.35)\quad (0.08)$
$\bar{R}^2 = -0.07$

a. Computed as arithmetic averages of monthly data. Each period represents a National Bureau of Economic Research cycle measured from trough to trough.

economic forces that affect short-term interest rates, there is every reason to suppose that u_t is correlated with π_t^e. The simultaneity in 5 cannot be avoided by the mechanical application of instrumental variables. Any variable that is correlated with inflationary expectations will also be correlated with real activity and therefore with interest rates. The problem with equation 5 is logical rather than statistical. One cannot usefully ask about the causal influence of one simultaneous determined variable on another.

In light of these considerations, it may not be surprising that equations like 5 yield results that do not appear to bear out the Fisher relationship. Nor is it surprising that the results are highly unstable through time. The estimated parameter β_1 does not bear any consistent relationship to the taste and technological parameters, which are usually assumed to be stable through time.

Some recent work on the Fisher effect has avoided specifications like equation 5. Fama estimates equations of the form in monthly data, using the one-month Treasury bill rate:[20]

$$(6) \qquad \pi_{t+1} = \alpha_0 + \alpha_1 r_t + u_t.$$

He shows that if one is willing to accept the assumption that the required expected real interest rate ρ is constant, then rational expectations implies that $\alpha_0 = -\rho$ and $\alpha_1 = 1$. He finds evidence consistent with these assumptions for the 1954–71 period. In the appendix to this paper, I show that his results are an artifact of his choice of sample period. This should not be surprising. It is well known that output fluctuates. In any model like the one presented in the first section of this paper, it is impossible to generate serially correlated fluctuations in output without also generating serially correlated movements in the ex ante real rate of interest, except by assuming arbitrary and unlikely correlations between the shocks. The success of Fama's tests for the 1954–71 period is probably closely related to the unprecedentedly minor business cycle fluctuations during this interval.

More recent work by Fama and Gibbons has applied the random coefficients technique to equation 6 and allowed α_0 to evolve according to a random walk.[21] This procedure, which amounts to imposing a particular serial correlation structure on the residuals u_t, does not avoid the logical problems just discussed. The procedure imposes the highly implausible restriction that variations in u_t and α_0 are uncorrelated. In fact, the same shocks that lead to changes in inflation also affect interest rates.

Yet another approach to studying the relationship between inflation and interest rates is suggested by the work of Mishkin, who studies the relationship between lagged inflation and the real ex post return on

20. Eugene F. Fama, "Short-Term Interest Rates as Predictors of Inflation," *American Economic Review*, vol. 65 (June 1975), pp. 269–82.

21. Eugene F. Fama and Michael R. Gibbons, "Inflation, Real Returns and Capital Investment," working paper (University of Chicago, Graduate School of Business, 1980).

Treasury bills. He is careful, however, to stress that no causal interpretation can be placed on his results.[22]

The analysis in the preceding section suggested that, while the short-run relationship between inflation and interest rates was arbitrary, theory yielded quite precise predictions about the relationship between interest rates and inflation across different steady states. Essentially this difference occurs because the model implies that steady state inflation is determined only by the rate of money growth. The model, like most well-specified macroeconomic models, exhibits approximate superneutrality in the absence of taxes. Hence real interest rates should be unaffected by changes in the rate of inflation. This suggests that, if each observation represented a steady state corresponding to some level of money growth, equation 5 should hold, with $\beta \cong 1$ in the absence of taxes. Of course, in time series data on a single country, observations corresponding to steady states under different monetary regimes cannot be isolated. However, statistical techniques are available that filter out the high-frequency movements in the variables. The band spectral regression procedure developed in Engle allows the user to estimate regression coefficients at different frequencies.[23] The hypothesis implied by the preceding discussion is that the long-run (low-frequency) relationship between interest rates and inflation is stronger than the high-frequency relationships that dominate movements over the course of the business cycle. Robert Lucas makes a similar argument to justify the testing of the quantity theory using filtered data.[24]

The central advantage of using band spectral techniques to study the relation between interest rates and inflation is that it makes it possible to filter out the high-frequency variance in the variables that is not explicable in terms of the underlying theory. Just as it is common to exclude some periods (such as wars and strikes) because one's theory is not expected to hold, it is reasonable to exclude frequencies to which the underlying theory is inapplicable. There are several other advantages as well. Because the variance in the right-hand-side variables in equation 5 comes only from low-frequency movements, the problem of modeling

22. Frederic S. Mishkin, "The Real Interest Rate: An Empirical Investigation," NBER Working Paper 622 (National Bureau of Economic Research, 1981).

23. Robert F. Engle, "Band Spectrum Regression," *International Economic Review*, vol. 15 (February 1974), pp. 1–11.

24. Robert E. Lucas, Jr., "Two Illustrations of the Quantity Theory of Money," *American Economic Review*, vol. 70 (December 1980), pp. 1005–14.

inflationary expectations vanishes. Low-frequency variations in the rate of inflation are almost completely forecastable, so the assumption that expected inflation can be proxied by actual inflation is warranted. Indeed, when the equations reported below were reestimated with various proxies for expected inflation, the results were not significantly affected. A further virtue of the band spectral technique is that the results are insensitive to problems of data alignment and errors in variables. The former problem leads Fama to despair of being able to test the Fisher effect using pre–World War II data.[25]

This discussion has so far been somewhat vague about the choice of interest rates. The argument that any high-frequency relation between interest rates and inflation is possible is best understood in terms of the short rate. The long rate, which reflects expected short rates over a long period, should be largely free of high-frequency fluctuations. It therefore seems surprising that more of the empirical work on interest rates and inflation has not used long rates. Probably the reason is the difficulty of measuring long-term inflationary expectations. At low frequencies one would expect long and short rates to exhibit similar movements. Both are exhibited in the empirical work represented below.

The 1860–1940 Period

Most discussions of prewar interest rates and inflation focus on the Gibson paradox, which is the observation that for this period in both the United States and Britain there appears to be a strong positive correlation between the *price level* and interest rates. Such a relationship is inconsistent with monetary theory, which holds that the units in which money is measured should have no real effect.

One potential resolution of the Gibson paradox is the Fisher effect discussed in this paper. If, as Fisher argues, inflation expectations are formed with very long lags, there will be a strong positive correlation between the price level and the expected rate of inflation. To see this, observe that

(7) $$P_t = \sum_{i=0}^{\infty} (p_{t-i} - p_{t-1-i}),$$

where p_t is the log of the price level. Equivalently,

(8) $$P_t = \sum_{i=0}^{\infty} \pi_{t-i}.$$

25. Fama, "Short-Term Interest Rates."

It follows immediately that the price level will be highly correlated with any long-term average of past rates of inflation.

This explanation of the Gibson paradox has been considered by several investigators.[26] These authors have tended to reject the Fisher explanation because the lag lengths required are regarded as implausible. Other explanations have been sought in terms of the Keynes-Wicksell effect and distributional effects. However, the logically separate question of the relationship, or lack thereof, between interest rates and inflation during this period has received much less attention. The relationship is of particular interest for this early period because the economy was relatively free of institutional interference. Taxes were negligible, countercyclical stabilization policy had not yet been attempted, and there were fewer interventions in wage and price flexibility. The conditions of classical macro models were much closer to being satisfied than they are today.

Before examining the data, it is instructive to review the results presented by Fisher.[27] He began by examining the contemporaneous correlation between inflation and nominal interest rates. He found that it was negligible but that it could be improved substantially by taking a long-run weighted average of past rates of inflation. Fisher, however, reported only on the correlation coefficient between his measure of expected inflation and the interest rate. He made no effort to estimate $dr/d\pi^e$. Replication of Fisher's work using his data and his procedure for estimating inflation expectations (essentially a first-degree Almon lag with an endpoint constraint at zero at twenty years) yields estimates of $dr/d\pi^e$ that range from 0.03 for short-term interest rates to 0.18 for long-term rates. Thus in no sense can his results be said to demonstrate the empirical validity of the theory that bears his name. As the quotations at the beginning of this paper attest, Fisher did not overstate his conclusions. It is later authors who have exaggerated the power of his evidence.

In tables 3 and 4 the relationship between inflation and short- and

26. Thomas J. Sargent, "Interest Rates and Prices in the Long Run: A Study of the Gibson Paradox," *Journal of Money, Credit and Banking*, vol. 5 (February 1973), pt. 2, pp. 385–449; Robert J. Shiller and Jeremy J. Siegel, "The Gibson Paradox and Historical Movements in Real Interest Rates," *Journal of Political Economy*, vol. 85 (October 1977), pp. 891–907; and Milton Friedman and Anna J. Schwartz, "Monetary Trends in the United States and the United Kingdom: Their Relation to Income, Prices, and Interest Rates, 1867–1975" (National Bureau of Economic Research, 1980).

27. Fisher, *The Theory of Interest*.

Table 3. *Commercial Paper Yield and Inflation, Selected Periods,*
1860–1939[a]

Interval	Length of cycle	Constant	Slope coef- ficient[b]	$\bar{R}^2$
1860–1939	Ordinary least squares	4.92	0.00 (0.00)	0.00
	Over 1 year	4.92	0.00 (0.01)	0.00
	Over 3 years	4.90	0.01 (0.02)	0.00
	Over 5 years	4.88	0.01 (0.03)	0.01
	Over 10 years	4.83	0.03 (0.05)	0.02
	Over 20 years	4.49	0.12 (0.10)	0.23
1870–1900	Ordinary least squares	5.36	−0.00 (0.00)	0.00
	Over 1 year	5.37	−0.02 (0.02)	0.01
	Over 3 years	5.31	−0.03 (0.05)	0.02
	Over 5 years	5.37	−0.03 (0.07)	0.02
	Over 10 years	5.41	−0.25 (0.15)	0.33
1900–39 (excluding 1914–18)	Ordinary least squares	3.97	0.00 (0.01)	0.00
	Over 1 year	3.98	−0.00 (0.03)	0.00
	Over 3 years	3.94	0.05 (0.08)	0.02
	Over 5 years	3.91	0.08 (0.14)	0.03
	Over 10 years	3.90	0.11 (0.30)	0.03
	Over 20 years	3.72	0.34 (0.57)	0.22

a. Regression results were obtained using the band spectral procedure in the Troll computer program. Data are described in the text.
b. Standard errors are shown in parentheses below the coefficients.

Table 4. *Long-Term Bond Yields and Inflation, Selected Periods, 1860–1939*[a]

Interval	Length of cycle	Constant	Slope coef-ficient[b]	$\bar{R}^2$
1860–1939	Ordinary least squares	4.48	−0.00 (0.00)	0.00
	Over 1 year	4.48	−0.00 (0.00)	0.00
	Over 3 years	4.49	−0.00 (0.01)	0.00
	Over 5 years	4.48	−0.00 (0.02)	0.00
	Over 10 years	4.43	0.01 (0.03)	0.01
	Over 20 years	4.31	0.05 (0.06)	0.09
1870–1900	Ordinary least squares	4.35	−0.00 (0.00)	0.01
	Over 1 year	4.36	−0.02 (0.01)	0.03
	Over 3 years	4.37	−0.05 (0.04)	0.09
	Over 5 years	4.37	−0.06 (0.06)	0.10
	Over 10 years	4.39	−0.19 (0.14)	0.33
1900–39 (excluding 1914–18)	Ordinary least squares	4.16	−0.01 (0.00)	0.01
	Over 1 year	4.17	−0.02 (0.01)	0.03
	Over 3 years	4.19	−0.04 (0.03)	0.06
	Over 5 years	4.23	−0.09 (0.06)	0.17
	Over 10 years	4.30	−0.19 (0.12)	0.36
	Over 20 years	4.28	−0.17 (0.25)	0.26

a. Regression results were obtained using the band spectral procedure in the Troll computer program. Data are described in the text.
b. Standard errors are shown in parentheses below the coefficients.

long-term interest rates at various frequencies is examined for the entire 1860–1940 period and for various subperiods. Data on the rate of inflation for 1860–1918 are based on the Warren-Pearson wholesale price index, the only price index available that goes back this far on a monthly basis. For the more recent part of the period, 1919–40, the consumer price index is used to estimate the rate of inflation. Data on short-term interest rates are the rates on commercial paper reported in MacCauley[28] for 1860–1918, and the Federal Reserve series for 1918–39. Long-term yields come from MacCauley's series on railroad bonds for 1860–1918 and the Federal Reserve series for 1918–39. The results were all obtained with monthly data. Only negligible changes were observed when the equations were reestimated using quarterly or annual data.

In estimating the equations movements above various frequencies are filtered out. As Engle shows, if the data interval is of length p, ordinary least squares estimates reflect the variance at all cycle lengths greater than $2p$.[29] Here the OLS estimates are reported along with the results for cycle lengths greater than one, three, five, ten, and twenty years. The frequency of business cycles is about five years, so the results should provide a good reflection of the long-run effects discussed in the preceding section.

No strong association between inflation and interest rates emerges at any frequency. While there is some tendency for the coefficient on inflation to increase as the cycle length rises, the differences are not statistically significant. For the entire 1860–1939 period, the highest estimate of the effect of inflation is in the low-frequency commercial paper equations where the estimated coefficient is only 0.12. For the 1870–1900 period, the relationship is actually negative for both the commercial paper rate and the long-term bond rate. In all the equations, the $\bar{R}^2$ is low, indicating that low-frequency movements in inflation explain only a small part of variations in interest rates.

In tests not reported here, a variety of other sample periods were chosen. While the results changed somewhat depending on the inclusion of World War I, there was no evidence in any of the equations of a strong Fisher effect. As a further check, some of the equations were reestimated using long, distributed lags on inflation. It is sometimes argued that the

28. Frederick MacCauley, *Some Theoretical Problems Suggested by the Movements of Interest Rates, Bond Yields and Stock Prices in the United States Since 1856* (National Bureau of Economic Research, 1938).

29. Engle, "Band Spectrum Regression."

failure of interest rates to adjust for inflation reflects the effects of deflation in conjunction with the zero floor on nominal interest rates. Dropping all years in which prices fell from the sample raised standard errors but had essentially no impact on the estimated coefficients. This had only a negligible effect on the results. The failure of interest to adjust to changes in inflationary expectations is confirmed in the appendix, with the use of more standard techniques.

It is frequently argued that the failure of interest rates to adjust and incorporate inflation premiums from 1860 to 1940 is the consequence of the different monetary standard that prevailed during that period. The argument, as expressed, for example, by Gordon,[30] is that under the gold standard a stable level of prices, rather than of inflation, was anticipated. Hence, the argument continues, inflation led, if anything, to expectations of future deflation. This argument provides a rationalization for the failure of regressions of interest rates on distributed lags of past inflation to yield estimates that imply significant Fisher effects. It does not apply to the results reported here that consider low-frequency movements in the rate of inflation. Such movements were an important feature of the period. Ten-year averages of the rate of inflation varied between 5.5 percent during the 1860s and -2 percent during the 1880s. Far larger variations existed at cyclical frequencies. These fluctuations are usually traced to monetary forces, arising indirectly from the gold standard, and they represent exactly the sort of exogenous disturbance that should give rise to the Fisher effect.

There are two subsidiary difficulties with the monetary standard explanation of the failure of the Fisher effect. The argument implies a negative correlation between the expected rate of inflation and the price level. Yet the Gibson paradox is the observation that the price level and interest are positively associated. The monetary standard explanation also fails to take account of agents' changing perceptions of the trend growth rate of prices. As Barsky and Summers argue, a rational observer's inflation forecast would in fact have varied as much or more in the gold standard era as in recent times.[31] It is difficult to understand why these variations were not reflected in movements in interest rates.

There are of course a number of problems with the data used here.

30. Robert J. Gordon, in *Journal of Money, Credit and Banking*, vol. 5 (February 1973), pt. 2, pp. 460–63.

31. Robert Barsky and Lawrence H. Summers, ''The Gold Standard and the Gibson Paradox'' (in preparation).

The interest rates may include default premiums and the inflation rate is unlikely to be measured accurately. However, these factors are probably unimportant in low-frequency movements. The strong evidence against the Fisher proposition presented here for the prewar period is particularly striking because of the laissez-faire character of the economy. Nominal rigidities caused by deposit ceilings, wage contracts, pension arrangements, or long-term wage contracts were virtually nonexistent. Taxes also were negligible. This suggests that the failure of interest rates to fully incorporate inflation premiums reflects something more fundamental than the effect of institutional nonneutralities.

The Postwar Period

The analysis in the first section of this paper suggests that it is reasonable to expect that $dr/d\pi^e \cong 1.3$ in the postwar period. Estimates of this parameter for various intervals after World War II, using both short- and long-term interest rates, are reported in tables 5 and 6. The short-term interest rate is the Treasury bill yield as reported by Ibbotsen and Sinquefield,[32] and the long-term interest rate is measured by the government bond yield. Inflation is measured by the CPI. Variation in the choice of interest rate and inflation measures had only a negligible effect on the results.

The results for both short- and long-term rates are broadly consistent. There is no evidence that interest rates have risen more than the rate of inflation. In almost every case the data reject quite decisively the hypothesis that $(dr/d\pi) = 1$. It appears that almost all the power in the Fisher relationship comes from the acceleration of inflation during the 1960s. When the equation is estimated for the 1970s or for the period before 1965 (not shown), a very weak relationship between interest rates and inflation emerges. Eliminating the controls period has little effect on the results.

It is noteworthy that the estimated impact of inflation on interest rates increases as the length of the cycle increases. For example, the coefficient on inflation in the long-term interest rate regressions rises from 0.24 to 0.73 for 1948–79. The hypothesis that the relation between interest rates and inflation is the same at all frequencies is decisively rejected by the

32. Roger G. Ibbotson and Rex A. Sinquefield, "Stocks, Bonds, Bills, and Inflation: Year-by-Year Historical Returns (1926–1974)," *Journal of Business,* vol. 49 (January 1976), pp. 11–47.

Table 5. *Inflation and Treasury Bill Yields, Selected Periods, 1948–80*[a]

Interval	Length of cycle	Constant	Coefficient of Π[b]	$\bar{R}^2$
1948–79	Ordinary least squares	2.71	0.29 (0.02)	0.34
	Over 1 year	2.01	0.47 (0.05)	0.57
	Over 3 years	1.62	0.57 (0.08)	0.71
	Over 5 years	1.46	0.62 (0.11)	0.75
	Over 10 years	1.22	0.68 (0.17)	0.80
	Over 20 years	1.22	0.68 (0.33)	0.90
1954–79	Ordinary least squares	2.70	0.41 (0.02)	0.55
	Over 1 year	2.00	0.57 (0.04)	0.82
	Over 3 years	1.88	0.60 (0.05)	0.89
	Over 5 years	1.92	0.59 (0.07)	0.89
	Over 10 years	1.90	0.60 (0.12)	0.89
1970–80	Ordinary least squares	3.71	0.38 (0.04)	0.43
	Over 1 year	2.21	0.58 (0.08)	0.75
	Over 3 years	1.71	0.64 (0.10)	0.89
	Over 5 years	1.64	0.65 (0.16)	0.89
1954–71	Ordinary least squares	2.68	0.31 (0.03)	0.29
	Over 1 year	1.80	0.68 (0.09)	0.64
	Over 3 years	1.53	0.79 (0.12)	0.81
	Over 5 years	1.49	0.81 (0.18)	0.81
	Over 10 years	1.38	0.86 (0.30)	0.86

a. Band spectral regressions were performed using the Troll computer program. Data are described in the text.
b. Standard errors are shown in parentheses below the coefficients.

Table 6. *Inflation and the Yield on Long-Term Government Bonds,
Selected Periods, 1948–79*[a]

Interval	Length of cycle	Constant	Coefficient of Π[b]	$\bar{R}^2$
1948–79	Ordinary least squares	3.97	0.24 (*)	0.30
	Over 1 year	3.36	0.40 (0.05)	0.50
	Over 3 years	2.98	0.50 (0.09)	0.63
	Over 5 years	2.65	0.59 (0.12)	0.70
	Over 10 years	2.13	0.73 (0.14)	0.87
1954–79	Ordinary least squares	4.03	0.34 (0.02)	0.52
	Over 1 year	3.44	0.49 (0.04)	0.76
	Over 3 years	3.29	0.52 (0.07)	0.80
	Over 5 years	3.10	0.56 (0.09)	0.84
	Over 10 years	2.76	0.65 (0.07)	0.97
1970–79	Ordinary least squares	6.57	0.15 (0.02)	0.29
	Over 1 year	5.95	0.23 (0.05)	0.52
	Over 3 years	5.74	0.26 (0.12)	0.56
	Over 5 years	5.68	0.26 (0.16)	0.61
1954–71	Ordinary least squares	3.88	0.21 (0.03)	0.25
	Over 1 year	3.27	0.47 (0.07)	0.56
	Over 3 years	3.10	0.53 (0.12)	0.65
	Over 5 years	2.96	0.59 (0.18)	0.70
	Over 10 years	2.82	0.65 (0.29)	0.79

* Less than 0.005.
a. Band spectral regressions were performed using the Troll computer program. Data are described in the text.
b. Standard errors are shown in parentheses below the coefficients.

data. However, even at ten-year cycle lengths the full Fisher effect is not observed, much less the effect that is predicted with high taxes.

One issue not yet addressed is simultaneity even at the low frequencies considered here. If interest rates and inflation are jointly determined, inflation and the error term may be correlated in the regressions reported here, leading to biased estimates of the effects of steady inflation on interest rates. For such bias to explain the anomalously low estimated effect of inflation on interest rates, inflation and the error term must be negatively correlated. In this case, the extent of simultaneity bias can be banded by running the regression in the opposite direction. However, Griliches and Ringstad show that the "reverse regression" coefficient $\hat{\sigma} = R^2/\hat{\beta}$.[33] An upper bound on the effect of inflation of interest rates is given by $1/\hat{\sigma} = \hat{\beta}/R^2$. In almost all cases, even this bound is less than unity. This suggests that simultaneous equations bias cannot account for the results obtained here.

It is natural to conjecture that the introduction of taxes has increased the value of $dr/d\pi^e$, explaining the difference between the prewar and postwar periods. However, until an explanation of its surprisingly low value is available, this conjecture remains speculative.

Inflation and Other Determinants of the Interest Rate

The results in the preceding section, which demonstrate that there is a very weak relationship between long swings in the rate of inflation and nominal interest rates, contradict the prediction of the standard macroeconomic model developed in the first section. That model holds that the long-run rate of inflation is determined by the rate of money growth, which is exogenous. It implicitly assumes that fluctuations in the long-run rate of growth of the money stock are independent of movements in the other forcing variables. This supposition may be warranted.

Equation 2b implies that the rate of interest in steady state is proximately determined by the risk premium β and the marginal product of capital. If inflation is correlated with real shocks, these should work through these two variables. When they are held constant, the Fisher

33. Zvi Griliches and V. Ringstad, *Economies of Scale and the Form of the Production Function: An Econometric Study of Norwegian Manufacturing Establishment Data* (North-Holland, 1971).

Table 7. *Inflation and Other Determinants of Interest Rates,*
Selected Periods, 1926–79[a]

Interval	Length of cycle	Constant	Coefficient of Π	Variable MARVAR		$\bar{R}^2$
1926–79	Ordinary least squares	2.68	0.06 (0.01)	−0.05 (0.01)		0.08
	Over 1 year	2.43	0.13 (0.05)	−0.03 (0.03)		0.12
	Over 3 years	2.32	0.16 (0.09)	−0.02 (0.06)		0.13
	Over 5 years	2.34	0.16 (0.15)	−0.03 (0.09)		0.13
	Over 10 years	2.38	0.18 (0.28)	−0.05 (0.09)		0.15
1954–79	Ordinary least squares	2.46	0.39 (0.02)	0.15 (0.06)		0.56
	Over 1 year	2.10	0.59 (0.04)	−0.07 (0.10)		0.82
	Over 3 years	2.02	0.63 (0.06)	−0.13 (0.15)		0.90
	Over 5 years	2.29	0.63 (0.09)	−0.26 (0.26)		0.90
	Over 10 years	2.82	0.71 (0.17)	−0.67 (0.69)		0.93
				BTRR	*VarGNP*	
1954–79	Ordinary least squares	−2.03	0.72 (0.10)	0.35 (0.18)	0.40 (0.42)	0.81
	Over 3 years	−2.65	0.75 (0.12)	0.39 (0.23)	−0.34 (0.51)	0.85
	Over 5 years	1.44	0.65 (0.12)	0.12 (0.23)	−1.02 (0.55)	0.94
	Over 10 years	3.20	0.63 (0.25)	0.00 (0.59)	−1.48 (1.75)	0.97
				ATRR	*VarGNP*	
1954–79	Ordinary least squares	0.85	0.68 (0.09)	0.00 (0.00)	−0.51 (0.42)	0.80
	Over 3 years	0.60	0.70 (0.12)	0.00 (0.00)	−0.49 (0.51)	0.84
	Over 5 years	1.64	0.67 (0.10)	0.00 (0.00)	−0.90 (0.47)	0.91
	Over 10 years	2.00	0.67 (0.19)	0.00 (0.01)	−1.10 (1.43)	0.97

a. Regressions were estimated using the band spectral procedure. Data are described in the text. Standard errors are shown in parentheses below the coefficients.

effect should hold. This proposition is tested in the results reported in table 7.

The major difficulty is finding proxies for the real return on capital and the level of risk. The top half of the table reports results using as a measure of risk the variance of real stock market returns, *MARVAR*, which was calculated according to the procedure suggested by Merton.[34] It is the mean squared real return for the twelve months bracketing each observation. The notion here is that the attractiveness of debt securities should increase as the equity risks rise. If inflation is associated with greater real variability, this could lead to the negative association between inflation and real interest rates demonstrated in the preceding section.

The results do not bear out this hypothesis. The data do tend to suggest that increases in risk depress nominal interest rates. However, this correlation cannot account for the nonadjustment of interest rates to inflation. The estimates of the effects of inflation are very close to those in the preceding section.

The bottom half of the table reports the results of including proxies for the real rate of return on capital and an alternative risk measure. This necessitated the use of annual data. The marginal product of capital is alternatively proxied by the real pretax marginal product, *BTRR*, and the posttax marginal product, *ATRR*.[35] These estimates are based only on the nonfinancial corporate sector. The risk measure is a moving eight-quarter variance of real GNP growth rates. The results suggest that real returns and risk measure had some effect on interest rates. Including these variables, however, had little impact on estimates of the effect of inflation on interest rates.

The results reported here are a very small sample of a large number of equations that were estimated in an effort to rescue the Fisher effect by including additional variables. All were unsuccessful. Perhaps there is some unmeasurable variable correlated with inflation that affects required real returns.

34. Robert C. Merton, "On Estimating the Expected Return on the Market: An Exploratory Investigation," *Journal of Financial Economics*, vol. 8 (December 1980), pp. 323–61.
35. Martin Feldstein and James Poterba, "State and Local Taxes and the Rate of Return on Nonfinancial Corporate Capital," Working Paper 508 (National Bureau of Economic Research, 1980).

Interest Rates and Equity Values

The empirical analysis in the previous section suggests that periods of high inflation are associated with low real interest rates. One line of explanation for this phenomenon holds that inflation is associated with the more fundamental factors that affect real interest rates. The examination of proxies for the real rate of profit and level of economic risk showed that they do not account for the anomalous relation between inflation and interest rates. A more indirect approach is through a study of the relation between inflation and alternative indicators of the real interest rate. The stock market provides a natural alternative indicator.

There are three possible ways to measure the real interest rate using stock market data. The standard approach is the use of holding period returns. The ex post return on stocks should equal the required ex ante rate plus a risk premium. The difficulty is that the enormous volatility of stock prices implies that ex post returns are noisy indicators. An alternative is the use of the ratio of earnings or dividends to prices, but these measures can be misleading if there are transitory movements in dividends or earnings. This should be less important in the low-frequency range studied here. The choice between dividends and earnings is somewhat unclear. Earnings would seem preferable since the value of a firm's assets is the present value of their earnings stream. The dividend–price ratio is also considered because it can be measured more accurately and because there is some evidence that dividends are set on the basis of "permanent earnings."

Evidence on the relationship between low-frequency movements in these variables and inflation is presented in table 8. All the regressions are estimated filtering out cycles shorter than five years. The results indicate that for all the sample periods there is no strong relation between inflation and dividend–price ratios or earnings–price ratios. During the postwar period the relationship is positive and in some cases statistically significant. The failure of the ratios to decline with inflation is surprising in light of the failure of nominal interest rates to adjust, especially in the postwar period, when increases in inflation have been associated with sharp decreases in after-tax real interest rates.

The bottom part of the table examines the relation between the holding-period return on stocks and inflation. Throughout the prewar period the relationship appears positive and statistically insignificant.

Table 8. *Inflation and Equity Yields, Selected Periods, 1871–1979*[a]

Sample period	Constant	Slope	$\bar{R}^2$
Earnings–price ratio			
1891–1914	7.21	0.06 (0.08)	0.03
1871–1940	7.58	−0.10 (0.06)	0.12
1919–40	6.97	−0.02 (0.11)	0.01
1948–79	6.91	0.36 (0.30)	0.12
1954–79	5.31	0.49 (0.16)	0.54
1871–1979	7.66	0.12 (0.05)	0.11
Dividend–price ratio			
1871–1914	4.74	−0.13 (0.04)	0.38
1871–1940	4.98	−0.03 (0.02)	0.05
1919–40	5.03	−0.03 (0.03)	0.11
1948–79	4.03	0.03 (0.13)	0.01
1954–79	3.24	0.10 (0.06)	0.30
1871–1979	4.82	−0.03 (0.02)	0.04
Holding-period returns			
1871–1914	7.44	1.33 (0.41)	0.41
1871–1940	8.33	0.82 (0.33)	0.20
1919–40	14.65	0.78 (0.81)	0.13
1948–79	18.72	−1.61 (0.57)	0.44
1954–79	17.65	−1.48 (0.71)	0.36
1871–1979	8.93	0.55 (0.27)	0.09

a. All regressions were estimated using a band spectral technique which filters out all cycles shorter than five years. Standard errors are shown in parentheses below the coefficients.

Table 9. *Real Interest and Equity Returns, 1955–78*

Year	After-tax real interest rate[a] (1)	Earnings– price ratio[b] (2)	Inflation- adjusted earnings– price ratio[c] (3)	After-tax market- value– income ratio[d] (4)
1955	0.83	.079	.060	.047
1956	1.30	.073	.053	.034
1957	1.24	.076	.058	.035
1958	1.00	.059	.043	.030
1959	1.38	.056	.046	.035
1960	1.38	.057	.046	.034
1961	1.70	.046	.036	.030
1962	1.57	.058	.053	.041
1963	1.68	.055	.051	.041
1964	1.78	.053	.048	.045
1965	1.73	.056	.053	.048
1966	1.81	.066	.065	.053
1967	1.71	.056	.054	.047
1968	1.15	.055	.057	.039
1969	2.16	.059	.059	.034
1970	2.27	.062	.059	.031
1971	1.14	.052	.047	.032
1972	1.10	.052	.044	.038
1973	0.65	.068	.064	.031
1974	−0.40	.109	.094	.010
1975	−0.36	.088	.069	.032
1976	−0.42	.086	.059	.036
1977	−1.02	.104	.087	.040
1978	−0.58	.115	.092	.039

a. Estimated as the municipal bond rate minus a weighted average of the CPI inflation rate of the five previous years.

b. Annual average of Standard & Poor's earnings–price ratio.

c. Standard & Poor's earnings–price ratio adjusted to calculate profits on an inflation-adjusted basis, as described in Lawrence H. Summers, "Capital Taxation and Accumulation in a Life Cycle Growth Model," *American Economic Review,* vol. 71 (September 1981), pp. 533–44.

d. Ratio of corporate and individual after-tax earnings (as calculated by Martin J. Feldstein and James Poterba, "State and Local Taxes and the Rate of Return on Nonfinancial Corporate Capital," Working Paper 508 [National Bureau of Economic Research, 1980]) to the market value of corporate debt and equity claims.

Surprisingly, it is negative after the war. This largely reflects the disastrous performance of the market during the high-inflation 1970s. These results provide weak support for the view that something depressed real rates of return during the 1970s. The behavior of earnings–price and dividend–price ratios, however, suggests the opposite.

The results raise the question of whether the puzzling behavior of the interest rates and the stock market are related. This is examined in table 9. The first column displays a crude proxy for the real after-tax interest rate. Its value has declined sharply in recent years. The second and third columns present estimates of the earnings–price ratio unadjusted and adjusted for inflation. The ratio in column 3 is derived from Standard & Poor's ratio of 500 common stocks, after making adjustment for historic cost depreciation, FIFO inventory accounting, and the deduction of nominal interest payments in calculating profits.[36] Both earnings–price ratios display significant increases in the recent high inflation years.

The increasing value of the earnings–price ratio coupled with the declining real interest rate have substantially widened the spread between the expected return on debt and equity. Whether the relationship of the total market value of the corporation to the stream of returns generated for investors has changed is answered in the fourth column of the table, which shows that this ratio has not risen in recent years. The decline in real stock prices has offset the rise in bond prices associated with lower interest rates, leaving the valuation of the corporate sector relative to the income it generates unchanged.

This phenomenon can be described in another way. The constancy of the income-value ratios in column 4 suggests that by historical standards the corporate sector is not misvalued. The spread between the relative valuation of the two types of claims on corporate income has widened substantially, from 3.1 percent in 1965 to 9.8 percent in 1978. The increase in this spread is puzzling. If the spread had remained constant at its 1965 values, the nominal municipal bond interest rate would have been 12.7 percent in 1978 rather than 6.9 percent. Since expected inflation rose by 5.5 percent between 1965 and 1978, and the interest rate was 3.3 in 1965, this figure implies that inflation had a very significant impact on interest rates.

The finding that inflation increases the spread between debt and equity yields strongly supports the view of Fisher and Modigliani and Cohn that investors suffer from money illusion.[37] If, as the latter suggest, they confuse nominal and real interest rates in valuing stock, stock prices could be expected to be undervalued. Similarly, bonds would be overvalued as their apparent attractiveness was overstated. An alternative explanation might hold that the risk premium required to get investors to hold equities increases with the rate of inflation. Efforts to explain

---

36. Details of the calculation are provided in Summers, "Inflation and the Valuation of Corporate Equities."

37. Fisher, *The Theory of Interest;* and Franco Modigliani and Richard A. Cohn, "Inflation, Rational Valuation, and the Market," *Financial Analysts Journal,* vol. 35 (March–April 1979), pp. 24–44.

earnings and dividend price ratios using the measures of risk discussed in the preceding section proved unsuccessful, casting some doubt on this conjecture. In any event, it is not clear that this hypothesis is operationally distinguishable from the inflation illusion hypothesis.

Conclusions

The empirical analysis in this paper demonstrates that U.S. interest rates do not appear to systematically incorporate inflation premiums in the way that classical monetary theories suggest. The data for 1860 to 1940 indicate no tendency for interest rates to increase with movements in expected inflation. Theory suggests that postwar interest rates should have increased much more than point for point with inflation in the presence of taxes. The data suggest some tendency for interest rates to adjust to changes in expected inflation, but far less than is predicted by theory. These conclusions hold at low frequencies and thus primarily reflect the effects of changes in inflation caused by movements in the long-run rate of money growth. The implied strong negative relationship between inflation and real interest rates is not explicable by changes in either proxies for the marginal product of capital or the risk premium. Furthermore, it appears that increases in the rate of inflation are associated with a widening of the spread between the real ex ante return on bonds and stocks.

These facts, taken together, at least raise the possibility that some form of money illusion infects financial markets. All are explicable by the hypothesis that before the war agents ignored inflation in making financial calculations. As the average inflation rate increased after the war, investors' sophistication increased and the market was partially though not fully affected by changes in inflation. This hypothesis also accounts for several other puzzles. Efforts to estimate Phillips curves on any data generated before 1965 consistently generate the conclusion that long-run inflation is not neutral. More generally, the failure of market participants to understand the effects of inflation is the most plausible explanation for the abundance of nominally rigid institutions. Do purchasers of annuities wish less insurance when the rate of inflation increases? Did borrowers and lenders in the mortgage market desire the effective shortening of maturities that has resulted from increasing inflation? These are just prominent examples of the general failure to adopt contractual provisions that are neutral to inflation. The absence of private indexing arrangements has not been satisfactorily explained.

How unlikely is it that market participants are unaware of the distinction between nominal and real interest rates? Not until the twentieth century was the distinction even introduced into economic analysis. Mainstream economic writings in the 1950s and 1960s exhibit little evidence of an awareness of this distinction. It was almost universally believed that low interest rates were both the short- and long-run consequences of easy money policies. The distinction between nominal and real interest rates is constantly confused in investors' sources of information. Modigliani and Cohn have described an informal survey of brokerage letters supporting this proposition.[38]

These considerations suggest the plausibility of some form of inflation illusion infecting financial markets. One major piece of evidence that casts doubt on the inflation illusion hypothesis is the behavior of house prices in recent years. James Poterba and I have suggested that the interaction of inflation and taxes can account for the boom in house prices.[39] If home buyers had displayed substantial inflation illusion, high nominal interest rates should have choked off housing demand and led to a decline in real prices. One would expect inflation illusion to be much more prevalent among the relatively unsophisticated, liquidity-constrained purchasers of homes than among the investors in the stock and bond markets. The failure of housing construction to increase, as predicted by models that emphasize tax effects, may imply that rising construction costs are the real reason for the appreciation in the prices of homes. Another possibility is that the boom in prices represents a speculative bubble. Furthermore, investors may form expectations about real interest rates on an asset from its past price behavior. This would imply a low real rate on housing and a high real rate on stocks.

In considering the suggestion that financial markets are inefficient because of inflation illusion, it is important to examine what market forces should be pushing toward the restoration of efficiency. The fundamental implication of the view developed in Modigliani and Cohn,[40] and supported here, is that as the rate of inflation increases, the expected

38. "Inflation, Rational Valuation, and the Market."
39. James M. Poterba, "Inflation, Income Taxes, and Owner-Occupied Housing," Working Paper 553 (National Bureau of Economic Research, 1980); and Summers, "Capital Taxation and Accumulation."
40. Modigliani and Cohn, "Inflation, Rational Valuation, and the Market."

real return on stocks relative to bonds should rise. This inefficiency would be corrected if increases in inflation led sophisticated investors to borrow and buy stock, or shift some of their portfolio to equity. Both of these strategies involve more risk. Indeed, it seems impossible to devise a strategy for profiting from inflation illusion that does not involve taking an additional risk because of the lack of safe real assets or nominal assets with risk characteristics similar to common stock. This factor limits the extent to which any individual will be willing to invest to take advantage of the inefficiency. If investors are fairly inflexible about the amount of risk they are willing to bear, it may require a very large number to eliminate the tendency of market prices to reflect inflation illusion.

Several other factors suggest that inflation illusion is not readily susceptible to elimination by market forces. The very set of financially sophisticated investors who could most profit from it have been trained to believe that it does not exist. More seriously, focusing on nominal yields may be individually rational, if collectively undesirable. The holder of a nominal mortgage should not purchase an indexed bond. For any individual it may be rational to compare nominal yields, particularly where there are constraints expressed in nominal terms. Examples include institutions or individuals who are permitted to spend "income" but not to "dip into capital." A third factor limiting the ability of market forces to overcome inflation illusion is the myriad constraints the capital market imposes on borrowing. By artificially limiting the demand for funds, these restrictions, which bite more sharply when inflation is high, tend to reduce interest rates below the level they would otherwise attain.

This analysis may help illuminate the reasons for the current high level of interest rates. In 1965 the AAA bond rate was 4 percent. The long-run model developed in the first section implies that the increase of eight points in the inflation rate since then should have raised bond rates by about eleven points. This yields a 15 percent rate. It is just possible that current high interest rates indicate that investors have finally shed their inflation illusion. The dismal performance of the stock market in recent months remains inexplicable, according to this view.

Appendix

A number of authors using data on the post–World War II period have estimated equations that they have interpreted as providing evidence in favor of the Fisher hypothesis. From the perspective of this paper, these equations are neither well specified nor likely to be stable. This appendix verifies this conjecture using two standard procedures for modeling expectations. It also demonstrates that the anomalous results obtained in the paper are not the consequence of the use of the band spectral technique.

The basic equation to be estimated is of the form:

$$(9) \qquad R_t = \beta_0 + \beta_1 \pi_t^e,$$

where the principal empirical difficulty is the measurement of π^e.

The Keynesian model holds that inflationary expectations at any one time are predominantly a function of past rates of inflation. This implies that

$$(10) \qquad \pi_t^e = \sum_0^T w_i \pi_{t-i}.$$

Under this assumption the relationship between interest rates and inflation can be inferred from the distributed lag relation

$$(11) \qquad r_t = \beta_0 + \beta_1 \sum_0^T w_i \pi_{t-i}$$

if the additional identifying restriction

$$(12) \qquad \sum_0^T w_i = 1$$

is imposed. This restriction is necessary if a constant rate of inflation maintained for T periods is to lead to an equal expected rate of inflation. However as Sargent and others have pointed out,[41] it may not be appropriate if inflation follows any other stationary stochastic process; for example, if inflation rates follow the process

$$(13) \qquad \pi_t = \rho \pi_{t-1} + u_t,$$

then the optimal autoregressive predictor of inflation will have $\Sigma w_i = \rho$. Since the assumption is that inflation expectations are based on arbitrary rules rather than on rational forecasts, this point is neglected here. Rational expectations are considered below. In estimating equation 11

41. Thomas J. Sargent, "A Note on the 'Accelerationist' Controversy," *Journal of Money, Credit and Banking,* vol. 3 (August 1971), pp. 721–25; and Sargent, "What Do Regressions of Interest on Inflation Show?" *Annals of Economic and Social Measurement,* vol. 2 (July 1973), pp. 289–301.

many investigators constrain the w_i to lie on some simple curve. This approach is undesirable if the goal is just to estimate the sum of the lag coefficients, as is the case here.

The second assumption about expectations examined in the empirical work below is that inflationary expectations are rational. This case can be treated easily using a procedure developed by McCallum.[42] The assumption of rationality implies that

$$(14) \qquad\qquad \pi_t = \pi^e_{t-1,t} + u_t,$$

where u_t is uncorrelated with any information available at time $t - 1$. If u_t were correlated with any information available at time t, such information could be used to improve the formation of π^e_t. Consider the regression equation where the realized rate of inflation π_t is used as a proxy for the expected rate. That is,

$$(15) \qquad\qquad R_t = \beta_0 + \beta_1\pi_t - u_t.$$

Equation 15 implies that 16 meets the conditions of the classical errors in variables problem. Consistent estimates are obtainable if instruments correlated with the expected rate of inflation but uncorrelated with any expectational errors exist. The assumption of rationality implies that any information available at time $t - 1$ meets these criteria. In particular, lagged values of inflation are suitable instruments. Thus the rational expectations assumption is implemented below by estimating equation 16 using lagged values of inflation as instruments.

Fama has developed an alternative approach to studying the relationship between interest rates and inflation.[43] He begins by postulating that the expected real interest rate is constant. In this case,

$$(16) \qquad\qquad r_t = \rho + \pi^e_t,$$

where ρ is the expected real interest rate. The assumption that ρ is constant enables us to write:

$$(17) \qquad\qquad \pi^e_t = r_t - \rho.$$

The assumption of rational expectations embodied in equation 14 allows us to estimate the relation

$$(18) \qquad\qquad \pi_t = \alpha_0 + \alpha_1 r_t + u_t.$$

42. Bennett T. McCallum, "Rational Expectations and the Estimation of Econometric Models: An Alternative Procedure," *International Economic Review*, vol. 17 (June 1976), pp. 484–90.

43. Fama, "Short-Term Interest Rates."

Table 10. *Ten-Year Estimates of dr/dπ^e before World War II*[a]

	Commercial paper		Long rate[d]	
Period	*Keynesian*[b]	*Rational*[c]	*Keynesian*	*Rational*
1860–69	−0.01	−0.01	−0.02	−0.01
	(0.02)	(0.02)	(0.01)	(0.03)
1870–79	0.34	−0.05	0.11	−0.23
	(0.07)	(0.05)	(0.06)	(0.10)
1880–89	0.04	−0.02	0.10	−0.26
	(0.02)	(0.02)	(0.01)	(0.06)
1890–99	0.01	−0.03	0.02	−0.14
	(0.07)	(0.04)	(0.02)	(0.02)
1900–09	0.03	−0.02	−0.12	−0.08
	(0.08)	(0.03)	(0.02)	(0.02)
1910–19	0.02	−0.01	0.06	−0.11
	(0.01)	(0.01)	(0.01)	(0.02)
1920–29	0.04	−0.16	−0.14	−0.86
	(0.05)	(0.03)	(0.03)	(0.27)
1930–39	−0.17	−0.10	−0.23	−0.30
	(0.03)	(0.02)	(0.03)	(0.05)
1860–1913	0.03	0.03	0.03	−0.31
	(0.01)	(0.02)	(0.01)	(0.08)
1914–39	0.07	0.02	0.05	−0.38
	(0.02)	(0.02)	(0.01)	(0.05)
1860–1939	0.04	0.04	0.04	−0.36
	(0.01)	(0.02)	(0.01)	(0.06)

a. Standard errors are shown in parentheses below the coefficients.
b. Indicates the sum of the coefficients in the ordinary least squares regression of the commerical paper rate on eight lagged quarters of inflation.
c. Coefficient yielded by regression of commercial paper on current inflation where eight lagged rates of inflation are used as instruments. This two-stage procedure, relevant to estimating an equation with an unobservable but rationally formed expectations variable, is described in the text.
d. Long rate used is represented by the railroad bond yield in MacCauley, *Some Theoretical Problems*, from 1860 to 1918, and the Federal Reserve AAA bond yield from 1919 to 1979. In the OLS regression, twenty lagged quarters of inflation were used. In the two-stage procedure, the realized ten-year inflation rate (annualized), starting at time t, was instrumented, using twenty lagged values of quarterly inflation.

The joint assumptions of a constant real rate and rational expectations imply that $\alpha_1 = 1$ and that u_t is serially uncorrelated. Fama reports that he obtains results consistent with these assumptions for the 1954–71 period.[44] The robustness of this conclusion is examined below by extending his tests to other sample periods.

In table 10 the relationship between inflation and short- and long-term interest rates is examined for the 1860–1940 period, using the techniques described above for measuring expectations.

Neither the results using the Keynesian assumptions nor those using the classical assumptions support the view that interest rates adjust fully

44. Ibid.

Table 11. *Regressions of the Inflation Rate, π_t, on the Short-Term Rate of Interest, by Decade, 1860–1939*[a]

Period	Constant	R_t	Summary statistic	
			$\bar{R}^2$	Durbin-Watson
1860–69	71.50	−8.66 (3.34)	0.13	1.57
1870–79	−1.11	0.02 (1.32)	−0.02	1.82
1880–89	5.17	−1.47 (2.27)	−0.01	1.76
1890–99	7.31	−1.25 (1.54)	−0.01	1.95
1900–09	14.40	−2.35 (1.49)	0.04	2.31
1910–19	51.90	−8.80 (2.96)	0.17	1.22
1920–29	13.80	−3.03 (0.47)	0.50	1.03
1930–39	3.20	−3.22 (0.75)	0.30	1.06
1860–1913	9.30	−1.30 (0.80)	0.01	1.55
1914–39	3.60	−0.25 (0.68)	−0.01	0.87

a. All regressions were run ordinary least squares. The relevant inflation rate for 1860 through 1918 is the realized three-month rate of change in prices. For 1919 to 1939, it is the realized six-month rate of change. Standard errors are in parentheses.

to incorporate inflation premiums. In no decade does the estimate of $dr/d\pi^e$ for commercial paper exceed 0.34. The estimate for the entire period is only 0.04 based on the Keynesian assumption; all eight ten-year-average estimates of $dr/d\pi^e$ are negative. The results for the longer period are almost as unfavorable: they are not substantially altered when longer lags are assumed in the formation of inflation expectations. The long-rate results are equally unfavorable to the Fisher effect. The rational expectations estimates are again consistently negative while the Keynesian expectations estimates are always statistically insignificant. Every equation for either the short or long rate rejects the conclusion that $dr/d\pi^e = 1$ with t-statistics in excess of 10. Thus the data overwhelmingly refute the hypothesis that nominal interest rates adjusted to ensure the neutrality of inflation.

Similar conclusions emerge from an extension of Fama's tests to the prewar period. Results of this exercise are reported in table 11. In seven

Table 12. *Postwar Estimates of* $dr/d\pi^e$, *Selected Periods, 1947–79*

Period	Three-month Treasury bills[a]		Period	AAA rate	
	Auto-regressive	Rational		Auto-regressive	Rational
1947–79	0.35	0.38	1946–69	−0.26	0.72
	(0.05)	(0.05)		(0.05)	(0.08)
Omitting controls[b]	0.33	0.35			
	(0.05)	(0.06)			
1947–55	−0.04	−0.03	1946–55	−0.08	−0.32
	(0.02)	(0.02)		(0.01)	(0.05)
1956–65	−0.16	0.05	1956–65	0.07	0.22
	(0.17)	(0.15)		(0.25)	(0.06)
1966–75	0.35	0.47			
	(0.66)	(0.07)			
Omitting controls[b]	0.38	0.51			
	(0.08)	(0.13)			
1950–59	0.00	0.00	1950–59	−0.07	0.55
	(0.10)	(0.08)		(0.07)	(0.37)
1960–69	0.85	0.77	1960–69	0.82	0.58
	(0.08)	(0.10)		(0.05)	(0.06)
1970–79	0.47	0.51			
	(0.08)	(0.06)			
Omitting controls[b]	0.49	0.55			
	(0.13)	(0.09)			

a. See table 11 for explanation of regression procedures. Three-month bills were used here in order to be consistent with table 5. The difference between these results and those obtained using the commercial paper rate are statistically insignificant. Standard errors are in parentheses.

b. For these regressions, the twelve observations 1971:3 through 1974:2 were omitted.

of the eight decades the coefficient on the interest rate is negative. Only the weakness of the statistical tests precludes rejection of the Fisher hypothesis. The predictive power of interest rates in explaining inflation is negligible. The estimated values of the ex ante real interest rate are ludicrous, ranging from −1.1 during the 1870s to 51.9 during the 1910–19 period.

The analysis in the first section of the paper suggests that one could expect $dr/d\pi^e > 1$ in the postwar period. Estimates of this parameter for intervals in this period are presented in table 12. The regression procedures are the same as those for the prewar analysis. The short rate is proxied by the rate on Treasury bills, and the AAA bond rate is used as a measure of the long rate. Reestimating the equations using alternative interest rates had no important effect on the results, nor did the use of monthly or annual data.

Table 13. *Regressions of Quarterly Inflation Rate on Three-Month Treasury Bill Rates, Selected Periods, 1947–79*[a]

Period	Constant	R_t	$\bar{R}^2$	Durbin-Watson
			Summary statistic	
1947–79	−0.31	1.14	0.37	1.18
		(0.12)		
Omitting				
controls[b]	−0.06	1.04	0.31	1.19
		(0.14)		
1947–55	6.33	−2.94	0.04	1.37
		(1.82)		
1956–65	0.85	0.32	0.00	1.80
		(0.33)		
1966–75	−3.32	1.59	0.51	1.53
		(0.24)		
Omitting				
controls[b]	−0.43	0.96	0.30	1.74
		(0.26)		
1950–59	2.06	−0.18	−0.02	1.06
1960–69	−1.82	1.12	0.61	2.07
		(0.14)		
1970–79	−2.78	1.66	0.65	1.87
		(0.19)		
Omitting				
controls[b]	−2.31	1.56	0.61	1.85
		(0.23)		

a. All regressions were estimated OLS, using quarterly data. Standard errors are in parentheses.
b. For these regressions, the twelve observations 1971:3 through 1974:2 were omitted.

The results for both the short and long rates are broadly consistent. There is no evidence that interest rates have risen more than the rate of inflation. In only a few instances are the data unable to reject the hypothesis that $dr/d\pi^e = 1$, and in no case is it impossible to reject $dr/d\pi^e = 1.3$ at a very high level of confidence. The results differ substantially across subperiods. It appears that almost all of the power in the interest rate–inflation relation comes from the acceleration of inflation during the 1960s. The data for the 1940s and 1950s reveal no statistically significant inflation effects. The regressions for the 1970s also exhibit effects of inflation significantly smaller than those found for the entire period. Fama argues that the price level is mismeasured during the controls period.[45] Omission of this interval has no significant effect on the results. Hence the inflation–interest rate nexus appears to be very

45. Ibid.

weak during the 1970s. It is difficult to escape the conclusion that even viewed from a purely postwar perspective the strong inflation–interest rate relationship during the 1960s was an aberration.

Somewhat more favorable results (table 13) were obtained using the Fama procedure. The results for the whole period are consistent with $dr/d\pi^e = 1$, although the low Durbin-Watson statistic is troublesome. The hypothesis that $dr/d\pi^e = 1.3$ as predicted by theory is again refuted. The failure of the Fisher relationship in the 1950s and 1970s again emerges clearly. These results do not exactly parallel Fama's because of the use of quarterly data. However, the results for sample periods comparable to these closely parallel those he reports. It seems reasonable, therefore, to conclude that the failure of these tests outside his sample period casts doubt on the robustness of his conclusion.

Comment by Franco Modigliani

LAWRENCE SUMMERS'S paper is, in my view, a valuable endeavor at systematically reexamining the questions of whether Fisher's law holds empirically for the United States, whether it should, and if not, why not.

The empirical analysis based on more than a century of data is generally convincing, and I am therefore ready to endorse his verdict against the empirical relevance of "a Fisher's law" in its narrow formulation, according to which interest rates tend to rise one for one with inflation. Summers's evidence is overwhelming for the period 1860 to 1940, when the nominal rate, whether short or long, seemed hardly to respond to inflation (and in the first half actually responded perversely). But even for the postwar period, though the response is appreciably positive, especially over longer spans of time, it remains well below unity—except for the subperiod 1954–71. This result is important since for a while the work of Fama based on the last-mentioned period seemed to support the validity of that law.

The next question Summers investigates is whether Fisher's law *should* hold. Here one must consider three broad issues: first, the effect of taxes on the inflation premium, or the spread between nominal and real rates; second, the effect of inflation on the real rate, through taxes or other real effects; and third, the effect of nominal institutions (other than fiscal) and of money illusion on both the first and second issues.

The first two questions are examined in the first section of the paper on the basis of a fairly standard, streamlined model. Though the relevant formulas would depend somewhat on the specific model, one can readily agree with his conclusions as follows. (1) The second question can be given a satisfactory answer only in the long run when the force driving inflation can be identified with the expansion of money (or other nominal monetary or credit aggregates) and when, I might add, redistributional effects of unanticipated inflation have subsided. In the short run, when inflation is largely the result of real shocks, there is in general no reason for any systematic relation between inflation, the real rate, and the inflation premium. (2) In the presence of personal taxes, which treat nominal rather than real returns as a taxable income and a deductible expense, the inflation premium added to the real rate should be above unity, that is, the narrow Fisher effect should be replaced by a more general "Fisher-plus" effect. If all (noncorporate) transactors had the same tax rate, and interest paid and received were treated with complete symmetry, the premium would be roughly equal to the rate of inflation times one plus *the* tax rate. Under more realistic circumstances, one must be satisfied with some measure of the average marginal tax rate. (3) In the presence of taxes, even aside from the effect of other nominal institutions, inflation is *not* neutral and in particular will affect the real rate. The main culprit is the taxation of income based on historical cost accounting and the corporate deductibility of net interest payments—at least where the corporation tax rate exceeds the "effective" personal tax rate, as in the United States. These two effects go in opposite directions but on balance are likely to have a mild negative impact on the real rate.

The consequences of other nominal institutions are hardly touched on by Summers. Yet they are widespread, and at least some could be of significance for the real rate. Two of these institutions are likely to exert a downward pressure on real rates. First is the continued reliance on conventional mortgages, even when modified to allow for some form of floating rate; either type results in the well-known tilt in the real payments schedule and high initial payments, which should reduce the demand for housing. The second is the enforcement of nominal deposit rate ceilings and related credit rationing, though its importance has been declining steadily. The impact on real rates of the opposite tilt implicit in pension contracts is, on the other hand, hard to gauge, as is that resulting from massive redistributions due to long-term nominal contracts. On the whole, nominal taxation and other nominal institutions would seem to make for a decline in real rates in response to inflation. But the decline would not be sufficient to change the conclusion that, with rational behavior, *nominal* rates should be expected to behave in accordance with a "Fisher-plus" effect. This is in sharp contrast with the actual behavior of nominal rates, which can best be described as "Fisher minus." Note also that nominal institutions could hardly be relevant to an understanding of the observed behavior of nominal rates in the period up to the First World War, when these institutions as well as income taxation were largely absent.

We are thus left with money illusion to account for the difference between observed behavior and the implications of rational behavior. This subject is considered in the fourth and fifth sections of the paper, though somewhat hurriedly, I feel. Instances of money illusion are pervasive, as Summers illustrates. I could add to his list my lack of success in persuading bankers to offer modifications of the mortgage instruments that would avoid the tilt problem. The idea that the debt may for a while rise in nominal terms seems to be anathema.

But I remain convinced that the most important instance of money illusion is to be found in the behavior of investors in equities. I was happy to see that my hypothesis about the irrational undervaluation of stocks receives some support in Summers's fourth section. However, in my view, the main reason for the tendency of the undervaluation to persist is not the unwillingness of "sophisticated" investors to exploit the bargains, because that would require additional risk. It is rather that the irrational valuation is self-fulfilling, as I have argued elsewhere; as long as inflation and nominal rates are on the rise, the persistence of the valuation error ensures the absence of abnormal returns, or even leads to losses, despite the mammoth earnings–price ratio. Those meaning to exploit the undervaluation would not make money; they would be more likely to lose their shirts.

The depressing effect of rising inflation on the stock market, in turn, can help to explain very low or negative real rates. First, the high required earning yield on equity capital should depress investment and the demand for debt funds. Second, the low holding yield on equities should reduce the required real rate on nominal assets.

I am not sure whether Summers's paper provides the final answer to the puzzle of why nominal and real rates behaved as they did in the United States, but it certainly makes important progress in that direction. In particular, the view that money illusion and nominal institutions play a major part is supported by the fact that both should tend to disappear if inflation is very persistent or very high. We have many indications of the shedding of money illusion and nominal institutions in high inflation, and I tend to agree with Summers's assessment that recent developments in the United States suggest that the world may well be on its way to fitting our models of rational behavior.

Macro Policy

WILLIAM D. NORDHAUS

Macroconfusion: The Dilemmas of Economic Policy

AMERICAN macroeconomists are in disarray. Like a shell-shocked army, barraged by criticism because of poor forecasts, wearied from fruitless battles with chronic inflation, confused because of divided intellectual leadership, they are unsure which way to retreat. Out of the ashes of defeat rises a new phalanx of competing theories, a ragtag collection of discarded ideas from the past as well as unproved fancies for the future.

In this period of reconstruction, the time has come to assert the superiority of the earlier, too quickly discarded views. I believe that the intellectual consensus of the late 1960s was basically sound. The synthesis of Keynesian and neoclassical economics—the "neo-Keynesian synthesis" for short—although oversimplified, is the best way to understand the puzzles of the economy as well as the dilemmas of policy. The neo-Keynesian synthesis is in critical condition today, not because it is flawed, but because it has too often been on the losing side of the battles against inflation and unemployment. The new phalanx of theorists— monetarists, supply siders, rational expectations, "deficists," goldbugs, and constitutionalists—have contributed little to resolving the dilemmas of economic policy. They only provide diversion from the real task of economic policymaking.

I sometimes wonder what Arthur Okun's view of the rise of the new army of macroeconomic theories would be. He remained a reconstructed Keynesian to the end. In his last paper, he criticized the rational expectations view as failing to explain many of the key features of the business cycle. His last book dismisses supply-side economists with one sentence in a footnote on page 353: "Their position simply cannot be taken seriously." I suspect Okun would have taken these theories increasingly seriously—as political happenings. But his rigorous demand that theory be consistent with reality would, I am sure, have left him untouched by their fanciful prescriptions.

The Central Problems for Economic Policy

The central problems for macroeconomic policy in the 1980s, while changed in nuance, are those of the 1970s—slow productivity growth, chronic inflation, high unemployment, and high vulnerability to volatile oil and foreign exchange markets remain the most important and durable issues. Contrary to much public discussion, we do *not* have a soaring budget deficit, public debt, or a runaway public sector. The task of macroeconomic theory is to understand the linkages between policy instruments and major economic problems so that policymakers can steer the economy in sensible directions.

The principal goals of macroeconomic policy are rapid growth in income, output, and consumption; high employment; price stability or low inflation; and external balance. As is shown in table 1, economic performance over the last decade has been depressing. In short, the goals have not been attained in the United States, or elsewhere.

As can be seen in the table, the last few years have witnessed a deterioration in all the major indexes of macroeconomic activity. Real growth of output, income, and consumption declined from one-third to one-half. Unemployment rates rose 2 percentage points. The inflation rate tripled, and the terms of trade deteriorated considerably after more than a decade of stability.

Having briefly suggested that the body economic is in critical condition—which few today would contest—I observe today little consensus about the diagnosis. There is deep division over the precise cause of the country's economic maladies. Was economic policy responsible for driving the economy off the road? I believe that the deterioration in economic performance did not result mainly from economic policy errors of the past.

It is useful to clarify what I mean by acquitting economic policy of responsibility for the current economic mess. It is not to deny, for example, that by ruthless anti-inflation policy chronic inflation could have been kept at a much lower level. But given the economic costs of erasing chronic inflation, it would not have been sensible economic policy to do so. In technical language, it is unlikely that an ex ante optimal macroeconomic policy would have improved markedly a reasonable objective function when taking into account the actual constraints under which the economy was operating in the 1970s.

Table 1. *Measures of Economic Performance in the United States, 1960–80*

Measure	1960–73	1974–80
Growth rate[a]		
Real GNP	4.2	2.4
Real consumption	4.2	2.8
Real national income[b]	4.5	2.1
Unemployment rate[c]	4.9	6.8
Inflation rate (CPI)[a]	3.2	9.2
Change in the terms of trade[a,d]	−0.1	−4.1

Source: *Economic Report of the President, January 1981;* and *Economic Indicators,* September 1981.
a. Growth rates are geometric averages, percent per year.
b. National income deflated by the consumption deflator.
c. Annual averages.
d. Ratio of implicit price of exports to implicit price of imports, 1960 = 100.

Two items can be used to illustrate the relative innocence of economic policy in the current economic mess, one concerning inflation, the other productivity growth.

An oft-repeated complaint about economic policy is that it has left the United States with a heritage of high inflation. In a recent study Otto Eckstein decomposes inflation into core, demand, and shock components.[1] He estimates the contribution each of these components made to the acceleration of inflation from 1960 to 1979. When all the demand shocks in this period are added up, the total contribution to inflation is minus 0.7 percentage point. In view of this result, it is hard to see how anyone could conclude that excessively expansionary policies were responsible for the acceleration of inflation over the last two decades.

A second myth concerning economic policy is that the slow productivity growth in the United States and abroad has been due to successive bouts of self-inflicted wounds. The most prominently mentioned problem is discouragement of capital formation. It is claimed that stop-go policies, high inflation, high taxes, loose money, tight money, and burdensome regulation have significantly weakened the incentive for investment.

Evidence on the role of disincentives can be obtained by examining international trends in investment behavior. The Organization for Economic Cooperation and Development has collected data on capital stocks and other determinants of productivity in major countries for the years 1960, 1973, and 1978. The results are shown in table 2.

The first column indicates the estimated share of pretax profits in

1. Otto Eckstein, *Core Inflation* (Prentice-Hall, 1981).

Table 2. *Contribution of Slowdown in Capital–Labor Ratio to Labor Productivity, 1960–73 and 1973–78*

Country	Pretax share of profits in GDP[a] (1)	Change in annual growth of capital–labor ratio[b] (2)	Contribution, slowdown to slowdown[c] (3)	Actual slowdown[b,d] (4)
Canada	0.34	+0.5	+0.2	−2.1
France	0.37	+1.0	+0.4	−1.7
Germany	0.33	−0.4	−0.1	−1.0
Italy	0.25	−2.4	−0.6	−4.3
Japan	0.31	−3.4	−1.1	−5.6
United Kingdom	0.29	−0.5	−0.1	−2.4
United States	0.29	−0.6	−0.2	−1.9

Source: William Nordhaus, "Economic Policy in the Face of Declining Productivity Growth," *European Economic Review* (forthcoming).
a. Taken to be the elasticity of output with respect to capital.
b. Annual growth rate, 1973–78, less annual growth rate, 1960–73 (percent).
c. Column 1 times column 2.
d. Output per employer, nonfarm business sectors.

gross domestic product (GDP)—conventionally taken as a good estimate of the elasticity of output with respect to capital services. The second column shows the acceleration or deceleration of the capital–labor ratio from the 1960–73 period to the 1973–78 period for each of seven industrial countries.

Multiplying column 1 by column 2 gives, in column 3, the growth-accounting estimate of the slowdown in labor productivity that should have come about because of the slowdown in the growth of the capital stock. This estimate is either of the wrong sign or very small in five of the countries, and above the noise levels only in Italy and Japan. But the major conclusion is clear: by the conventional analysis, in no country could the slowdown in investment and capital formation plausibly be a major part of the productivity slowdown. Indeed, in no country is the estimated contribution of capital more than one-fifth the size of the productivity slowdown.

While crude, these calculations give the same qualitative answers as the more careful estimates for the United States. In a review of recent studies of productivity behavior, I concluded that perhaps one-fifth of the slowdown in productivity in the United States could be attributed to economic mismanagement. It is a puzzle, best left to the political scientists, how so small a factor can have become the major popular explanation for the slowdown.

So I conclude that some of the claims about the failure of economic policy are groundless. This is not saying much. You don't get a medal for good driving by making it around the block without a crash, but at least you stay out of jail.

Of course, even agreement that policy played a relatively unimportant part in the dismal performance of the 1970s provides little guidance about the appropriate role for policy in the 1980s. Appropriate policy will depend more on which of the shards of the fragmented consensus one examines. The next two sections review some of today's theories, and the final section attempts to provide some prescriptions for economic policy.

The Fragmented Consensus

Since the central paradigm of macroeconomics today is the neo-Keynesian synthesis, I will first outline its elements, with particular attention focused on elements that are central to economic policy, and then compare it with the major competing paradigms—monetarism, rational expectations, and supply side views.

It is obviously impossible to summarize the complex body of neo-Keynesian thinking in a few pages. In what follows I will concentrate on the aspects most clearly related to economic policy. These are the distinction between, as well as the determination of, actual and potential output; the role of monetary and fiscal policies in the determination of output; and the division of the growth of nominal output between prices and quantities.

The first element in the neo-Keynesian synthesis is the distinction between actual and potential output. Actual output is whatever is produced in a given period. Potential output is what the economy could produce if resource utilization were at a high or benchmark level—today taken as a 5 percent unemployment rate for labor. It is not an oversim-plification to think of actual output as "demand" and potential output as "supply"; and further to regard the forces determining supply and demand as quite distinct, acting with quite different time lags. One of the central elements of the neo-Keynesian synthesis—clearly laid out in the 1962 *Economic Report of the President,* but since then often forgot-ten by policymakers—is that both the demand and supply sides of the economy require attention from economic policy. But the kinds of policies that affect the two are very different, and there is only a weak link between actual and potential output, particularly in the short run.

The need to keep an eye on improving the performance of both actual and potential output has proven a rigorous requirement. Central economic policy treatises of the 1970s—the McCracken report, Okun's *Prices and Quantities*,[2] most issues of the *Economic Report of the President*—largely ignore the problem of increasing potential growth. If there is any justification for "supply-side" criticism, it lies in the tendency of Keynesian thinking in the 1970s to forget the lessons of growth theory of the 1960s.

It should be noted in passing that the intellectual foundation of the distinction between actual and potential output has never been well articulated from a theoretical point of view. Its roots lie in the "fix-price" view of the world, that is, one in which prices and nominal wages are viewed as largely exogenous in the short run. The distinction would not make much sense in a "flex-price" world, where all markets are auction markets like corn or silver. In the flex-price world the short-run outcomes closely approximate a competitive outcome, and there is little reason to think output would be far from the level of output that would be produced by a competitive economy with auction markets ("ideal output" for short). In the fix-price world, in my view, output is often far from ideal and probably has a secular bias below the ideal output. In this case, if potential output is in the neighborhood of ideal output, the gap between potential output is a measure of the deviation of actual from ideal output. (Because of asymmetries in fix-price markets, ideal output may even be considerably above potential output.) The infirm foundation of fix-price behavior has been pounced on by critics from the rational expectations school and will be returned to below.

The second feature of the neo-Keynesian synthesis relates to the determination of potential output. In current thinking potential output is determined in a way that is best described by neoclassical growth theory. That is, output is determined by a production function with labor, capital, energy, and other material inputs. This production function is often described as exhibiting constant or modestly increasing returns to scale and having a variable rate of technological change.

---

2. Paul McCracken and others, *Towards Full Employment and Price Stability*, Report to the Organization for Economic Cooperation and Development (Paris: OECD, 1977); Arthur M. Okun, *Prices and Quantities: A Macroeconomic Analysis* (Brookings Institution, 1981).

Assuming that the rate of technological change is exogenously given, potential output growth is determined by the growth of factor inputs. Policy affects potential output growth chiefly by raising or lowering the rate of formation of human or reproducible tangible capital.

This feature of the neo-Keynesian synthesis is not subject to much debate by the critics. With the minor provisos discussed in the final section of this paper, the view of the growth of potential just outlined is shared by all the major schools of thought reviewed here. Indeed, sometimes other paradigms accept the neoclassical growth model as applying to the short run as well as to the long run.

One of the major findings of empirical economic growth theory, however, is the great difficulty of increasing the rate of growth of potential output by policy. (This is a corollary of the earlier proposition that policy has little to do with the productivity slowdown.) Edward Denison estimated that a large increase in private net investment (raising it one-quarter above what it would otherwise be) would raise the growth of potential output only 0.1 percentage point a year.[3] Given this very modest response of potential output to policy, it may be understandable that policymakers, particularly those with short time horizons, have generally ignored the goal of increased potential output and focused instead on stabilization policy.

The short-run determination of actual output is the major difference between the new paradigms today. The differences arise from views about the determination of nominal GNP and views about how nominal GNP is split between prices and quantities.

The view of the neo-Keynesian synthesis of the determination of the level of actual output has changed little since the 1930s—though it has been refined and given considerable empirical flesh. In this view output is basically determined by aggregate spending, as in the Hicksian IS-LM curve. Of course, reality and the embodiment of this vision or reality in large-scale econometric models are much more complicated than the simple IS-LM framework, but the increased realism of the 1,000-plus equation econometric models mainly adds to the distinction between the impacts of different taxes or financial policies and better determination of the time lags. With the exception of the greater power currently given to money, there appear to be no major differences between the behavior

3. Edward F. Denison, *The Sources of Economic Growth in the United States and the Alternatives Before Us* (New York: Committee for Economic Development, 1962).

of the large models today and that of the earliest econometric Keynesian models.

The best way of summarizing the beliefs of the neo-Keynesian synthesis is by examining simulations of the major models—the DRI, Wharton, Chase, MIT-Penn-SSRC models. From model simulations and comparisons, the major features of the neo-Keynesian synthesis models emerge, as follows: fiscal policy appears to have substantial impact on actual output, at least in the short run, and the multipliers do not differ much among major models. Monetary policy also has substantial effects on output, but the money multipliers differ enormously among econometric models. Thus both money and fiscal policy matter, but the uncertainty is much greater for the former than the latter.

The final important feature of the neo-Keynesian synthesis concerns the split of impulses to demand between output and prices. In other words, what is the view of aggregate price determination? No issue has produced more intellectual turmoil among macroeconomists than inflation theory; and the evolution of thinking from the 1930s to today is considerable.

It seems a reasonable approximation to say that some early Keynesian thinking held prices and wages to be approximately constant up to the point where the economy hit full employment. Today the view is quite different. Inflation is taken to be the sum of inertial, cyclical, and volatile or random forces. The inertial element is the inherited "underlying" rate of inflation, particularly from wages, which changes slowly in response to experience and expectations. Cyclical elements include a very modest response of wage inflation to unemployment as well as some response of markups and material prices to the cycle. Volatile forces include such elements as oil and food prices, as well as the effects of interest rates.

In the view of the neo-Keynesian synthesis, inertial or chronic inflation poses one of the most difficult problems for economic policy. This is because chronic inflation is extremely costly to erase, while the benefits of lower inflation are subtle. According to Okun's calculations of the short-run trade-off between unemployment and inflation, but with the use of an up-to-date Okun's Law coefficient, it would cost two-thirds of one year's GNP to lower chronic inflation by 10 percentage points. The high cost of reducing inflation, or the stubbornness of the inertial element in inflation, arises because inflation is so firmly embedded in our institutions in formal and informal contracts.

Put differently, a shock that lowers spending has its major short-run impact on output. Evidence indicates that around 90 percent of the first-year response to a spending shock shows up in output, while 10 percent is in prices. As the time period lengthens, this split changes, moving more toward price response and away from output response. Although econometric evidence is obviously unavailable, it seems likely that after several decades all the response is in prices. These numbers are, it must be emphasized, not known with certainty, nor are they independent of space, time, or expectations. But the evidence for the United States is that the short-run division of nominal demand shocks between quantities and prices is closer to 90–10 than the 10–90 or 0–100 envisaged by the other paradigms.

Alternative Paradigms

It will be useful to describe briefly the major alternative schools of thought that have affected thinking about economic policy in the United States. It should be emphasized that the summary below, as for the neo-Keynesian synthesis, cannot fairly represent the full richness of these theories. Moreover, I have emphasized only those aspects of the theories that relate to economic policy.

Monetarism

Monetarism is a venerable doctrine going back for centuries. It is, in my view, best interpreted as a special case of the neo-Keynesian synthesis. Monetarists accept the distinction between actual and potential output, as well as the view of the determination of potential output of the neo-Keynesian synthesis. The major difference lies in the view of output determination and the inflation process.

In the strict monetarist view, money velocity is interest-inelastic, so nominal GNP is determined by the money stock (although the definition of "the" money stock is quite volatile). In the standard Hicksian framework, such a proposition can be interpreted as a vertical LM curve. Fiscal policy affects the composition but not the level of nominal GNP. The money multiplier is large and stable, while the fiscal multipliers are zero. Today, most monetarists have backed off from the extreme view of the insensitivity of velocity to monetary and fiscal policy of earlier periods. The fallback position is sometimes "constitutional monetarism" and sometimes the "new classical macroeconomics."

The second major aspect, perhaps less generally agreed upon by monetarists, is their view of the inflationary process. Along with all the other non-Keynesian paradigms adhering to the Walrasian conception of markets, monetarists believe that prices adjust relatively rapidly to demand or supply shocks. Thus any shock to aggregate demand ends up mainly in price shocks rather than in output shocks.

While they are optimistic compared to most neo-Keynesians, monetarists still diverge widely on the costs of disinflation. In testimony before a British select committee on monetary policy, Milton Friedman stated that he thought there would be virtually no loss of output from a program of monetary restraint, and David Laidler provided an estimate of the response of inflation to slack ten times greater than that cited above.[4] On the other hand, work by Philip Cagan and Jerome Stein provides estimates that are from two to four times more optimistic.[5]

The two basic propositions of monetarism—interest-inelastic demand for money and quick price adjustment—have received scant empirical support in most careful structural statistical studies. Once an exogenous velocity is abandoned, however, it becomes virtually impossible to distinguish the implications of monetarism from those of the neo-Keynesian synthesis.

New Classical Macroeconomics

A second major school of thought today is the rational expectations or new classical macroeconomics (NCM) view. This view has been developed by Robert E. Lucas, Jr., Thomas J. Sargent, and Neil Wallace over the last ten years.

The NCM school is based on two central premises. The first, and less controversial, is that economic agents form expectations on the basis of all available information. This premise has been a provocative tool for challenging established techniques for modeling expectations. It has led,

4. Milton Friedman, in United Kingdom, *Third Report from the Treasury and Civil Service Committee of the House of Commons*, Session 1980–81, *Monetary Policy*, vol. 1, p. xxxvi; and David Laidler, in ibid.

5. Phillip Cagan, "The Reduction of Inflation by Slack Demand," in William Fellner, Project Director, *Contemporary Economic Problems in 1978* (American Enterprise Institute for Public Policy Research, 1978), pp. 13–45; and Jerome L. Stein, "Inflation, Employment and Stagflation," *Journal of Monetary Economics*, vol. 4 (April 1978), pp. 193–228.

for example, to much better understanding of why financial markets appear to behave perversely—why "good news" looks like "bad news." It has also led to an understanding of why "unstable" structural equations are to be expected in, say, price and wage behavior.

The second, more controversial premise is that all markets clear in the very short run, that is to say, prices are perfectly flexible. This premise is more an assumption than an empirical finding; moreover, it is at variance with considerable empirical work on actual price and wage behavior.

These two assumptions provide a rich set of propositions concerning behavior and policy. An early result—outdoing monetarist thinking— was to suggest that the Phillips curve is vertical in the short run as well as in the long run. A more general result was the "policy ineffectiveness theorem," which states that anticipated policies affect only prices, not real output.

One way of interpreting the NCM view is that it accepts the long-run but not the short-run half of the neo-Keynesian synthesis. That is, it views the economy as in neoclassical equilibrium, though subject to random shocks. According to this interpretation, the NCM view would share the prescriptions concerning acceleration of the growth of potential output, but not those concerning short-run stabilization policy. Thus actual output never deviates from potential except when there are random shocks. The division of output between prices and quantities is at the extreme end of the spectrum, with 100 percent of anticipated changes in spending on nominal GNP going into prices. In this view, disinflation is an easy and costless process that simply involves an announced and credible reduction in aggregate demand.

The professional verdict on the NCM is still out. Given the dubious nature of the fundamental flexible price assumption, many of the policy prescriptions of the NCM have been widely and correctly viewed as elegant but irrelevant. Thus while the NCM school has been extremely influential inside the economics profession, it has been adopted reluctantly by practitioners. Perhaps the idea that policy cannot affect the real economy is as foreign to policymakers as random walk theories of stock prices are to stockbrokers.

Supply-Side Economics

Conceived on a cocktail napkin, carried by an ambitious ex-quarter-back congressman, and midwifed by a skillful president, supply-side economics burst upon the economic scene physically full-grown but intellectually dwarfed. In contrast to the other major paradigms, particularly the new classical macroeconomics school, supply-side economics is fundamentally a political inspiration without serious scientific support. In this respect it resembles the limits-to-growth movement of a decade ago.

The major tenet of supply-side economics is that economic activity responds quickly to relative prices, particularly to changes in tax rates, but that income effects are unimportant. Supply siders predicted that the reductions in the personal tax rates in the Laffer-Kemp-Roth proposal enacted in the 1981 Revenue Act would lead to greatly expanded supplies of labor and capital, and thus to rapid economic growth. Therefore, ignoring the pessimism engendered by the work of Denison discussed above, supply siders appear to believe that the growth in potential output can be readily increased.

Aside from this central tenet of the supply-side school, it is difficult to glean a comprehensive (or even comprehensible) view of economic policy. The major problem, apparent even in the central proposition, is the failure to distinguish between actual and potential output. Thus the supply siders like to point to the Kennedy tax cuts of 1964 and 1965 as evidence of the validity of their views. Yet the Kennedy cuts were designed to increase actual output—and they clearly did so—and were only incidentally aimed at potential output.

Does this indicate that supply siders are simply closet Keynesians, assuming a new mantle of respectability for revving up the economy? Not likely. A more plausible interpretation is that the supply siders have failed to grasp the analytical distinction between aggregate supply and demand.

Since they do not distinguish between actual and potential output, it is easy to understand why the supply siders have difficulty articulating a consistent view of the inflationary process. If markets clear instantaneously, as the new classical macroeconomists believe, inflation can be quickly erased. If, on the other hand, inflation persists because wage and price behavior is sticky, then a notion of excess demand or supply is necessary to provide a mechanism by which inertial inflation accelerates or decelerates. Without either the market-clearing or the sticky-behavior model, inflation seems completely ad hoc. I have not seen any of the major supply-side enthusiasts outline a theory of inflation. This lack of theory has recently been compensated for by a new bold proposal to lick inflation—a return to the gold standard.

Policy Dilemmas

Over the coming years five issues must be faced by policymakers. Almost all of them have been part of the internal dialogue of macroeconomics for decades. But the economic turmoil of the 1970s has made the dilemmas more painful and the trade-offs more intractable.

Economic Constitutionalism

A pervasive issue concerns the movement that imposes on economic decisionmakers stricter economic discipline, such as fixed monetary rules or constitutional amendments. I call this trend "economic constitutionalism." Examples of such a trend are legion. Perhaps the first was the congressional resolution that required the Federal Reserve to announce monetary targets. More recent are proposals for constitutional amendments on the budget balance, expenditure limitations, and money growth, as well as a number of more informal operating rules for the fiscal and monetary authorities.

From an analytical point of view, there are two reasons for economic constitutionalism. The first is the need for credibility. Assume that we accept the view that a credible disinflation policy would lead to little output loss. What we need to find is a cheap way of being credible. As Thomas C. Schelling has shown, the best way to establish the credibility of a decision is for the decisionmaker to put himself in a position where changing the policy would be extremely costly to him. Thus by announcing, legislating, constitutionalizing policies—why not shoot inconsistent politicians?—credibility can be enhanced.

If credibility is the key to better policies, however, why do we need to impose stricter discipline to be credible? I would generally expect optimal credible policies to be the same as optimal incredible policies (although counterexamples do exist). In this case the worrisome element in economic policies would be—and this is the second point—that the optimal credible policy differs from likely *actual* policy.

According to this second interpretation, economic constitutionalism is necessary because political leaders are perceived as untrustworthy. This perception has many roots. One of the most general is the well-documented decline in respect for authority, particularly of political figures. This has spilled over into the economic debate in the form of distrust of discretionary political management of the economy. Another would be the failed promises of the "new economics" of the 1960s, the impression that hard on the heels of the belated but short-lived Keynesian revolution in U.S. macroeconomic policy came the economic disasters of the 1970s. Perhaps a third source would be growing political conservatism, part of which is the result of earlier "liberal" programs' lack of success.

Many of the most radical proposals for management of the economy—particularly the monetarism and "deficism" discussed below—can be interpreted as reflecting a profound mistrust in the institutions of American democracy. The movement for economic constitutionalism is sometimes rationalized as a retreat from "fine-tuning" the economy, but this is inaccurate. It is rather a desire to abjure all discretionary management of the economy.

Recent economic theory has begun to incorporate explicitly some formal theory of the interaction between political and economic forces, as in the theory of the political business cycle. This line of thought suggests the possibility that elected policymakers will manipulate economic policy in ways that exacerbate business cycles.

The revulsion against democratic policymaking among economists has generally led them to suggest adding legal constraints to the policy process. Two of the most popular doctrines suggesting constraint are monetarism and deficism, discussed further below. These are attempts to substitute suboptimal but nonmanipulable rules for manipulable but potentially optimal policies as a way of inserting backbone into spineless politicians.

Not to be outdone, the supply siders have suggested a different economic rule that will discipline policymakers' return to the gold standard. The rationale for this is that by returning to a "high-quality money" inflation will automatically (and painlessly?) cease. Without the discipline of the convertibility of the dollar into gold, it is argued, policymakers will be subject to the temptation to use inflation as a way of resolving political conflicts.

Not all procedural reforms are without intrinsic merit. There are other and more constructive uses of procedures to remove the defects of current institutions, particularly piecemeal decisionmaking. The Congressional Budget and Impoundment Control Act of 1974 is a way of ensuring that Congress acts on the budget as a whole rather than bidding up the total budget in small increments. A similar proposal has been suggested for regulation—the so-called regulatory budget.

What is the economist's judgment on constitutionalism? These approaches have both an economic and political component. From a purely economic point of view, however, it seems clear that the use of general rules, like a fixed money growth or a balanced budget rule, is at best a second-best solution to stabilizing the economy or promoting the appropriate balance between public and private sector. One academic defender has labeled strict monetary constraints as "the half-blind leading the blind." A more apt analogy is that economic constitutionalism represents the lame leading the sometimes wicked.

If we accept the view that political management of the economy will be subject to impure motivation and incomplete knowledge, real dilemmas arise in the optimal design of economic policy institutions. Surely there are better institutional arrangements, however, than imposing rigid rules with little economic justification. Economic constitutionalism also reflects a conservative view of the role of government, a view that much of government nondefense spending is wasteful. With roadblocks to slow government spending or prevent deficits, social programs are likely to wither on the vine. The acid test of whether these programs are simply procedural or reflect an underlying conservative stance lies in their treatment of national defense: most proposals have an "escape clause" that exempts defense from their stringencies—a sure sign of the philosophical origin of the idea.

Deficism

In 1863 a man from Las Vegas, New Mexico, was found guilty of having murdered a witch who had supposedly given him tuberculosis. In 1925 John Scopes was convicted of having illegally taught the theory of evolution. By 1980 thirty-one of the states had passed resolutions calling for a constitutional convention to impose a balanced budget on the federal government. What these events have in common is that they exhibit the triumph of scientifically unsupported theories over the accumulated evidence.

Many economists and policymakers are calling for a balanced federal budget to cure high interest rates, high inflation, and swollen government. The movement, which I call "deficism," is fundamentally flawed as an economic doctrine, for the federal deficit has major shortcomings both as an accounting measure and as a device for controlling the economy. The only serious intellectual support for deficism can be found in its use as an indirect constraint on the political process, as explained above in the section on constitutionalism. But it must be emphasized that it is highly defective as a constitutionalist constraint.

The first defect of deficism is its reliance on an imperfect instrument for controlling economic activity, this problem being similar to the reliance of monetarists on an endlessly evolving concept of the money supply. An examination of the January 1981 estimates for the 1981 federal budget illustrates the problems. The "official" budget deficit was estimated to be a frightening $55 billion. However, this figure excluded two sets of programs: off-budget entities like the Tennessee Valley Authority and interest subsidies on various loan programs. After correcting for these omitted programs, the deficit became $105 billion.

However, the official deficit does not correct for two standard accounting concepts, investment and capital gains. The projection for 1981 was that $143 billion of outlays would be investment-type activities, like filling the strategic petroleum reserve. Also, capital gains on the debt (or, in accountants' jargon, correction for the real value of monetary assets) reduced outlays by $78 billion. With these four corrections the federal government was estimated to run a surplus of $116 billion for fiscal 1981.

Of course, even this "corrected" federal surplus is an inadequate measure. But the point is that conventional measurement tools are highly imperfect, underestimating federal deficits just as they overestimate corporate profits. How can we seriously consider using as a control variable a tool whose conceptual and measurement uncertainty is on the order of 10 percent of GNP?

Deficism also suffers from an inadequate grounding in economic theory, for deficits and surpluses per se play no direct role in attaining any of our major economic goals. The federal budget deficit itself does not enter into any of the major behavior equations of the economy—into the determination of inflation, aggregate demand, potential output, or interest rates. Rather, the level and composition of spending and taxes, as well as other off-budget programs, are the major channels by which the budget affects economic activity. And even for these variables the route by which taxes and expenditures affect the economy is almost wholly through their influence on aggregate demand or potential output. Only when one enters into much more complicated general-equilibrium models of financial markets can a separate influence of federal debt and its growth be found, and even here the sign of the effect is ambiguous.

In sum, the current emphasis on bringing the federal deficit under control can be considered misguided at best, disingenuous at worst, but in the end irrational.

Monetarism

Above I discussed briefly the monetarist economic philosophy. I will be even briefer in an analysis of the monetarist policy solutions, mainly because there is nothing new to add. The pros and cons of monetarism have been discussed ad nauseam. Two of the most illuminating debates were that between Milton Friedman and Walter Heller in the early 1970s, and that between James Tobin and David Laidler in the *Economic Journal* in 1981.[6]

The views of monetarists place a distinctive stamp on their policy proposals. Clearly monetarists look mainly to the central bank for policy execution. Moreover, since they estimate the output cost of reducing chronic inflation to be modest, they are less reluctant to recommend slow money and output growth as effective and inexpensive cures for chronic inflation. Finally, monetarists believe that the money demand function is stable; this reasoning leads to the conclusion that a stable path of money growth of 3 to 4 percent annually will lead quickly to stable, noninflationary growth paths.

For an outsider, the most striking feature of the debate is that it continues. With the several glaring weaknesses of the monetarist doctrine—the evidence of interest-sensitivity of the demand for money, the instability of the very definition of money, the highly unreliable nature of the relationship between interest rates and output—it is difficult to understand how the belief in the monetarist solution can survive and thrive.

The Productivity Slowdown

Over a period of a decade or more the growth of potential output will be the principal determinant of real economic performance, and the growth of total factor productivity, along with labor force participation patterns, the key to future growth in potential output. With some

6. Milton Friedman and Walter W. Heller, *Monetary vs. Fiscal Policy* (Norton, 1969); James Tobin, "The Monetarist Counter-Revolution Today—An Appraisal," *Economic Journal,* vol. 91 (March 1981), pp. 29–42; and David Laidler, "Monetarism: An Interpretation and an Assessment," *Economic Journal,* vol. 91 (March 1981), pp. 1–28, 43–57.

provisos, there is no real controversy among the major macroeconomic schools about the appropriate policy to spur productivity. The main way that an economy can increase the growth in potential is by increasing the fraction of output devoted to human and tangible capital formation. Virtually all economists have called for one of an assortment of pro-saving or pro-investment policies, from tax relief for investment to policies designed to spur personal savings to monetary policies that lower real interest rates.

The major dissenters from this consensus are the supply siders and the neo-Malthusians. The supply siders have extremely unrealistic notions about how easy it is to increase savings and investment. For example, supply siders suggest that personal tax rate cuts will have a significant impact on productivity growth. A careful review of the evidence indicates that there may well be a positive impact on produc-tivity if the growth of actual output is accelerated; but this is clearly a "demand-side" effect, not a supply-side effect. It is highly unlikely that personal tax cuts will have a positive impact on the growth of cyclically corrected output per person-hour employed; indeed, given the labor force responses of different demographic groups, the impact on potential productivity is likely to be negative rather than positive.

On the other side the neo-Malthusians paint a pessimistic picture in which economic growth will be constrained by limitations of resources or energy. One might have predicted that this view would land on fertile soil during the turbulent 1970s, but it appears to have received little serious attention either by economists or by policymakers.

Chronic Inflation

The final policy dilemma is the enduring issue of chronic inflation. Arthur Okun devoted the last years of his professional life to the diagnosis and cure of chronic inflation. He had something to say about every economic issue, but he said everything worth saying about inflation theory and policy.

One of the ironies of economic history is that, while Keynesians have often been thought insouciant about inflation, most of the recent inquiry into the mechanics of the inflation process and the dilemmas of policy have been undertaken in the framework of the neo-Keynesian synthesis. This apparent paradox is understandable, given the views of the other major paradigms about price adjustment. Only when wage and price adjustment is slow relative to the pace of other economic forces, as in the neo-Keynesian synthesis, does it become interesting to study inflation. It is also in just this circumstance of slow price adjustment that policy faces the problem of the Phillips curve trade-off in which inflation control involves significant economic costs.

To understand the dilemmas of anti-inflation policy it is necessary to restate an earlier point: the orthodox way to slow chronic inflation is by inducing slack in product and labor markets, and such a cure is extremely costly. To repeat the calculation given above, to reduce an underlying annual inflation rate of 10 percent to 0 would require forgoing approximately two-thirds of a year's GNP, although it might be spread over an extended period of time. This embedded chronic inflation is akin to an external national debt of $2.0 trillion—a debt that we must either live with in the form of high chronic inflation (with the "interest payments" being inefficiencies, misallocations, and shoe leather) or pay off in lower economic activity. The fact that occasionally fortune allows actual inflation to drop quickly and painlessly, as it has over the last year, confuses markets about the causes and costs of disinflation. An occasional run of good luck, in economic policy as in roulette, should not blind us to the fact that substituting chance for a deliberate anti-inflation policy leads to central bankers' ruin.

Since reducing chronic inflation is so costly, inflation has become the major constraint on economic activity in the United States over the last decade. The main reason policymakers have been unwilling to set higher targets for output and employment is simply their fear that higher targets would risk increasing inflation. It is difficult to guess how much higher output might have been without an inflation constraint; unemployment rates in the 2 to 3 percent range, and hence output 8 to 10 percent higher, would surely have been much closer to the ideal output than the outcome shown in table 1 was.

Once inflation is accepted as the major constraint on high levels of utilization of labor and capital, economists will have to think about economic problems in a novel and paradoxical way. This was the topic of the last two chapters of Okun's *Prices and Quantities*. In such a world, the social cost of public- or private-sector activities is measured not only by their resource costs but also by their inflationary impacts. Thus, when considering alternative ways of cutting taxes, the differential impacts of taxes on the price level should enter into the cost-benefit calculation along with more Keynesian considerations of aggregate demand or neoclassical strictures of resource allocation. Or in weighing alternative energy policies, it would be necessary to calculate the "energy price externality," the impact of different energy price trajectories on prices and thus on overall economic activity.

Given the view that inflation is the major constraint on economic activity in the short run, it is clear that much more thought should be given to devising "efficient" anti-inflation policies. An efficient policy is one that imposes lower economic costs than the orthodox anti-inflation policy of inducing economic slack.

Two classes of more efficient policies have been identified: cost-reducing policies and incomes policies. Cost-reducing policies consist of government actions, such as cutting indirect taxes or promoting productivity, that lower the normal costs of doing business. These provide one-shot reductions in the price level, but some fraction of them probably end up in a lower underlying inflation rate. There is little controversy about such measures, but the stock of cost-reducing actions is small and probably largely depleted.

Incomes policies are direct interventions in markets to moderate the pace of price and wage increases. A more modern version of incomes policies, relying on a marketlike mechanism, is "tax-based incomes policy," or TIP. TIPs continue to be the most promising of the "efficient" anti-inflation strategies.

Yet another efficient anti-inflation policy would be a monetary reform, such as that suggested by Jeffrey Shafer. This approach would revise all contracts and financial instruments (except currency) by reducing both future prices and nominal interest rates by a given amount, say, 6 percent a year compounded from today. A labor contract that contained annual increases of $2 an hour now and $1 an hour two years hence would thereby have these increases reduced to $2/(1.06) and $1/(1.06)^2, respectively. Such a scheme is complicated and might involve thorny issues of the extraterritorial impact of U.S. law on dollar-denominated foreign contracts. It has the advantage, unlike other price-wage policies, that such a monetary reform would in principle reduce inflation painlessly, that is, without changing relative prices.

Thinking about the efficient allocation of resources in a macroeconomic framework where inflation is the major constraint on economic activity has proved to be an arduous task. Like physics after relativity theory, the world seems upside down when the short-run marginal cost of an action is its effect on dollar prices rather than its opportunity cost in diverting resources from other uses. The construction of a theory of value in which the impact of inflation is a central part of the cost of an economic event, along with detailed analysis of the kinds of policies that would efficiently reduce chronic inflation or prevent its accelerating inflation, were the tasks that Arthur Okun had undertaken before his untimely death. Much further work remains to be done to synthesize Okun's theoretical and policy insights on the topic of chronic inflation into the body of modern macroeconomic thinking.

Comment by Stanley Fischer

THE NORDHAUS paper is refreshing for its boldness. Nordhaus presents a spirited defense of a currently unfashionable view: that the neo-Keynesian synthesis of the late 1960s constitutes an adequate foundation for understanding the behavior of the economy and for policymaking. Like any good strategist, he makes an active offense part of the defense. His sallies against monetarism, goldbugs, rational expectations, and especially supply siders provide entertainment along with instruction.

Many of Nordhaus's arguments are appealing. His evaluations of the current interest in the gold standard, of capital fetishism, and of supply-side economics are compelling. So is his view that the productivity slowdown is the most important macroeconomic phenomenon of the 1970s. I agree too with his belief that the neo-Keynesian synthesis of the 1960s remains a useful component of our understanding of the economy. But my comments will center on points of disagreement. Specifically I will argue, first, that Nordhaus substantially underestimates the intellectual coherence and cogency of the attack on the neo-Keynesian synthesis of the late 1960s that was mounted by Robert Lucas and others in the 1970s, that he therefore underestimates the extent to which the younger generation of macroeconomists have moved away from the view of the economy that he takes for granted, and that he underestimates the depth of the defense of his views that he has to mount; and second, that for policy purposes there is indeed a useful neo-Keynesian–Friedman–Phelps-Lucas synthesis, but that there remains an awkward gap between sensible policy advice and sound theory.[7]

7. This was the situation deplored by John Maynard Keynes in *The General Theory of Employment, Interest and Money* (London: Macmillan, 1936), p. 20.

Macroeconomics of the 1960s and 1970s

The neo-Keynesian synthesis of the late 1960s consisted of the IS-LM apparatus writ large (very large) with a wage-price sector appended. The Phillips curve was not yet vertical; perhaps there was an expected inflation term on the right-hand side of the reduced-form price-price Phillips curve, but its coefficient was certainly less than one. Progress was expected to come from further refinement, meaning enlargement, of the large econometric models. The models were confidently being used for policy simulations.

Three subsequent developments have affected professional views of the working of the economy and policy.

1. The rational expectations equilibrium with misperceptions (REEM) view of the economy has been worked out.

2. The Lucas econometric policy evaluation critique[8] is accepted by many as invalidating any claims to usefulness of policy simulations in existing econometric models, or at least those of the late 1960s.

3. The notion of dynamic inconsistency of policy has been developed to justify the need for policy rules rather than discretion.

Nordhaus well describes the REEM approach to economics. He dismisses it as elegant but irrelevant on the grounds of its dubious assumption of price flexibility. He argues further that the approach implies both that output should not deviate persistently from the potential level and that changes in the inflation rate can easily be achieved through the implementation of a credible slower money growth policy. He also notes that it has had virtually no effect on policy: "Perhaps the idea that policy cannot affect the real economy is as foreign to policymakers as random walk theories of stock prices are to stockbrokers."

Like Nordhaus, I believe that the price-flexibility assumption of REEM is a crucial weakness. But the approach is dismissed too quickly. First, REEM treats unemployment as search related, attaches no great significance to the unemployment rate, and does not regard itself as destroyed by the serial correlation of unemployment. The well-known early criticism that REEM could not explain the serial correlation of output is clearly false: once the economy is moved away from a particular

8. Robert E. Lucas, Jr., "Econometric Policy Evaluation: A Critique," in Karl Brunner and Allan H. Meltzer, eds., *The Phillips Curve and Labor Markets,* Carnegie-Rochester Conference Series on Public Policy, vol. 1 (North-Holland, 1976), pp. 19–46.

output path, various sources of persistence, like capital accumulation or inventory accumulation or slow labor adjustment, can keep it away from that path for some time.

Indeed, I am not sure that REEM accepts the distinction between potential and actual output in the same sense as Nordhaus. The full employment level of output that appears in the Lucas supply function is usually subscripted with a t. That level of output is probably best interpreted as the level the economy would attain in a given period if there were no shocks in that period and all past shocks were taken into account. If a variety of mechanisms keep output serially correlated and if unemployment is generated by search behavior, then changing short-run wage prospects associated with output fluctuations can certainly be interpreted as producing serially correlated unemployment rates in REEM models.

As an aside, the 1970s were not easy on the notion of potential output, important though it may be. The decade saw a rising time series of estimates of the full employment rate of unemployment, along with changing Okun's Law coefficients. In 1970 it was quite clear that the natural, or full employment, rate of unemployment was around 4.5 percent; now estimates range from 5 percent to above 6 percent. In 1970 the Okun coefficient was 3, today it is 2. Confidence in estimates of potential output must be lower than it was ten years ago.

Nordhaus's second criticism of REEM concerns its implication that disinflation is easy as long as policy changes are credible. Credibility is the REEM dummy variable that explains the failure of disinflation policies to work rapidly. But it is not for that reason an empty argument. There are reasons other than credibility that a sharp reduction in money growth would not produce immediate disinflation and would produce unemployment. Nonetheless, the adjustment process would indeed be quicker if the policy change were credible. Given credibility as an economic variable, REEM can survive Mrs. Thatcher and probably even President Reagan's failure to produce quick disinflation.

Finally, there are arguments that price stickiness is not a fatal flaw in REEM. It has been argued—for instance, by Robert Barro and Robert Hall—that prices and wages can be irrelevant to the allocation of resources, which magically arrange themselves into a Pareto optimum.[9]

9. Robert J. Barro, "Long-Term Contracting, Sticky Prices and Monetary Policy," *Journal of Monetary Economics*, vol. 3 (July 1977), pp. 305–16; and Robert E. Hall, "Employment Fluctuations and Wage Rigidity," *Brookings Papers on Economic Activity*, *1:1980*, pp. 91–123.

The reason for this is that otherwise some people could be made better off without anyone being made worse off, a situation that proponents of the argument find it hard to believe could exist. The important point made in this argument is that, without having a theory that explains price inflexibility, it is difficult to know what policy or other implications follow from that fact. It is certainly possible to build models with price inflexibility in which anticipated monetary policy is irrelevant to output determination, as Bennett McCallum has shown.[10]

The objections to REEM that Nordhaus raises have thus been discussed in the literature and countered with arguments of varying persuasiveness. Nordhaus and I both find some of the arguments unpersuasive, but that certainly does not dispose of the REEM approach. At this stage, many of the best and brightest young macroeconomists are working within that approach, trying to build a new paradigm to replace the one that existed at the end of the 1960s.

Indeed, the situation bears all the marks of the counterrevolutionary stage set out in Harry Johnson's remarkable 1971 Ely lecture.[11] The approach has spawned new theoretical and empirical techniques that can be applied to old problems but that need further technical development before they can reasonably be expected to deliver on their promise. Too much remains to be done to give up the REEM approach soon, especially in favor of a comparatively recent orthodoxy.

It is in this context that I believe Nordhaus substantially underestimates the impact of the second leg of the REEM triad—the Lucas

10. Bennett T. McCallum, "A Monetary Policy Ineffectiveness Result in a Model with a Predetermined Price Level," *Economics Letters*, vol. 3, no. 1 (1979), pp. 1–4.

11. Harry G. Johnson, "The Keynesian Revolution and the Monetarist Counter-Revolution," *American Economic Review*, vol. 61 (May 1971, *Papers and Proceedings, 1970*), pp. 1–14. Johnson was of course discussing the monetarist counterrevolution, which he correctly predicted would fail. But his arguments can be adapted with very little change to describe the more successful REEM counterrevolution. One even sees—for instance, in Robert E. Lucas, Jr., "Understanding Business Cycles," in Karl Brunner and Allan H. Meltzer, eds., *Stabilization of the Domestic and International Economy*, Carnegie-Rochester Conference Series on Public Policy, vol. 5 (North-Holland, 1977), pp. 7–29— the claim to continuity with the prerevolutionary situation that Johnson described as necessary for the legitimacy of the counterrevolution. The reason the REEM counterrevolution is more successful than monetarism is that it is theoretically far more innovative.

Johnson argued that monetarism would fail because the problem on which it focuses, and which it was better equipped than Keynesianism to handle—namely, inflation—was inherently less important than unemployment. The prediction was right for the wrong reasons. Unemployment is now politically less important than inflation, but monetarism has lost ground because of its difficulty in solving the inflation problem.

econometric policy evaluation critique. The role of the critique in undermining the public's confidence in econometric models is no doubt minimal. But within the profession it is now possible, and increasingly common, for researchers to dismiss large econometric models as providing evidence on anything. Thus when Nordhaus cites Otto Eckstein's calculations as showing how little policy had to do with poor economic performance in the 1970s, he persuades no one who did not already believe that, nor does he even move their priors or posteriors one iota.

It is indeed remarkable that the Lucas policy evaluation critique has triumphed without any detailed empirical support beyond Lucas's accusation that macroeconometric models in the 1960s all predicted too little inflation for the 1970s. The general point made by the critique is correct and was known before it was so eloquently and forcefully propounded by Lucas. That the point has been important empirically, however, is something that should have been demonstrated rather than asserted.

The underprediction of inflation in the 1970s is a result of the omission of the expected inflation rate, or momentum, from the Phillips curves of the econometric models rather than of their failure to allow structure to change with policy. Subsequent breakdowns of important equations, such as the demand for money, perhaps come closer to justifying the policy evaluation critique dismissal of old-fashioned econometric models. In any event, it is now too late for most large econometric models to stage a comeback. It will be some years before we know whether any of the coming generation of models will fare better. It is by no means certain that they will, for there are many sources of misspecification in any econometric model and no evidence that current research is directed at overcoming a particularly serious one.

What Difference Does It Make?

So what if younger members of the profession are attracted in large number to the REEM approach? After all, as Nordhaus notes, the approach has had no effect on policy. However, the links between theory and policy work with long and variable lags. The reason that madmen in authority hear the voices of academic scribblers of a few years back is that both the madmen and the scribblers take time to rise through the ranks. Today's REEMers are tomorrow's Nordhauses.

Nordhaus remarks that the notion that policy can do nothing is as strange to policymakers as random walk theories of stock prices are to stockbrokers. But the REEM approach does not assert that all anticipated policy actions have no real effects. Certainly, anticipated changes in fiscal policy will have real effects. And in an economy that has not fully adapted to inflation, anticipated changes in monetary policy that affect the expected inflation rate will also have real effects. Nor does the truth of random walk theories of stock prices require that stockbrokers accept them.

The third leg of the REEM triad—dynamic inconsistency—also receives too little attention from Nordhaus. The notion, developed by Kydland and Prescott,[12] provides the most serious backing for the use of rules rather than discretion that has appeared to date. Their most important result is that a sequence of policy decisions, each of which is made optimally, looking forward over an infinite horizon, may lead to outcomes inferior to those obtained by sticking to an optimal policy rule.

The point is best made by example. Consider a model in which taxes may be raised by taxing capital or labor, or both. In the current period, in which the existing capital stock is already in place, it is optimal to tax only capital. An optimal plan will have implied tax rates for all future periods, which will in general tax both capital and labor. To produce optimal private sector behavior, these future rates should be announced. But of course, when the future arrives, it is optimal to tax only capital. So long as the public believes that this is the last time capital will be taxed, all is well. Once it believes that capital will be taxed heavily each period, trouble sets in, for capital accumulation is discouraged. On the average, the economy will do better if the authorities adhere to the rule calculated at the beginning rather than trying each period to do what is best.

This analysis should help clarify some of the real difficulties of democratic decisionmaking. For instance, consider the inflation-unemployment trade-off. From today's viewpoint, it is never better to have more unemployment to get rid of inflation. Rather, given the dynamics of inflation and unemployment, inflation is best left to be reduced slowly in the future. But when the future arrives, it is no longer sensible to incur more unemployment to fight inflation.

The argument may help explain how the economy reached a core

12. Finn E. Kydland and Edward C. Prescott, "Rules Rather Than Discretion: The Inconsistency of Optimal Plans," *Journal of Political Economy,* vol. 85 (June 1977), pp. 473–91.

inflation rate of around 8 to 9 percent rather than zero. The sense in which policy was not responsible for the inflation of the 1970s—a view that I have also argued—is a special one. Given the core inflation rate of the early 1970s, monetary and fiscal policy was not responsible for most of the variations in the inflation rate observed through the decade. Monetary policy was too expansionary by far in 1971–73, and less obviously so in 1978–79. But energy price shocks and the productivity decline deserve most of the blame.

Nonetheless, there remains the question of why we are now talking of getting the inflation rate down from 8 to 9 percent rather than down from 4 to 5 percent. And the answer is that we have chosen, when there has been a choice, not to try to get the inflation rate down at the expense of employment. Perhaps this was on each occasion a rational decision. And perhaps inflation does not have much cost. But that is not the perception of most of the public.[13] The feeling that 8 to 9 percent inflation is intolerable and that the normal processes of democratic decisionmaking have resulted, and will continue to result, in inflation of that level or higher is a driving force behind constitutionalism. So is the feeling that big government is the result of present processes of economic decisionmaking. There are serious arguments behind these views, and they are not disposed of by saying that the preferences for rules, constitutional amendments, and so forth, reflect distrust of democratic ways of making policy. Democracies make decisions in a variety of ways, including through the judiciary and executive branches. It is reasonable to discuss the question of whether some set of decisions is better made more or less frequently, more or less regularly, how, and by whom.

Is There a Post-Keynesian Synthesis of the 1980s?

The preceding discussion is not intended to convince anyone that the REEM approach to theory and policy is correct, but rather to argue that the approach has more depth than Nordhaus allows, to agree with him that the approach has become influential within the profession, and to suggest that it may influence policy much more in the future than it has so far.

13. The public opinion polls do not provide unambiguous support for the view that inflation is more costly than unemployment. When asked, most people say that it is *not* desirable to incur more unemployment in order to reduce inflation. See Stanley Fischer and John Huizinga, "Inflation, Unemployment, and Public Opinion Polls," *Journal of Money, Credit and Banking,* vol. 14 (February 1982), pp. 1–19.

On the issue of how useful the pure REEM approach is for understanding the behavior of the economy and for policy, I come out close to where Nordhaus does. The implication of the flexible-price REEM model that inflation should respond quickly to changes in monetary policy is palpably as far from accurate as the inflation predictions of macroeconometric models in the late 1960s were. Of course, credibility is an excuse, but invoking the credibility of policy as an argument explaining wage-price behavior brings us back close to an augmented neo-Keynesian synthesis.

There is a useful neo-Keynesian–Friedman-Phelps-Lucas synthesis that has (at least) the following elements.

1. In the long run the Phillips curve is vertical. Lower monetary growth, applied long enough, will eventually reduce the inflation rate and restore the unemployment rate to its natural level.

2. In the short run the Phillips curve is not vertical. The short-run nonverticality arises from several factors, among them nominal contracting, concern about relative wages, and expectational errors. The proportions in which these factors matter depend heavily on the state of the economy and the types of policy being followed. In normal times prices will be quite sticky, and policy can rely on the type of responses that Keynesian sticky price-wage models suggest. But radical policy changes could reduce stickiness rapidly. Price stickiness is not a structural characteristic of the economy. It can be relied on only so long as policy actions not too different from those of the past are undertaken.

3. Uncertainty about the structure of the economy and its robustness in the face of changes in policy is considerable, certainly more than the neo-Keynesian synthesis of the late 1960s realized.

4. Optimal policymaking is best viewed as a cooperative game in which the government maximizes a welfare function that is positively associated with the utilities of private agents. Actual policy may deviate from the optimum, and it is important both to study actual policymaking and to discuss institutional arrangements to improve its performance.

What is wrong with the synthesis, and why would it not command instant assent from the entire macroeconometrics profession? The major difficulty is that there is no convincing theoretical basis for the policy conclusions I draw from the existence of price stickiness. Until there is—if there ever is, for price stickiness is not an immutable fact of nature—views on policy and on appropriate macro modeling will continue to differ. This is the source of the embarrassing gap between sound theory and what Nordhaus and I believe to be sound policy, referred to at the beginning of my comments.

There is one other important issue on which there is likely to be substantial disagreement, and that is the importance of inflation. The neo-Keynesian synthesis of the late 1960s was that inflation was not a serious problem. There is agreement on this point from parts of the Chicago school, which argues that if inflation was a serious problem, far more private and public arrangements to deal with it would have been developed. This is not the place to discuss the merits of the arguments. But it is clear that disagreement within the profession on the relative importance of inflation and unemployment is a source of differing views on desirable policy, which are played up so extensively by those outside the profession.

On the State of Macroeconomics

When the outside world tells us that no two economists ever agree on anything, it is talking about macroeconomists. When colleagues announce that it is impossible to teach macroeconomics with a straight face, they are sending a similar message about the state of the field.

Should we macroeconomists bow our heads in shame, throw in the towel, and retire to the purity of the ivory tower, or should we cheerfully continue inflicting untold harm on the profession and the economy? The answer, obviously, is none of the above.

Macroeconomists are characteristically heard disagreeing in public because no one is interested in hearing them agree. There is, in fact, substantial agreement within the profession on many of the important issues. For instance, no reputable economists supported the supply-side claims underlying the recent Reagan budget. As many have observed, differences on policy matters where they exist stem in large part from differing value judgments.

A return of the academics to the ivory tower is unlikely to help the economy. Economic policy will continue to be made, whether or not academics participate in the process. The real issue is whether policy will be made better with or without their participation. It is difficult to see how a retreat by academics would help, particularly since they more than others know what it is they don't know.

What about our colleagues? It is a good idea to start with a little questioning. Typically it turns out that the complainers are ill-informed and can easily be answered. To restore balance it is helpful to ask about unresolved issues in the critic's field—for if there were no unresolved issues there would be no field worth working in. But sometimes the complaint is about the difficulty of modeling price stickiness and price dynamics. Here we can all agree that we need a more satisfactory theory to explain the facts—and that the issue is central to macroeconomics and our understanding of the behavior of the economy.

Comment by Larry A. Sjaastad

AFTER providing a description of the problems facing the U.S. economy, which include slow economic growth, high inflation, high unemployment, and sluggish productivity, Nordhaus concludes that chronic inflation is the principal problem in that inflation constitutes *the* overriding constraint on economic policy. In between, Nordhaus covers a lot of territory and has something to say about almost everything. He finds the neo-Keynesian synthesis alive and well (presumably somewhere east of Chicago). Monetarism becomes a special case of the neo-Keynesian synthesis, rational expectations are dismissed as "elegant but irrelevant" to policymaking, and supply-side economics is characterized as essentially a political phenomenon. While not an advocate of supply-side economics, I think that it is more correctly (and fairly) described as a collection of unsubstantiated empirical assertions and, as such, just could turn out to be right, although in my view, this is quite unlikely. The disturbing aspect of the supply-side discussion is that it is a debate about the facts, with neither side doing the hard work required to resolve the issue.

There is much in the Nordhaus paper with which I disagree and little with which I can agree. The central assertion that the neo-Keynesian synthesis has merely suffered a setback is debatable at best, but it remains a proposition that can (and will) be tested only over time. His cavalier treatment of rational expectations is unfortunate, particularly because he attributes to that approach a foundation that is quite incorrect. Nordhaus states that the second premise of rational expectations is that "all markets clear in the very short run." Neither Lucas nor Sargent nor Wallace would subscribe to that; indeed, no one denies that inventories fluctuate, unemployment exists, and so forth. The novelty of the rational expectations approach lies in the suggestion that these disequilibria are probably far less amenable to resolution by policy actions than is thought to be the case under the neo-Keynesian approach. Far from being irrelevant, the implications of the rational expectations approach to economic policy are fundamental.

Returning to the serious problems facing macroeconomists here and now, I suggest, at some risk of sounding complacent, that some of the problems may be less serious than Nordhaus suggests. For slow growth of output (and productivity), it is evident that the 1970s were far worse than the 1960s, but not very far out of line with the long-term experience of the United States. I submit that it is not that the 1970s were so bad, but rather that the previous decade was a particularly good one. Viewed that way, the interesting issue is why the 1960s were so far above the norm of historical experience.

The problem of inflation is, of course, a very real one, particularly under the Nordhaus interpretation. But again I disagree with his emphasis, as his concern with the short-run cost of stopping inflation does not extend to the long-run cost of living with inflation. It seems to me that one of the main reasons that inflation is a "problem" is that the rate of inflation is positively correlated with its variability, so that anticipating the rate of price rise becomes increasingly difficult as that rate goes up. The efficiency of markets—particularly long-term markets—suffers as a consequence. Nordhaus ignores the widely held view that these long-run costs can overshadow even exaggerated estimates of the short-run stabilization costs. In this context, I emphasize that stopping inflation obviously *can* be very expensive, but there is also evidence that it need not always be so. After all, there have been cases in which the inflation rate has fallen sharply without aggravating unemployment—the usual measure of the cost of stabilization. Thomas Sargent's recent work on post–World War I stabilizations is instructive here.

There are also some very recent experiences to draw on in Latin America, particularly those of Chile during the 1978–81 period and Argentina since 1979. Both countries had experienced extremely high (500 to 1,000 percent per year) rates of inflation that were rooted in enormous fiscal deficits, and both countries drastically reduced those inflations by what is best described as "scorched-earth" policies of demand reduction (1975–76 in Chile and 1977–78 in Argentina). The results were similar—large reductions in real output, particularly in the Chilean case, which appear to support the Nordhaus-Okun thesis that stopping inflation is terribly costly. Subsequently, however, both countries were able to all but eliminate the residual inflation without loss of output by a more subtle policy, one aimed at influencing expectations. The exchange-rate-based stabilization policy began in Chile at the end of 1977, with good results. The inflation rate fell from 65–70 percent a year to about 10 percent during calendar 1981; meanwhile the measured unemployment rate fell from 16 percent to between 7 and 8 percent. Argentina adopted a similar policy at the beginning of 1979 and induced a decline in the rate of inflation from 30 percent to 9 percent per *quarter,* with the unemployment rate both low and steady. Both examples fly in the face of the Nordhaus assertion.

The similarity between Argentina and Chile ends there, however. The Argentine policy terminated in disaster, with the rate of inflation during 1981 returning to its 1978 level, accompanied by a sharp drop in output and a rise in unemployment. The apparent explanation for the difference between the two experiments is relevant to the problem of inflation control in the United States. It is my contention that Chile succeeded, and Argentina ultimately failed, because a successful stabilization policy must have both coherence and continuity. One of the important differences is that Chile began the experiment with a balanced fiscal budget, whereas Argentina had a large deficit. I submit that economic agents in countries experiencing chronic inflation ultimately come to the view that, in the final analysis, fiscal deficits are always monetized and that a stabilization policy that does not incorporate fiscal reform is doomed to failure. Both Chile and Argentina were able to stabilize in the short run with virtually no unemployment cost, but the persistent fiscal deficit in the latter country eroded confidence in that stabilization so much that it was not only abandoned but totally reversed. The U.S. fiscal disaster that may well be waiting at the end of the supply-side tunnel has, I think, convinced a lot of people that the U.S. inflation is not about to disappear. Here I am in full agreement with Nordhaus and others that a scorched-earth monetary policy would entail mainly costs and few benefits unless the deficit was dealt with. While we can quibble about the definition of the deficit, my point is that the prospect for monetization of the debt is always enhanced whenever the Treasury is required to go to the market on a systematic basis.

The relevance of these episodes is not, of course, that we should adopt Argentine or Chilean exchange-rate policy (which we cannot do in any case), but rather that there is something important to be learned from them. Both were initially successful, measured by indicators acceptable even at Brookings, but one failed largely because of insufficient attention to the fiscal deficit. It goes without saying, of course, that if a fiscal deficit destroyed the Argentine attempt to adopt the dollar standard, our own fiscal deficit might well do the same if we were to restore the gold standard. Indeed, it seems to me most unusual to be contemplating a return to gold when thirty-year Treasury bonds carry a yield of 15 percent. If there is any lesson from history, it is the following: without systematic fiscal deficits, the gold standard is unnecessary, and with those deficits, it is impossible.

In conclusion, I point out that Nordhaus is vulnerable to the Friedman syndrome. Some years ago it was popular to say that if you began with Milton's assumptions, you always got Milton's results. Similarly, if you begin with the premise that it is incredibly expensive to stop inflation, you are driven to find ways to live with it or to devise schemes, such as incomes policies, that at least appear to be doing something about it. (I submit in passing, however, that the track record of incomes policies is not an enviable one.) But if we look outside the recent and narrow experience of the United States, we find a rather rich set of alternatives. Unfortunately, few nations demonstrate the ability to learn from the experiences of other countries; indeed, in some cases, we even fail to learn from our own. My own view is that we stand to gain at least as much by the historical approach as by devising new but untested techniques for dealing with old problems.

Comment by Robert M. Solow

NORDHAUS is right, and it needed saying. I agree with him that the "neoclassical synthesis" is a good way of understanding the level of economic activity and its evolution. Perhaps eventually we will be able to share the same confidence about the price level and its evolution, but clearly there is still some way to go.

Why, then, is macroeconomics in disarray? "Disarray" is an understatement. Thoughtful people in other university departments look on with wonder. Professional disagreements exist in their fields too—at the frontier there is always disagreement—but as outsiders they are shocked at the way alternative schools of thought in macroeconomics describe each other as wrong from the ground up. They wonder what kind of subject economics is. (Some of them are not above a little *Schadenfreude* either.) The fathers-in-law of economics graduate students must be even worse because, unlike good scholars in other subjects, they regard themselves as entitled to pontificate about macroeconomics. The person in the street would probably regard Nordhaus as just another special pleader, another candidate for alderman.

Two questions arise. How did we get into this fix? And how can we get out of it? Nordhaus has a lot to say about the first question. I will only supplement his comments. He has almost nothing to say about the second question. By implication he seems to be saying: if the neoclassical synthesis is essentially right, our duty is to keep the faith, to improve our understanding of the economy bit by bit, and to wait for the pendulum to swing our way again. I do not disagree, but I think part of the problem is not in our stars but in ourselves. So we could mend our ways a bit.

Why are we in a spot like this? Nordhaus has talked about some of the causes and hinted at others. Here are my marginal notes.

People have been stoning the messenger bearing bad news for millennia. When the economy is in trouble, so are economists. In fact, the reaction goes a little deeper. In the popular mind, economics is *expected* always to have a policy answer, whatever the current problem. The public is not prepared to take "You can't get there from here" or "There is no acceptable and costless way to end the inflation" as an answer. We may complain that they don't go after the biology department because death persists as a problem or even after doctors for not curing cancer or migraine. That will not get us off the hook.

Part of the crop of the 1973–80 inflation was planted in the financing of the Vietnam War. There is an important sense in which "we" are not to blame for that. Gardner Ackley and Arthur Okun warned Lyndon Johnson, and he disregarded them for reasons of his own. Outside commentators from within the profession expressed their misgivings; you could undoubtedly find *Newsweek* columns by Paul Samuelson urging that if we desired to bomb Vietnam into the Stone Age it would be better to do it with a smaller full employment deficit. But no one resigned from the Council of Economic Advisers and, as I remember, there were only half-hearted attempts to lobby public opinion and even less to lobby Congress.

As for that part of the inflation that stemmed from OPEC in 1974 and again in 1979, it may be that there was *no* practical way to avoid a very bad outcome in the second half of the 1970s. I think there is a passage in Nordhaus to suggest that he shares my suspicion. Unfortunately for us, the articulate public is unwilling to accept the notion that American society may for occasional intervals be at the mercy of forces it cannot overcome. We might only ask ourselves whether the science of economics might not be better off if we played a smaller role in practical policy. Would society be better off? That depends, I suppose, on how much harm one thinks Ronald Reagan can inflict on the economy, and whether any of it could have been fended off by a more detached, less involved economics profession.

There is another way in which we may be to blame for the poor opinion the world has of us. I think we suffer from econometric illusion. We overestimate the accuracy and reliability of our models. Too few econometric routines can respond to a question with "Don't ask." If you are honest you will agree that, although you are fundamentally right and monetarists and new-classical theorists are wrong, they can always find sample periods, data sets, econometric specifications, and time series methods according to which they are at least as good as you (we) are. This is again a piece of unavoidable bad luck—the collinearity of the world, the shortness of stationary time series, the inapplicability of the experimental method. But the result is Babel, or even babble.

The low power of econometric tests combines with political involvement to give the profession a very bad image. Every reporter knows that two well-known economists can be found who will say exactly opposite things about any current event. There was an example just the other day in the *New York Times*. The question was, "Is monetary policy too tight?" There, on the first page of the business section, were side-by-side photographs of Allan Meltzer and James Tobin saying not quite opposite things, but opposite enough. There are probably few top economists who have not contributed to the world's bemusement in this way. I know which statement I agreed with, but what is the ordinary reader of the *Times* to think? Of course, it would be infinitely better if the accompanying story had gone something like this. Meltzer and Tobin disagree about this because Meltzer thinks that most substantial deviations from Walrasian equilibrium are caused by misperceptions of the course of monetary policy, and so on and so forth, whereas Tobin believes that wages and prices are sticky for institutional, historical, and other reasons, so that persistent deviations from Walrasian equilibrium can arise from any change in the environment, and so forth. But that would be asking for scholarship, not politics. What is suitable for the *American Economic Review* is not suitable for the *New York Times*.

It may be that the solution here is to keep our mouths shut more often. I am learning to discipline myself to say to reporters, "No, I'd rather not comment on that because to make sense I would have to explain a five-equation model, for which you do not have the space or your readers the time." It has, of course, occurred to me that if responsible people adopt this policy, only the unscrupulous will be quoted in the *Times*.

There is a deeper and in some ways more disturbing connection that Nordhaus makes. What about the flood of simple-minded monetarists or, worse yet, the Laffers, the Wanniskis, the Claremonts, the goldbugs, the constitutionalists, the others? Why just now? I have mentioned two reasons—bad times and our own contribution to the undermining of the scientific character of economics. Nordhaus adds that this spate of snake oil is a by-product of the widespread loss of confidence in authority. I see what he means, but I am not sure that is the best way to put it. Many of the people who support constitutional amendments to balance the budget or require steady growth of some—any—monetary aggregate seem instead to be seeking authority. They are—with exceptions, of course—the same people who want constitutional amendments to prohibit abortion or to prohibit busing. They are motivated in all sorts of ways, often by a sense that they have been betrayed or conspired against. The kernel of truth in Nordhaus's view is that sometimes they feel that political or judicial authority has betrayed them. But not always: sometimes it is others, strangers. It is too simple to describe this movement as antidemocratic, though clearly there is a sense in which that is so. But what could be more democratic than a constitutional amendment duly passed? The bad thing, from our narrow point of view, would be for technical issues of economic analysis and policy to get caught up in people's acting out of their frustrations with their children, other races, sexual behavior, and so on.

So far I have been talking mainly about the state of macroeconomics as seen from the outside. How about the view from the inside? Nordhaus says very little on this subject. Fischer argues in his comment that the intellectual force of the attack on the neoclassical, neo-Keynesian synthesis is greater than Nordhaus admits, although it is not clear from his own exposition why that should be so.

I think we have learned something from the new classical macroeconomics of the past six or seven years, though I also think it becomes clearer with each passing day that equilibrium theory is simply incapable of providing a satisfactory explanation of what is happening out in the world. Baily's paper in this book demonstrates that failure for the 1930s, with something to spare. But it is proving to be true even for humdrum, everyday economic fluctuations. The notion that observed data are points of intersection of the relevant perceived Walrasian supply and demand curves for labor and goods is not self-evident and does not appear to be consistent with the results of exploratory data analysis.

The fruitful idea to emerge from the new classical macroeconomics, I think, is the notion that economic policy is really a game in which private agents have strategies too. As in any game, participants will react to perceived changes in others' policies, including those of the government. It offends neither common sense nor casual observation to suppose that this sort of behavior can have important consequences for the operating characteristics of the system and the effects of public policy. The new classical school has also been the source of nice technical improvements in the treatment of equilibrium dynamics with random disturbances in the environment, and there may be occasions when that is the appropriate setting for conducting analysis.

But this is hardly enough to explain why, in Fischer's words, so "many of the best and brightest young macroeconomists are working within that approach." Fischer's comments seem intended to explain why that has happened. In the end, however, he leaves the mystery unresolved even on his own grounds. He is aware that the new classical school has no single empirical success to its credit, nothing that could count as a statistical verification, no "cross-equation restrictions" satisfied. No one has discovered a Phelpsian island or even a message in a bottle. No one has bothered to check if misperception is rife, in the right sequence, in the right direction, with the right people. I am not sure that anyone wants to.

The neoclassical synthesis is better off, but only slightly better off, on this account. I doubt that the track record of the large econometric models, good or bad, is even relevant. Fischer is probably right on this, not primarily because of the "econometric policy critique" but because the record is so snarled by add factors, judgment calls, telephone calls, and fudging that it is incapable of providing a test of anything but the Bell System. Ray Fair is an exemplary exception to this judgment. Also, it is only fair to say that the neoclassical, neo-Keynesian mainstream has produced acres of small and partial models, which have been checked and estimated against data. Some of this is well done, some not, but at least there is a record to be evaluated. That is more than one can say for equilibrium theory.

Perhaps I should add that the importance, as distinct from the elegance, of the "econometric policy critique" is an empirical matter. Even where it applies, it could make little quantitative difference or a lot. Is anyone trying to find out?

Whatever it is that attracts so many bright young macroeconomists to the new classical model, it cannot be its demonstrated superiority as a model of the world. Is it merely a better toy—new, shiny, unfamiliar, full of tabs A to be inserted into slots B, requiring and generating new skills that not everybody has? I spent too much of my youth being told by my elders that I was captivated by mere technique to be prepared to accept that explanation out of hand. Here is another puzzle in the sociology of science, a subject in which I have already demonstrated my amateur status. I think Fischer has not drawn the conclusions implicit in his own arguments and judgments.

Let me mention one last possibility that plays a key role in Fischer's argument. Perhaps the vogue for the new classical equilibrium theory is based not on its own merits, which appear to be limited, but on a yawning gap in the mainstream synthesis, the fact that "there is no convincing theoretical basis for the policy conclusions [drawn] from the existence of price stickiness." And again, "Price stickiness is not a structural characteristic of the economy. It can be relied on only so long as policy actions not too different from those of the past are undertaken." I do not want to argue about the substance of price and wage stickiness here; it is a worthwhile subject for a research program. But I do want to point out the methodological peculiarity of this argument. Why is it not symmetrical? Is price and wage flexibility a structural characteristic of the economy? It is surely a structural characteristic of the Walrasian model, but that points to the question, not the answer. Nothing Fischer says excludes the possibility that the changes from past policy needed to restore wage and price flexibility might include the abolition of trade unions and whispered conversations at work, the prosecution of all firms with a market share bigger than 3 percent, and the prohibition of all long-term buying-and-selling relationships, formal or informal. I do not argue that those minor differences in policy would actually be required to restore price flexibility. I do not even argue that the restoration of price flexibility ought to be regarded as the economist's equivalent of the Second Coming. It seems to me that equilibrium theorists are saying: the world *must* be like the Walrasian model because that is the model we have. Those who are more in touch with reality seem to say: the world is not like the Walrasian model, but perhaps the resemblance could be made closer. That is real progress. I would like to argue for even a little more imagination: the world may have its reasons for being non-Walrasian.

ROBERT A. MUNDELL

International Monetary Reform:
The Optimal Mix in Big Countries

ECONOMIC theory is studied from the standpoint of a closed economy but economic policy must deal with open economies.

If the world economy were organized within the political framework of a world government, the theoretical treatises of the early masters of economic science would have direct policy relevance. Our planet, however, is organized around the political framework of interacting nation-states. The economic interaction is manifested in the imports and exports of goods, services, factors, claims, and money, the major categories of the balance of payments.

The balance-of-payments accounts of a country summarize its economic dependence on the rest of the world. This is as obvious in monetary and fiscal policy analysis as it is in problems of tariffs and quotas, foreign aid lending and investment, and international currency relations. The international monetary framework must therefore be the starting point for applicable monetary analysis for every economy.

The need to focus on the international monetary environment was well known in the early days of economic theorizing when ideal monetary standards were first debated. Plato, for example, favored national monetary standards, a token currency for each state convertible into hard money (gold and silver) at arbitrary prices fixed by the government under a disciplined exchange-control arrangement. His pupil, Aristotle, favored a convertible hard money like gold or silver, as valuable inside a country as it was outside. Aeschines, the founder of the School of Rhodes, favored something in between, like the ambiguous lottery money of Carthage, with either a precious stone or a piece of gravel (known only to the maker) sealed in leather. The different solutions were inspired by the life experiences of the three philosophers, one as monetary adviser to the kings of Syracuse, one as teacher of Alexander

285

in the era of Philip II, and the third as monetary historian of the Mediterranean.

In the twentieth century monetary proposals have also developed out of the peculiarities of time and place. Fisher in 1912, envisioning the problems of an emerging monetary superpower, favored cutting loose from the gold standard and gearing monetary policy to a stable price level, achieving a compensated dollar. Keynes, from the perspective of a declining monetary superpower in post–World War I Britain, rejected the deflationary solutions of a restoration of the centuries-old traditional gold price in 1925 and eventually, in the wake of the collapse of sterling in 1931 and the Great Depression, favored in 1935 a wage standard. Cassel and von Mises, economists brought up in small countries, favored (like Aristotle) an international standard based on gold, as did Rueff. Friedman, from the vantage of a mature superpower, advocated stable monetary aggregates with floating rates and more recently fixed exchange rates (currencies pegged to one or another of the monetary leaders) for the less developed countries. What these alternatives have in common, and what links the solutions to the different monetary schemes of Plato, Aristotle, and Aeschines, is the parochialism of the designers. Economists have a tendency to generalize from their own experience or knowledge of a particular time and place to situations to which the experience is not relevant.

A similar problem emerges at the global level. The world economy has experienced many different forms of international monetary system in the past. The monetary systems of the ancient world changed with political solutions. The currencies of the great empires of antiquity "overflowed" to neighboring countries and frequently provided the base of the international currency system of the time. At one time or another, the daric, stater, solidus-besant, drachma, dinar, maravedi, florin, ducat, sequin, écu, carlino, lira, livre, franc, pound, rupee, dirham, daler, rupee, thaler, peso, mark, ruble, sovereign, yen, and dollar are outcomes of the process by which the dominant currencies of the time reflect the historic importance of the international power structure and the role of trade within and between the great empires. The connecting link of these currencies is the substance of which it is made: at the international level the precious metals provided the common material out of which international money was made before the invention of paper, telegraphic transfers, and electronic money. Monometallism, bimetallism, and even trimetallism formed the basis of monetary theory in the great treatises on money of the past, of which one of the examples that still retains relevance is *De Moneta* of Nicole Oresme, the discoverer in the middle ages of Gresham's law.

The bimetallic standard established by Napoleon in 1803 gave the world a monetary unity until the pivot country dropped silver after 1870–71, leaving in its wake a deflationary gold bloc organized around the city of London, and an inflationary silver standard in much of the nonmetropolitan world. The heyday of gold from 1870 to 1914 gave a monetary unity to a comparatively tranquil and innovative European civilization ordered around imperialism and colonialism when Europe was "mistress of the world." When European unity became unhinged between 1914 and 1945, the vast subcontinents on the wings of European culture flapped into their superpower preeminence and the dollar era began in earnest. Neither emulation of nor nostalgia for a past tranquillity could restore the monetary system that assisted in its creation. The decentralized European gold standard provided the cement for great power economic interaction, but there is no way now that the circumstances of the past can be revived to fulfill the characteristics of the political environment needed to perpetuate that destiny. The old gold standard is as dead as a doornail. The rise of America killed it.

The Bretton Woods system was based on the U.S. dollar at a time when the U.S. economy was the manufactory of the world. But we cannot, and would not, restore the temporary conditions of that time. From 1945 to 1982 more than one hundred newly independent nations were born while only a few were aborted (chiefly in the Baltic region). The gross national product of the United States is only one-fifth of world GNP. The other four-fifths of the world economy does not want a world monetary system based solely on the U.S. dollar, subject to the vicissitudes of U.S. politics and arbitrary mismanagement. A global dollar standard would work only under an American imperium not wanted by the rest of the world or the overwhelming majority of U.S. citizens.

A combination of the attributes of a gold standard and a dollar standard would be more appealing than either a pure gold standard or a pure dollar standard. In the first amendment to the International Monetary Fund Articles of Agreement promulgated in 1968, which established a gold-backed special drawing right (SDR) worth, like the dollar, $\frac{1}{35}$ of an ounce, the concept of "paper gold" became popular. But the solid foundation of the SDR collapsed with the convertibility of the dollar on August 15, 1971. The SDR proved to be a close substitute neither for the dollar nor for gold. From a reserve asset that was a "ghost" of both gold and the dollar, it degenerated into a basket of sixteen currencies, which was not satisfactory to the less developed countries (because it lacked universality and its allocation was not linked to foreign aid), nor was it satisfactory as a unit of account; to predict its value one had to predict the monetary policies of the sixteen countries. The latest version of the SDR is a basket of five currencies, which makes it less universal but more operational; it is still complicated as a unit of account by the need to forecast the monetary policies of five countries, the United States, Japan, Germany, Britain, and France. In 1976 at Jamaica the nations agreed to endorse the already existing "managed flexible exchange rate system," to reduce the role of gold, and to enhance the role of the SDR. This second amendment to the IMF Articles revealed the gap in international theorizing on matters of monetary reform. The lessons of the 1970s were negative, showing how *not* to create an international substitute for gold or the dollar. The regional solutions attempted in various parts of the world—the Gulf of Mexico, Arabia-Persia, and Eastern and Western Europe—have not fared much better. The failures to create effective collective new currencies do not make one optimistic about the future.

Both history and the political condition of the world have combined to make a special role in international finance for gold and the dollar, the two "perennial" assets that have continued to dominate international reserves. The misconceptions that have become explicit in the failure of the experiments with international reserve creation in the 1970s should alert us to the possibility that, far back in the past, serious mistakes were made in the field of international currency theory. To err is human; to err twice is forgiveable; but to err again and again makes a mockery of belief in the progress of man's collective intelligence.

The gold standard broke down in 1914 when all major nations withdrew gold from circulation and centralized it in treasuries to form the basis for wartime inflationary finance. After the war the value of gold had fallen precipitously, even in U.S. dollars, and the supply was insufficient for the world's needs despite greatly increased production by South Africa. When Germany, Britain, and France spearheaded the return to gold in the 1920s, the scarcity of gold became obvious. When Churchill in 1925 abolished the use of gold coins in circulation, he said that such a use of gold "would be an unwarranted extravagance which our present financial stringency by no means allows us to indulge in." This policy set a bad precedent for President Roosevelt, who did the same thing in 1934, when the United States restored gold at the new parity of 13⁵⁄₇ grains, equivalent to $35 an ounce. The entrance of France into the system in June 1928 at a value of 3.92 cents instead of the prewar parity of 19.30 cents undervalued the franc relative to its purchasing power and enabled France to draw gold away from the United States and Britain. From the end of 1925 to the end of 1929 U.S. gold reserves not only failed to rise but fell (from $4 billion to $3.9 billion), which certainly helped create the monetary stringency that caused the crash on Wall Street. French gold reserves, on the other hand, went from $0.7 billion in December 1926 to $2.3 billion in August 1931. Britain dropped gold in the following month, but the United States hung on to its overvalued dollar for almost two years of a sickening slide into the slough of stagnation. Even today people have trouble understanding the crash of 1929 and its link to the undervaluation of gold throughout the 1920s.

With the new price of gold after 1934, gold was still considered scarce enough to prohibit Americans from holding it or using it as coinage. The U.S. reserve ratio was 40 percent behind notes and 35 percent behind deposits. With the inflationary expansion of World War II the Treasury, as early as 1945, considered it prudent to reduce the reserve cover to 25 percent behind both notes and deposits. By 1965 the backing for deposits was reduced to zero, and in 1968 the cover behind the notes was also eliminated. Thus all formal semblance of the national gold standard discipline had broken down by 1968.

The shortage of gold in the world monetary system had become apparent early in the 1920s, and in retrospect it would have been better to raise the price of gold after World War I in order to spare the world economy the painful adjustment of deflation that caught up with the system in the next decade. Instead, the palliative of the gold exchange standard propped the system up for another decade.

When the system broke down in 1931 with the fall of sterling and 1933 with the fall of the dollar, a new price of gold was set up, but the increase in price was not sufficient to restore a full gold standard. In the Great Depression each country was hungry, but the excess of surpluses over deficits in the world as a whole has to equal the increase in the value of gold stocks, which in 1938, for example, constituted 93 percent of world reserves. A higher gold price than actually took place would have raised the excess of surpluses over deficits and had multiplier effects, spurring recovery from the depression.

The world economy did repeat after World War II some of the mistakes authorities had made after World War I. The symptoms of gold shortage appeared early, not only in the prohibition on gold in the United States or the high dollar black market price, but by the need felt by the United States to increase "free" reserves by lowering Federal Reserve gold cover requirements to 25 percent while continuing to prohibit gold for American citizens. When the London gold market opened in 1954, the drain of gold started, dollar interest rates began to climb, and by 1960, during the U.S. election campaign, gold had climbed in the free market to $40 an ounce. Gold losses imposed a constraint on expansionary monetary policies, a fact that many considered a serious defect of the gold standard. Perhaps we should admit with the hindsight of the present that Sir Roy Harrod and Professor Rueff, who eloquently advocated a higher gold price in the 1950s, were closer to the mark than those who in the 1950s and 1960s objected to it. By then, however, the infectious enthusiasm for international monetary reform and a world central bank along the lines of a Keynes-Triffin plan had caught on, and this hope for an alternative to gold stood in the way of the retrospectively attractive option of raising the price of gold. The better makes the best its enemy.

Instead, circumstances led to the "third solution" of a free gold price and floating exchange rates. The basic argument for floating exchange rates had been that the U.S. balance-of-payments deficit would disappear, so that monetary and fiscal policies would be freed to preserve internal balance, with full employment and a stable price level. The monetary disequilibrium of the 1970s showed how wrongly conceived or badly implemented this solution was.

No theory can be further from the facts. The balance-of-payments deficits of the reserve countries have not been eliminated; they have multiplied ten times since floating rates came into existence. From 1952 to 1969 foreign exchange reserves, mainly dollars and sterling, rose from $16 billion to $33 billion, a little more than doubling over seventeen years. Then from 1969 to 1981 they rose by $272 billion, to $305 billion, almost a *tenfold* increase in only twelve years, feeding the inflation of the 1970s and the steady depreciation of the dollar in terms of goods. It was not just the explosion of official holdings of foreign exchange, however, that led to the inflation. The expansion of international liquidity held by the international deposit money banks (Eurodollars, and so forth), which amounted to $30 billion in 1963 and $117 billion in 1969, rose to $2,098 billion at the end of 1981, a figure indicative of an enormous inflation even if it does involve double counting. To this phenomenal expansion must be added the increase in the dollar value of gold reserves from $35 billion in 1971 to over ten times that amount in 1981. With the liquidity onslaught of the combined forces of foreign exchange, Euro-dollars, and gold, it is surprising that world inflation and the commodity depreciation of the dollar have not been greater than they have.

It is important for economists, bankers, and officials to realize how grossly erroneous were the calculations of those who advocated the breakdown of both the gold reserve standard and the systems of fixed exchange rate parities. The discipline of a currency system convertible at fixed exchange rates into one or a few major currencies that are in turn convertible directly into gold or an internationally stable world asset (such as a gold-backed SDR) offers far better prospects for a stable world economy in the future.

The IMF was actually set up to provide the framework to avoid fluctuations in exchange rates, which were believed to have smashed the international lending mechanisms, driven countries into economic nationalism, exchange controls, and protection, and deepened the de-pression, leaving the road open to the work of totalitarian forces that spread across the continent of Europe in the 1930s. The IMF system, however, was weakened from its birth by an inadequate level of gold liquidity, and soon came to rely on the U.S. dollar. This inadequacy was concealed by the magnificent growth of the United States as a superpower of colossal dimensions, generously spreading technological bounty to the rest of the world on a scale never before offered so freely. The miracles of growth on the continent of Europe, in Japan, and in the Soviet Union were based on the catch-up possibilities inherent in the new technology of American corporate capitalism, laying a basis for a new epoch in computers, electronics, communications, and outer space. The breakdown in the gold exchange standard and the monetary insta-bility of the 1970s were dismal, but should not conceal the improvements that continued despite rather than because of flexible rates. The errors were forgiveable: undervaluing gold in the Bretton Woods arrangements, failing to specify the meaning of "fundamental disequilibrium," lacking a coherent theory of "currencies in need," and not elaborating a sufficiently accurate analysis of the adjustment process or understanding the theory of key or dominant currencies. The basic concept of a workable framework for a kind of humanized gold standard based on the dollar and a revolving bag of other currencies was not in error. Today the IMF and the World Bank Group are a durable reminder of the idealistic intentions of the time to forswear the relapse into the chaotic jungle of fluctuating currencies.

It is for that reason that progress in the future, I believe, lies in the development of a monetary standard combining the virtues of gold and the amalgam of currencies making up a possibly revised SDR, defined in a third amendment of the IMF Articles of Agreement. A genuine convertible world reserve currency unit composed, say, of half gold and half SDRs would provide a more stable compromise that could last for several decades. This unit should be acceptable everywhere and accorded the status of legal tender in every member country. Some other suggestions follow.

First, countries should stabilize currencies (within margins) to gold, a major currency, or the new composite basket, allowing changes in reserve positions to affect monetary policies and thus give the new system features of an adjustment process for correcting the balance of payments along the theoretical lines of the monetary approach to the balance of payments.

Second, allocation of the new composite basket should increase at a definable target rate announced in advance after being agreed upon by the Committee of Twenty and endorsed by the Executive Board under the instructions of the Board of Governors.

Third, the price of gold in terms of the dollar and perhaps a few other currencies should be kept as stable as possible. Federal Reserve policy can make it consistent with the needs of internal balance. In an interim transitional period a crawling peg around gold established by a reformed gold pool would be a desirable transitional feature.

Fourth, budgetary policy in the United States should be geared to the preservation of internal balance to the extent that it is consistent with optimal public debt policies and interest rate objectives.

This approach envisages a new constitutional convention of the IMF governors, prepared in advance by committees of the IMF, member governments, and the interested community of bankers, academics, officials, and other relevant parties in the private sector.

Reform of the IMF is only a starting point for generating the new international monetary system needed to replace the one currently damaging prosperity and threatening the fabric of the international society that played so useful a role in the institutions created after World War II. Because of the new demands on the system arising from international debt problems, prompt action is needed.

International monetary reform is not the only answer, however. In the interim the immediate problems facing the world economy must be tackled, particularly the high unemployment of the current recession, and a noninflationary way found to increase the supply of jobs in the world economy. The approach I favor is to alter the fiscal policy mix toward supply-and-demand-promoting reduction in key tax rates and an accommodating monetary policy to accompany employment-enhancing growth without accelerating inflation.

The mistakes of "Reaganomics" were in failing to press forward with international monetary reform, a necessary prerequisite for efficient long-run reduction in the interest rates, and in tightening monetary policy before the tax stimulus had been allowed to take effect. Tight money is the best solution to inflation only if it is accompanied by employment-fostering reduction in tax rates and adaptive fiscal policy. Budgetary and monetary policies have differential effects on the inflation-unemployment target mix.

The mistakes of the recent past are correctable. When planned saving exceeds planned investment at full employment, it is desirable for the budget deficit to take up the slack. When this lesson, attributable to Keynes, is recalled, new policies can rise out of the ashes of sole reliance on balanced budgets and monetary aggregates. Budget deficits alone are not the cause of high interest rates. In the long run, international monetary reform must be accomplished to provide rational prediction of future monetary policy. It would be better to produce that reform in a climate of world prosperity than in the exigencies of global depression.

It is time for policymakers in the major countries and in the IMF to get back to work.

Comment by Pentti J. K. Kouri

ROBERT MUNDELL's discussion of monetary history and history of thought is insightful and interesting. I am sympathetic with his historical perspective and admire him for keeping alive the big issues of international monetary reform. Many economists, unfortunately, follow a random walk in their intellectual processes, always taking today as the point of reference for thinking about tomorrow in the mistaken belief that today always incorporates all the relevant information about the past. No one can accuse Mundell of this. Some may find his advocacy of world monetary reform radical and even eccentric. I think he has a strong case in arguing for the return to fixed exchange rates but a much weaker case in advocating the return to gold. Certainly, neither position is particularly radical. From the perspective of the 1960s Mundell's views are conservative and conventional.

Let me first take up the question of gold. As I understand it Mundell wants to return to gold as a means of stabilizing the price level. It may be true that the relative price of gold has remained constant since the Roman Empire (how could we possibly measure it?), but it does not appear very stable if we think in terms of decades rather than centuries. We know ex post that the purchasing power of gold in, say, 1915 was close to what it was in 1822, but no one could have known that ex ante. Fluctuations in the purchasing power of gold were a major cause of instability throughout the nineteenth century and in the early part of the twentieth century. The purchasing power of gold would be unstable even if the fundamentals were completely stable. An increase in the demand for money, for example, would still lead to price deflation because only a small part of the shift in liquidity preference would be directly affected by central bank purchases of gold. Presumably, price deflation would lead gradually to an excess supply of gold at the fixed price and even to an increase in the supply of money at an unchanged price level. But in today's economy the adjustment process would be so large as to be irrelevant. A return to gold might well be inflationary at first if the decline in private gold demand was not affected by an equal increase in money demand but was instead channeled to Treasury bills, for example.

The gold standard does not give a firm anchor to the purchasing power of money. I agree with Mundell that Friedman's monetary rule does not effectively stabilize the value of money either. Indeed, financial innovations and deregulation of banks will make it increasingly difficult, if not impossible, to exercise any reliable control on nominal magnitudes through the control of M1 or other such aggregates. The closer we move to a Wicksellian credit economy, the more irrelevant monetarism becomes.

One way out of this dilemma is to specify monetary rules directly in terms of either a price level target, as Wicksell, Davidson, and Lindahl advocate, or a nominal GNP target, and adjust the nominal interest rate so as to achieve that objective. Such a control mechanism would not be perfect either, but it would make it possible to proceed with deregulation of financial markets without sacrificing macroeconomic objectives. It would also enable a more orderly transition to price stability than the current monetarist strategy, which is keeping interest rates too high and forcing unnecessary deflation on the economy.

I agree with Mundell's reservations about flexible exchange rates. Unfortunately, a return to fixed rates is not imminent even though all the major countries have a basic agreement on the objectives of macroeconomic policy. There is no question that achieving price stability with sustained growth would be easier for everyone if the United States, Germany, and Japan decided to stabilize the dollar-mark and the dollar-yen exchange rate and to pursue monetary policies consistent with these objectives.

JAMES TOBIN

Okun on Macroeconomic Policy: A Final Comment

ON THE LAST PAGE of Arthur Okun's book he says:

> I expect the era of chronic inflation to end in the eighties. I am not particularly optimistic, however, that the era will be terminated by a coordinated program that combines a deceleration of nominal income growth with the cost-reducing elements and the incentives to wage and price restraint that the analysis of this book has highlighted. Viewing the world objectively, I believe it is more probable that the era of chronic inflation will end with a deep and prolonged recession or with a protracted period of rigid mandatory price and wage controls. I am not resigned to that conclusion, and I hope economists will work hard to prevent it.[1]

The United States, like the United Kingdom, has embarked on the course of disinflation via gradual destruction of monetary demand. Like Okun, I would expect the process to be lengthy and costly, characterized by deep recessions, stunted recoveries, and high and rising unemployment. The external environment is likely to be more benign in the 1980s than in the previous decade, when our economies suffered external shocks of severity unprecedented in peacetime. Therefore the orthodox cure, monetary starvation, will probably triumph in the end, at least if the political and social fabric holds together.

I think the experience, under Paul Volcker as well as Margaret Thatcher, will also vindicate Okun's skepticism, and my own, of claims that threatening advertising can make the process quick and painless. Our profession is in no small measure responsible for the confidently held view that public announcement of resolute irreversible monetary disinflation will so alter expectations in the private sector that our inherited wage and price inflation will melt like snow in spring sunshine. This proposition is not based on empirical evidence, of which there is

1. Arthur M. Okun, *Prices and Quantities: A Macroeconomic Analysis* (Brookings Institution, 1981), p. 359.

precious little, but on the a priori view that only misinformation prevents labor and product markets from arriving at market-clearing wages and prices. If in the past monetary disinflation has had a disappointingly small impact on prices and a large impact on output, the reason given is the expectation, based on experience over the postwar decades, of countercyclical reversals of monetary and fiscal policy. These make it unnecessary for workers and firms to disinflate in order to protect and restore their jobs and sales. Although Okun agreed that public perception of abandonment of compensatory policy would work in the direction claimed, he was skeptical of the quantitative magnitude of the shift.

He had several reasons. First, he doubted that a democratic government could make very credible a stance of indifference to the real state of the economy—unemployment, production, bankruptcy, and other symptoms of distress. In confirmation we may note that, unlike Mrs. Thatcher, President Reagan has not risked his prestige on the strategy of credible threat. He has promised disinflation without tears, along with simultaneous reduction of unemployment, rapid and full recovery, accelerated growth, and balance in the budget, to boot. Chairman Volcker is firm and clear enough, but his message may not penetrate to the level where wage and price decisions are actually made. Okun himself regarded a Volcker-Thatcher policy as indefensible:

I would be morally outraged by a local ordinance designed to promote fire prevention by prohibiting the fire department from responding to any alarms for a month. This is a strong analogy to attempting to prevent inflation by committing the government not to deal with a recession no matter how deep it becomes. A democratic society must have better cooperative ways to instill such socially desirable efforts than by threat and fear.[2]

Second, Okun's whole book explains why and how there are good business reasons for price and wage stickiness, for absorbing variations in demand in quantities rather than in prices and wages, at least in the first instance. The phenomenon is not solely due to misinformation and to errors of forecast perpetuated in contracts. There is some tangency between Okun's approach and that of Lucas and company. Rules of behavior adopted for local microeconomic reasons affect the response of a decentralized economy to macroeconomic events and policies, and will indeed be modified when the macroeconomic environment appreciably changes. The difference is that Okun was considering monopolistic

2. Ibid., p. 358.

rather than pure competition. (It is, by the way, both puzzling and unfortunate that Keynes, in spite of the Chamberlin-Robinson revolution that was occurring in microeconomics at the same time he was making his macro revolution, chose to challenge orthodoxy on its own microeconomic ground of competitive markets.) In "customer markets" with administered or negotiated prices, the micro rules of behavior leave room for quantities to adjust to demand, anticipated and unanticipated, and thus leave room for macro policies that control monetary demand.

From his unparalleled command of the facts of real world business fluctuations, Okun was able to muster a list of observations that contradict the implications of so-called equilibrium business cycle theory. See his marvelously cogent paper in the American Enterprise Institute Symposium on Rational Expectations, the last one of his published.[3] Nowadays theorists are busy trying to amend and elaborate rational expectations models to reconcile them with Okun's facts. I suspect that this process will result in a synthesis in which rational behavior and rational expectations are divorced from competitive markets simply and continuously cleared by price. When this synthesis matures into a new mainstream theory, I suspect it will be capable of explaining Okun's observations and will also allow room for compensatory stabilization policies.

Third, Okun saw the conquest and control of inflation as a problem of externality. What we need today, for example, is mutually assured disinflation. Resistance to departures from the existing inflationary pattern is due to the fear of each group, workers and firms, that others will not disinflate simultaneously or subsequently. If these fears are correct, the group will lose real and relative terms of trade for very little gain in demand. But if everyone disinflates, no one will lose in terms of trade, and everyone will gain the benefits of low inflation or price stability. Those benefits, I must say, Okun rated more highly than I do. But it is sufficient now to say that inflation has serious social costs because society, for reasons some of which are valid and some invalid, regards it as a prime social malady, and its continuation cripples society in dealing with other serious economic problems.

Coordinated and mutually assured disinflation is difficult to arrange in an economy with decentralized and staggered wage-setting. The tax-

---

3. "Rational Expectations with Misperceptions as a Theory of the Business Cycle," *Journal of Money, Credit and Banking,* vol. 12 (November 1980), pt. 2, pp. 817–25.

based incomes policies that Okun, I, and many others have advocated have their own costs and distortions, but their justification is the public good of achieving disinflation without severe cost in employment and production. At the same time, a supportive consensus of labor and management must be engineered by presidential leadership, fostered more by the promise of real economic gains than by the threat of disaster. The incomes policies must be in place during a transition long enough to unwind the previous history of contracts, patterns, and expectations. Monetary and fiscal policy must not, of course, overheat the economy during the transition and, indeed, should err on the cautious side. But Okun would certainly not approve a game plan that I fear will be the likely sequel to any successful monetary campaign against inflation, namely, that the economy will be run permanently at the high transitional unemployment rates in order to avoid all risk of the resurgence of inflation.

I have devoted this comment to recalling what Arthur Okun thought and said about the issues of science and policy discussed in this book. I have done so not only because the book is the result of a conference held in his memory and honor, but also because I think he was wise and right.

Index

301